P9-DHM-067

Uruguay
a country study

Federal Research Division
Library of Congress
Edited by
Rex A. Hudson and
Sandra W. Meditz
Research Completed
December 1990

On the cover: A gaucho displays an ornamental saddle and harness at a festival.

Second Edition, First Printing, 1992.

Library of Congress Cataloging-in-Publication Data

Uruguay : a country study / Federal Research Division, Library of
Congress ; edited by Rex A. Hudson and Sandra W. Meditz. —
2nd ed.
    p. cm. — (Area handbook series, ISSN 1057-5294) (DA
pam ; 550-97)
    "Supersedes the 1971 edition of Area handbook for Uruguay
written by Thomas E. Weil, et al."—T.p. verso.
    "Research completed December 1990."
    Includes bibliographical references (pp. 249-272) and index.
    ISBN 0-8444-0737-2
-------Copy 3. Z663.275 . U78 1992
    1. Uruguay. I. Hudson, Rex A., 1947- . II. Meditz, Sandra
W., 1950- .   III. Library of Congress. Federal Research Division. IV. Area handbook for Uruguay. V. Series. VI. Series:
DA pam ; 550-97.
F2708.U855   1992   92-6702
989.5—dc20   CIP

Headquarters, Department of the Army
DA Pam 550-97

For sale by the Superintendent of Documents, U.S. Government Printing Office
Washington, D.C. 20402

Foreword

This volume is one in a continuing series of books prepared by the Federal Research Division of the Library of Congress under the Country Studies/Area Handbook Program sponsored by the Department of the Army. The last page of this book lists the other published studies.

Most books in the series deal with a particular foreign country, describing and analyzing its political, economic, social, and national security systems and institutions, and examining the interrelationships of those systems and the ways they are shaped by cultural factors. Each study is written by a multidisciplinary team of social scientists. The authors seek to provide a basic understanding of the observed society, striving for a dynamic rather than a static portrayal. Particular attention is devoted to the people who make up the society, their origins, dominant beliefs and values, their common interests and the issues on which they are divided, the nature and extent of their involvement with national institutions, and their attitudes toward each other and toward their social system and political order.

The books represent the analysis of the authors and should not be construed as an expression of an official United States government position, policy, or decision. The authors have sought to adhere to accepted standards of scholarly objectivity. Corrections, additions, and suggestions for changes from readers will be welcomed for use in future editions.

Louis R. Mortimer
Chief
Federal Research Division
Library of Congress
Washington, D.C. 20540

Acknowledgments

The authors would like to acknowledge the contributions of Thomas E. Weil, Jan Knippers Black, Kenneth W. Martindale, David S. McMorris, Sally Engle Merry, and Frederick P. Munson, who wrote the 1971 first edition of *Uruguay: A Country Study*. The present volume incorporates portions of their work.

The authors are grateful to individuals in various agencies of the United States government, private institutions, and Uruguayan diplomatic offices, particularly the Uruguayan Mission to the Organization of American States, who gave their time, research materials, and special knowledge to provide information and perspective. These individuals include Ralph K. Benesch, who oversees the Country Studies/Area Handbook Program for the Department of the Army. None of these individuals, however, is in any way responsible for the work of the authors.

The authors also would like to thank those who contributed directly to the preparation of the manuscript. These include Lynne Shaner, who edited the chapters; Marilyn L. Majeska, who managed the editing; Andrea T. Merrill, who performed the final prepublication editorial review and managed production; Barbara Edgerton, Janie L. Gilchrist, and Izella Watson, who did the word processing; and Tim L. Merrill, who provided geographical assistance. In addition, Joan C. Cook compiled the index, and Malinda B. Neale and Linda Peterson of the Library of Congress Printing and Processing Section performed the phototypesetting, under the supervision of Peggy Pixley.

David P. Cabitto, assisted by Sandra K. Ferrell and Kimberly A. Lord, provided invaluable graphics support. Sandra K. Ferrell prepared the ranks and insignia charts; Kimberly A. Lord prepared the illustrations and all the maps except for the topography and drainage map, which was prepared by Harriett R. Blood.

Finally, the authors acknowledge the generosity of the individuals and the public and private agencies who allowed their photographs to be used in this study.

Acknowledgments

Contents

Chapter 3. The Economy 95

Brian D. McFeeters

Bibliography 249

Glossary 273

Index 277

List of Figures

Preface

Like its predecessor, this study is an attempt to examine objectively and concisely the dominant historical, social, economic, political, and military aspects of contemporary Uruguay. Sources of information included scholarly books, journals, monographs, official reports of governments and international organizations, and numerous periodicals. Chapter bibliographies appear at the end of the book; brief comments on sources recommended for further reading appear at the end of each chapter. To the extent possible, place-names follow the system adopted by the United States Board on Geographic Names. Measurements are given in the metric system; a conversion table is provided to assist readers unfamiliar with metric measurements (see table 1, Appendix). A glossary is also included.

Although there are numerous variations, Spanish surnames generally are composed of both the father's and the mother's family names, in that order. In the instance of José Batlle y Ordóñez, for example, Batlle is his patronymic, and Ordóñez is his mother's maiden name. In informal use, the matronymic is often dropped, a practice that has usually been followed in this book, except in cases where the individual could easily be confused with a relative.

The body of the text reflects information available as of December 1990. Certain other portions of the text, however, have been updated. The Introduction discusses significant events that have occurred since the completion of research; the Country Profile includes updated information as available; and the Bibliography lists recently published sources thought to be particularly helpful to the reader.

Country Profile

Country

Formal Name: Oriental Republic of Uruguay (República Oriental del Uruguay).

Short Form: Uruguay.

Term for Citizens: Uruguayan(s).

Capital: Montevideo.

Date of Independence: August 27, 1828. August 25 celebrated as a national holiday (Independence Day).

NOTE—The Country Profile contains updated information as available.

Geography

Size: 176,220 square kilometers.

Topography: Country consists mostly (75 percent) of gently rolling plateau, interrupted at two points by low hilly ridges (*cuchillas*). Remainder fertile coastal lowlands, including narrow coastal plain—sandy and marshy, occasionally broken by lagoons—and somewhat broader littorals of Río de la Plata and Río Uruguay.

Climate: Country situated in temperate zone (only Latin American country lying wholly outside tropics). Climate mild and fairly uniform nationwide, although northwestern area farther inland has warmer summers and drier winters than rest of country. Seasonal variations pronounced, but freezing temperatures almost unknown. High humidity, high winds, and fog common. Winter warm spells can be abruptly broken by a strong *pampero,* a chilly and occasionally violent wind from Argentine pampas.

Society

Population: In 1991 estimated at 3.1 million; annual rate of growth averaged 0.7 percent during 1981–88 period but fell to 0.6 percent in 1990–91. Relatively low birth rate (17 per 1,000 population in 1991). According to 1985 census, 87 percent of population lived in urban areas, Latin America's highest percentage.

Literacy and Education: In 1990 literacy rate 96 percent (highest in Latin America). System of universal, free, and secular education required total of nine years of compulsory school attendance, from ages six to fourteen. By 1985 an estimated 70 percent of secondary school-age children enrolled in secondary school (also highest rate in Latin America). Despite inadequate teaching resources, quality of education generally high.

Health: In 1984 total health care spending represented 8.1 percent of gross domestic product (GDP—see Glossary). In 1985 number of inhabitants per physician 466 (proportion similar to developed countries). In 1987 Montevideo had over sixty public health facilities, including seven major public hospitals. Total mortality rate just below 10 per 1,000 population in 1980s. In 1990 infant mortality 22 deaths per 1,000 population. Average life expectancy at birth in 1991 sixty-nine years for men and seventy-six years for women.

Language: Spanish.

Ethnic Groups: Largely homogeneous society. In 1990 about 88 percent of population white and of European descent; 8 percent mestizo; and 4 percent black.

Religion: In 1990 about 66 percent were professed Roman Catholics; 2 percent Protestants; and 2 percent Jews. Remainder nonprofessing or other (less than half of adult population attended church regularly).

Economy

Gross Domestic Product (GDP): Approximately US$9.2 billion in 1990, or US$2,970 per capita, making it one of highest-income countries in Latin America. As result of severe recession, real GDP declined by almost 17 percent during 1981–84 but increased after 1985. Led by growth in agriculture and fishing sectors, GDP grew by 6.6 percent in 1986 and 4.9 percent in 1987 but slowed to 0.5 percent in 1988, 1.5 percent in 1989, and 0.9 percent in 1990.

Agriculture: Self-sufficient in most basic foodstuffs. About 90 percent of country, including 8 percent arable land, can be used for some kind of agriculture, mainly for extensive livestock grazing, wheat, rice, corn, and sorghum. In 1988 agricultural activity, including fishing, directly generated 13 percent of GDP and provided over half of value of exports. Although sector's growth rate in 1989 was low (1 percent), its output increased an estimated 3.5 percent in 1990.

Industry: Accounted for 33 percent of GDP in 1988. Industrial sector geared mostly to small domestic market. Industries included meat processing, wool and hides, sugar, textiles, footwear, leather apparel, tires, cement, fishing, petroleum refining, and wine making. Industrial production growth rate in 1988 about –2.9 percent.

Mining and Energy: Exports granite and marble. Semiprecious stones also have been found in quantity. Primary sources of energy hydroelectricity and imported petroleum (mostly crude oil).

Services: Accounted for 42 percent of GDP in 1988, including 6 percent for transportation, storage, and communications and 15 percent for banking and commerce.

Currency and Exchange Rate: Uruguayan new peso. In 1990 average exchange rate was US$1 = N$Ur1,171. On December 31, 1990, buying and selling interbank rates were N$Ur1,573 and N$Ur1,594, respectively, per US$1. On March 2, 1992, average exchange rate was US$1 = N$Ur2,674.

Trade: Exports wool, meat, hides, manufactured goods, and rice (total about US$1.6 billion in 1989). Imports fuels and lubricants, metals, machinery, transportation equipment, and industrial chemicals (total about US$1.1 billion in 1989). Main export markets and sources of imports Brazil, Argentina, United States, and European Community.

Balance of Payments: Trade balance positive and steadily improving during most of 1980s. Current account balance negative until mid-1980s, owing to burden of debt service (reduced from US$613 million in 1988 to US$449 million in 1989). Foreign debt to United States in 1989 about US$6.2 billion of total US$6.7 billion foreign debt (one of developing world's highest per capita). Capital account balance positive for most of 1980s.

Fiscal Year: Calendar year.

Fiscal Policy: Stabilization plan of Julio María Sanguinetti (president, 1985–90)—designed to reduce deficit and inflation and improve balance of payments—had mixed results. Public-sector deficit declined, but inflation continued unabated, reaching at least 85 percent by 1989, owing to monetary and exchange-rate policies. Luis Alberto Lacalle de Herrera (president, 1990–) attempted to further cut fiscal deficit and tighten monetary policy by introducing new taxes on wages and increasing value-added tax (VAT— see Glossary) rate, gasoline prices, and public-sector tariffs. Nevertheless, inflation rose to 129 percent in 1990 but then dropped to 106 percent in 1991.

Transportation and Communications

Roads: One of best highway systems in Latin America. In 1989 about 50,000 kilometers total, including 6,800 kilometers paved roads, 3,000 kilometers gravel roads, and over 40,200 kilometers dirt roads.

Railroads: One of best rail systems in Latin America (but passenger service discontinued in 1988 because of declining ridership). In 1989 about 3,000 kilometers total, all 1.435-meter standard gauge and government owned.

Ports: Montevideo, Punta del Este, Colonia, Fray Bentos, Paysandú, and Salto principal ports.

Airports: Two international airports (Montevideo and Punte del Este) and fourteen other primarily commercial airports with permanent-surface runways.

Telecommunications: Most modern facilities concentrated in Montevideo. New nationwide radio-relay network. Total telephones in 1990 over 345,000 (highest per capita in South America). In

1990 ninety-nine AM (ten of them shortwave) radio stations, twenty-six television stations, and two satellite earth stations.

Government and Politics

Government: Republic with three separate branches of government. Constitution of 1967 institutionalized strong presidency, subject to legislative and judicial checks. Executive power exercised by president (elected for five-year term by simple majority of the people through unique voting system), vice president (who served as president of bicameral General Assembly), and Council of Ministers. General Assembly consisted of thirty-member Senate and ninety-nine-member Chamber of Representatives; members of both chambers elected to five-year terms through proportional representation system. Independent judicial branch headed by Supreme Court of Justice. Country's administrative subdivisions consisted of nineteen departments, each headed by a governor, subordinate to central government and responsible for local administration. Unusual electoral system combined primaries and a general election in one event characterized by a "double simultaneous vote," allowing each party's factions to run rival lists of candidates.

Politics: Civilian government restored in 1985 after twelve years of military rule. Lacalle of conservative National Party (Partido Nacional, usually referred to as Blancos)—elected president in November 1989 in country's first free election since 1971—succeeded Sanguinetti of liberal Colorado Party (Partido Colorado) on March 1, 1990. Two-party system of these rival parties had dominated since nineteenth century but was dealt strong challenge in November 1989 elections by win of mayorship of Montevideo by Broad Front (Frente Amplio), a leftist coalition. Other parties in 1989 elections included various factions of Colorado Party and National Party and new left-of-center, social democratic coalition, New Sector (Nuevo Espacio).

International Relations: Guided historically by principles of nonintervention, respect for national sovereignty, and reliance on rule of law to settle disputes. Traditionally an active participant in international and regional organizations. During 1973–85 period of military rule, "military diplomacy" focused on national and regional subversion and geopolitical concerns. Sanguinetti renewed relations with Cuba, Nicaragua, and China and strengthened relations with Soviet Union. Excellent bilateral relations with United States during 1985–90 period. Lacalle continued traditional guidelines of Uruguayan foreign policy and placed emphasis on regional integration, especially with Argentina and Brazil. Although somewhat ambivalent toward United States policy on drug trafficking, Lacalle strongly endorsed President George H.W. Bush's free-trade Enterprise for the Americas Initiative of June 1990.

International Agreements and Memberships: Member of at least thirty-two international organizations, including Organization of American States, United Nations and most of its specialized agencies, World Bank (see Glossary), International Monetary Fund (IMF—see Glossary), General Agreement on Tariffs and Trade, International Telecommunications Satellite Organization, Latin American Economic System, and Latin American Integration Association. Signatory of Inter-American Treaty of Reciprocal Assistance (Rio Treaty), Treaty for the Prohibition of Nuclear Weapons in Latin America (Tlatelolco Treaty), and Río de la Plata Basin Treaty.

National Security

Armed Forces: Total strength in 1991 estimated at 22,900: army, 16,000; navy, 3,500; and air force, 3,400.

Organization: Country divided into four military regions headquartered in Montevideo (I), San José (II), Paso de los Toros (III), and Maldonado (IV). Each military region headquarters hosted one of four administrative army corps headquarters. Montevideo's First Corps traditionally most powerful of army's main command elements. Army had one independent infantry brigade, fifteen infantry battalions, six engineer battalions, six artillery battalions, and ten cavalry battalions. Navy organized into one fleet command divided into one escort division and one patrol division. Navy also commanded naval air, coast guard, marines, and National Maritime Police. Air force organized into tactical, training, and matériel commands, principally Tactical Air Command.

Equipment: Services had mostly obsolete United States equipment in 1991. Army had sixty-seven United States-made light tanks; armored vehicles from Belgium, Brazil, United States, and Federal Republic of Germany (West Germany); and Swedish-, Argentine-, and United States-made artillery pieces. Navy's former United States equipment included one frigate, one destroyer escort, one corvette, and two large patrol craft. French-made equipment included three frigates and three large patrol craft. Fleet included one minesweeper, five amphibious landing craft, and one training vessel. Air force had thirty-three combat aircraft (seven of them trainers).

Police: Total strength in 1990 estimated at 17,500. About 40 percent of police assigned to urban areas (with at least 20 percent in Montevideo). National Police subordinate to Ministry of the Interior and organized into four operating agencies: Montevideo Police, Interior Police, National Traffic Police, and National Corps of Firemen. Two police paramilitary organizations—Republican Guard and Metropolitan Guard—assigned to capital area for ceremonial and guard or riot-control duties, respectively.

Figure 1. Administrative Divisions of Uruguay, 1990

Introduction

URUGUAY USED TO BE KNOWN as the "Switzerland of South America," but clearly not because of any geographical similarity. Although it is the second smallest republic in South America (after Suriname), Uruguay is more than four times larger than landlocked Switzerland, and its highest peak is only 501 meters. Rather, the analogy was made because Uruguay enjoyed other Swiss-like attributes. It was a peaceful, conservative country with a bountiful, livestock-based economy. It was also home to South America's first social democracy; a cradle-to-grave welfare system; and a largely urban, homogeneous, and relatively well-educated population. A political slogan of the 1940s proudly boasted, "There's no place like Uruguay."

Beginning with the prolonged stagnation of their country's industrial and livestock sectors in the mid-1950s, however, Uruguayans began losing their economic well-being, civility, and tranquillity. By the late 1960s, Uruguay was suffering from high inflation and public deficits and was governed by an authoritarian president, instead of by the former revolving collegial executive (*colegiado*) that had been modeled on the Swiss system and designed to avoid a concentration of power. In 1973 Uruguayans also lost their cherished freedom and their democratic system when the country was plunged into one of Latin America's most repressive military dictatorships (1973–85). The country's democratic system was not fully restored until 1990.

Having fallen far behind many countries economically, Uruguayans could only reminisce about their former welfare state. In a discussion of Uruguay's global ranking, the late political scientist and Uruguay specialist Charles Guy Gillespie noted that "Uruguayan society in 1990 presented a rather contradictory picture of advanced social indicators and declining economic status." Since Gillespie's research was completed, Uruguay has risen to be the highest ranking country in South America and Central America on the United Nations Development Programme's 1991 Human Development Index (HDI), a measure that combines per capita gross domestic product (GDP—see Glossary) with such factors as longevity and access to education. In world HDI ranking, however, Uruguay slipped from twenty-ninth place in 1990 to thirty-first place in the 1991 report.

The assumption of the presidency by Luis Alberto Lacalle de Herrera in 1990 improved the country's political development index by marking the success of Uruguay's five-year transition back to democracy. Undeterred by their nation's serious economic problems, tens of thousands of the Uruguayans who had fled the country during the military regime returned home. Instead of the old Uruguay, however, they found their traditionally statist society undergoing privatization and sharp cutbacks in social services under the Lacalle government's plan to turn the nation into a South American "Singapore."

Yet, unlike the Swiss, for whom modernization and traditionalism were mutually compatible, Uruguayans in general were stubbornly resistant to Lacalle's vision of a free-market economy, which had been much talked about during the previous administration of Julio María Sanguinetti Cairolo (1985–90), and to changing their old ways, which still included horse-and-buggy milk deliveries in Montevideo. This predilection for traditionalism over modernism was explained in part by the fact that Uruguay, a country with a low birth rate and long life expectancy, had Latin America's oldest population. With a work force of 1.4 million in 1990, Uruguay had 650,000 people receiving pensions. Another explanation was a general uncertainty as to whether modernization offered a better future. As Jorge Batlle Ibáñez, a 1989 presidential candidate, explained in the weekly news magazine *Búsqueda:*

> Uruguay is the most difficult country in Latin America to change because, being the smallest [sic] country, it lacks masses that could switch rapidly or violently from one side to the other, and it has a relatively prosperous middle class that feels there are few opportunities for easily finding another destiny without losing what they already have.

Nevertheless, the new destiny as a regional free-trade and financial center envisioned for the nation by Lacalle seemed designed to make better use of the country's existing geographic and economic advantages, as well as its historical role as gatekeeper to the Río de la Plata Basin trade region.

Although not a maritime nation, Uruguay is surrounded on three sides by water. Three rivers (the Río de la Plata, one of the widest rivers in the world; the Río Uruguay; and the Río Yaguarón), a lake (Laguna Merín), and the Atlantic Ocean border the country. The main port and capital city of Montevideo, founded in 1726, is situated on strategic trade routes.

Even the name of Uruguay, first applied to the Río Uruguay, has river-related origins. Its etymology derives from either *urugua,* a Guaraní Indian word meaning a species of mussel, thus Río

Uruguay, "the river of shellfish"; or the Guaraní word components *uru* (a kind of bird that lived near the river); *gua* ("to proceed from"); and *y* ("water").

Uruguay also has long been associated with cattle and sheep and the gauchos who have herded them, as well as with verdant grasslands. The country's traditional beef and wool exports have been well known in world markets. A land of gentle hills and rolling plateau covered by tall prairie grass, Uruguay has been often referred to in travel books as "the purple land" since the publication in 1885 of a book by British naturalist and travel writer W.H. Hudson. In addition to the purple verbena wildflowers (*margaritas*) that populate the grasslands from December through March, the red sandstone in the northern area has a faint purplish hue.

When discovered by Spanish conquistador Juan Díaz de Solís in 1516, the Río de la Plata region was inhabited only by fierce Charrúa and Guaraní Indians and an enormous wildlife population, including ostrich-like birds called rheas. The region disappointed Spaniards in search of gold and silver riches. As a consequence, the first Spanish settlement, in Soriano at the mouth of the Río Negro in the southwest, was not established until 1624, after the gold fever had cooled. Unlike elsewhere in Latin America, the native population, which remained hostile to settlers, was left relatively undisturbed, at least until the beginning of the seventeenth century.

Jesuit and Franciscan missionaries proselytized among the Indians, but with limited success. Most of the Indians in fact remained hostile and eventually perished in battles with Spanish and Portuguese forces (but not, as in other places in the Americas, in working the land or mines as serfs). Because the native population was relatively small and so few Indians survived (the last Charrúa Indian died in 1948), present-day Uruguay, unlike most Latin American countries, has only an 8 percent mestizo presence.

With the separation of their thrones in the mid-seventeenth century after sixty years of joint rule, Spain and Portugal began an intense rivalry for control of the Río de la Plata region, mainly because of its strategic trade location. From 1680, when the Portuguese established their first settlement at Colonia del Sacramento, to 1827, the forces of Spain and Portugal fought over the region known as the Banda Oriental (eastern side, or bank), the fertile plain east of the Río Uruguay that would later become known as Uruguay.

Much of Uruguay's nineteenth-century history featured an endless succession of invasions, coups, dictatorships, and civil wars. However, the half-year-long occupation of Montevideo by British forces in 1807, followed by an invasion of British merchants, left the city with an enduring cultural legacy. It included the country's first printing press and an English/Spanish weekly newspaper, *The Southern Star/La Estrella del Sur,* which introduced Montevideans to British democracy and strengthened a desire among them for self-government and independence from Spain. Accordingly, their resentment of being subordinate to the viceroyalty capital of Buenos Aires grew.

The nine-year campaign (1811–20) by José Gervasio Artigas to take control of Montevideo successively from the Spanish, the Argentines, and the Portuguese engendered a new sense of nationality among the residents of the Banda Oriental. The announcement by the Portuguese in 1821 that Brazil was annexing the Banda Oriental and renaming it the Cisplatine Province prompted Juan Antonio Lavalleja to launch a guerrilla war against Brazilian forces. Lavalleja and his fellow revolutionaries (later called the Thirty-Three Heroes), assisted by Argentine troops, sparked a countrywide insurgency that escalated into a war between Argentina and Brazil (1825–28). Aided by Britain's mediation, both Argentina and Brazil renounced their claims to the Banda Oriental, at least in theory, and the Oriental Republic of Uruguay (República Oriental del Uruguay) became officially independent on August 27, 1828. Uruguay was the last nation in South America to be created from the Spanish colonies.

The new nation's first constitution, a liberal document, was adopted on July 18, 1830, and would remain unchanged for eighty-seven years. Shortly after its adoption, Uruguay's two main political parties—the Colorado Party (Partido Colorado) and the National Party (Partido Nacional, usually referred to as the Blancos)—emerged from armed clashes. The Colorado Party was composed of Montevideo-based middle-class liberals, whereas the National Party was made up of rural-based conservative landowners and merchants. Their mutual hostility erupted into the Great War (Guerra Grande, 1843–52), in which Colorado-held Montevideo was once again besieged in another nine-year war, this time involving Uruguayan, Argentine, Brazilian, French, British, and Italian forces (including Italian patriot Giuseppe Garibaldi). Following the war, which was economically disastrous for Uruguay, a policy of fusion (*fusión*), in which the Colorado and National parties agreed to cooperate, created the political framework and stability that were conducive to economic recovery and growth.

The fusion policy was cast aside with the onset of the War of the Triple Alliance (1865–70), in which Colorado-ruled Uruguay was, ironically, an ally of Argentina and Brazil against hopelessly outmatched Paraguay. The war ended armed foreign intervention in Uruguayan affairs, but fighting between the gaucho forces of the ruling Colorados and the opposition Blancos resumed. In 1872, however, the two parties reached an accord under which the National Party was given control of four of the country's departments, but the Colorado Party remained in power. This new policy of coparticipation (*coparticipación*) represented a compromise between the two parties and was a policy that would continue in Uruguayan politics. A political watershed in Uruguay's struggle for stability was another interparty accord reached in 1897, following a civil war, under which all citizens were guaranteed political rights and the National Party increased the number of departments under its control to six.

In the last quarter of the nineteenth century, heavy immigration from Europe, either directly or by way of Argentina or Brazil, propelled social and political changes, and Uruguay made progress toward becoming a more stable and peaceful state. By 1872 one-fourth of the population was foreign born and by 1900, one-third. The European immigration produced an urban and secular society that was largely middle class, with European values. The northern European immigrants tended to be of middle-class origin, whereas the predominant Spaniards and Italians were more often of working-class origin.

Uruguay adopted free, compulsory, and secular education in 1876, thanks to the efforts of educator José Pedro Varela (president, 1875–76), who was influenced by Horace Mann of the United States. Varela lived only thirty-five years, but his basic principles of education, which were incorporated into the 1877 Law of Common Education, have endured, allowing Uruguay to become one of the most literate of Latin American nations.

The foundations of the modern state and of the governmental institutions and political traditions were laid in the first two decades of the twentieth century, but particularly during the second presidential term of the Colorado Party's José Batlle y Ordóñez (1903–07, 1911–15). Under Batlle y Ordóñez's influence, Uruguay implemented even more profound social reforms—becoming Latin America's first country to adopt a minimum wage scale for its agricultural workers, obligatory voting, and women's suffrage—and became a stable social democracy modeled on the Swiss system, which Batlle y Ordóñez had studied in Switzerland between terms. Batlle y Ordóñez also instituted a Swiss-style presidency designed to prevent dictatorships. Under it, the nine members of the National Council of Administration (Consejo Nacional de Administración), or collegial executive (*colegiado*), rotated the presidency for one-year terms. Batlle y Ordóñez's new executive system and social reforms were adopted in the 1917 constitution.

With revenue generated from their country's vast wool and beef exports, Uruguayans enjoyed Latin America's highest standard of living, which included free public education through the university level, expanded public-sector employment, and a generous social welfare system that permitted people (with the exception of the rural poor) to retire in middle age. Uruguay was so prosperous that in 1920 it forgave France a US$100 million debt.

The "welfare state" system limited the appeal of revolutionary ideologies and parties by co-opting their programs, minimizing social and economic stratification, and giving the majority of the population a stake in the existing order. These and other factors, such as racial and ethnic homogeneity and the high level of mobility within the predominantly middle-class social structure, all contributed to the relative stability of the country's democratic system. Uruguay ranked with Chile and Costa Rica as one of the most stable democracies in Latin America, although it, like most countries, suffered from the Great Depression. Uruguay was subjected to dictatorial rule only once during the first half of the twentieth century (1933–38). Even then, the ad hoc regime was headed by a civilian, Gabriel Terra, who had been elected president, at least initially. Moreover, Terra preserved the country's social reforms.

Uruguay enjoyed a boom in wool and meat exports during World War II and the Korean War. Unlike Argentina, it sided with the Allies during World War II and hosted United States air and naval bases. Economic stagnation and decline, however, followed the post-Korean War drop in world demand for livestock products. Pressures created by those developments—combined with growing political lethargy, sectarianism, and governmental inefficiency and corruption—unraveled the nation's delicate social fabric and precipitated rising levels of class conflict. In the second half of the 1960s, Uruguay was racked by continual labor militancy and urban terrorism by the National Liberation Movement-Tupamaros (Movimiento de Liberación Nacional-Tupamaros—MLN-T) that propelled the military increasingly into the political arena.

Jorge Pacheco Areco (1967–72) and Juan María Bordaberry Arocena (1972–76), both members of the Colorado Party, governed under increasingly frequent states of siege and allowed the military to pursue its national security goals without regard for constitutional safeguards or laws. Put in charge of fighting the Tupamaros in late 1971, the armed forces defeated the urban guerrillas within six months. Nevertheless, repression continued, and the military assumed a greater political role, in effect making

Bordaberry little more than a figurehead president. Opposing these Colorado Party regimes were the National Party and the newly formed Broad Front (Frente Amplio), a coalition of disaffected Colorados, socialists, communists, and other left-of-center parties. When the General Assembly (the legislature) resisted final approval of draconian national security measures imposed by the military, Bordaberry abolished the General Assembly on June 27, 1973, thereby commencing the dictatorship. The regime prohibited all political party activity, suppressed the opposition press, disbanded the National Convention of Workers (Convención Nacional de Trabajadores—CNT) as well as all parties in the Broad Front, arrested left-of-center political and union leaders, and prohibited all labor union activities. In June 1976, after forcing Bordaberry to resign, the military assumed total control of the country.

According to Amnesty International, a private human rights organization, under the military regime Uruguay had the world's highest per capita ratio of political prisoners: one in every 500 citizens. By 1980 many citizens had been detained and tortured at some point, and one in every 500 had received a sentence of six years or longer. Between 300,000 and 400,000 Uruguayans went into exile.

Fortunately for Uruguayan democracy, the military's attempt to institutionalize its rule by submitting its proposed constitutional reform to a national referendum in November 1980 backfired. By a vote of 57 percent to 43 percent, Uruguayans rejected the proposed national security state. As a result, Lieutenant General (retired) Gregorio Alvarez Armelino (1981–85) was obliged to transfer power to an elected civilian, Julio María Sanguinetti.

During the first half of the Sanguinetti administration, Uruguay became an atypical island of economic stability and, thanks to a deregulated financial system, a refuge for capital fleeing Argentina and Brazil. Although Uruguay bore a heavy foreign debt load, it never stopped paying on its debt. Uruguay also had important gold reserves, one of the largest in proportion to its indebtedness and economic potential. During the final two years of Sanguinetti's administration, however, the economy suffered a downturn. In 1989 inflation had increased to 85 percent, the foreign debt to US$6.7 billion, and the fiscal deficit to 8.5 percent of GDP, and the purchasing power of salaries had fallen.

During Sanguinetti's administration, Uruguay, like other Latin American countries undergoing a transition from military dictatorship to democracy, found itself confronted with the dilemma of having to decide between prosecuting military officers for crimes committed during the period of military rule, and thereby risk antagonizing civil-military relations, or granting them a blanket amnesty. Sanguinetti had noted that every conflict in Uruguayan history was followed by a generous amnesty law. Nevertheless, a 1986 law granting amnesty to the military was so controversial that a national referendum on the issue had to be held. In a 1989 referendum, a majority of the population upheld the law exempting military officers from human rights prosecutions.

Thus, Lacalle was spared from having to contend with the amnesty issue after assuming office as Uruguay's president. Yet, he quickly caused grumbling within the armed forces by asserting his presidential prerogative and naming two trusted officers to head the navy and air force, thereby sidestepping the order of military seniority. The military was already unhappy with its shrinking size and the reduction in the military budget during the Sanguinetti administration.

Although the military reaffirmed its subservience to the nation's democracy, Lacalle ordered the Ministry of National Defense in May 1990 to formulate a new armed forces doctrine "within the framework of the Constitution and current laws." The guidelines were to restrict its scope of action by excluding the military from responding to ordinary internal conflicts that came within the sphere of the police. Nevertheless, Army Commander Lieutenant General Guillermo de Nava raised concerns among Uruguayan politicians because of his public endorsement of a retired general's statements in April 1991 warning of a comeback by the Tupamaros and the Communist Party of Uruguay and calling for Uruguayan society to be placed on a "red alert."

Lacalle also embarked on an austere economic adjustment program that had two main components: a reduction in public spending and the inflation rate, as well as an increase in certain taxes. He succeeded in his first year in office in cutting spending by 10 percent and increasing revenue by 9 percent. Nevertheless, real wages in the public sector fell by 9 percent and in the private sector, by 6 percent; GDP growth in 1990 was negligible; and inflation reached 129 percent by year's end.

The popularity of the Blancos plummeted from about 38 percent at the time of the 1989 election to 21 percent in December 1990, according to a public opinion poll published by *Búsqueda*. Lacalle at least shared company with the Marxist mayor of Montevideo, the Broad Front's Tabaré Vázquez, whose popularity fell from 35 to 30 percent; national support for the Broad Front slipped from 26 to 24 percent. Essentially, in the wake of the 1989 elections the two traditional parties no longer dominated Uruguay, and Montevideo in particular. (Vázquez even assumed a diplomatic role by paying a five-day visit to Cuba in June 1991 and signing a five-year agreement of intent for bilateral cooperation with Havana.)

Lacking a parliamentary majority, Lacalle formed a governing coalition, National Coincidence (Coincidencia Nacional), with the Colorados but encountered strong resistance to his proposed austerity and privatization programs. Labor union opposition to these plans and support of wage claims increased during 1991, taking the form of work stoppages, slowdowns, and, in May, a one-day general strike (the third since Lacalle took office). Instead of using the unpopular term *privatization* to describe his economic policy agenda, Lacalle called instead for a redefinition of the role of the state, deregulation, and elimination of monopolies.

In the first of a number of proposed privatizations (which included the telephone company, the state airline, and state monopolies on insurance, port services, and production of alcohol), the government sold the state-owned Commercial Bank (Banco Commercial) in July 1990 to a group of international investors. They and other multinational investors regarded Uruguay as an increasingly important regional financial market because of its liberal foreign investment exchange and banking regulations, strategic location, stable political climate, and relatively predictable economic policies.

Like Switzerland, Uruguay in 1990 continued to serve as an international meeting place and a banking center. Uruguay has long been known as a location for international economic conferences. The eleven-member Latin American Integration Association (Asociación Latinoamericana de Integración—ALADI; see Glossary) has been headquartered in Montevideo since its inception in 1980. For many of the West's economists, in the early 1990s the word *Uruguay* was synonymous with the Uruguay Round of negotiations of the General Agreement on Tariffs and Trade (GATT—see Glossary). International meetings often have been held in Punta del Este, a popular resort city.

Aided by its bank secrecy laws first implemented by the military regime in the early 1980s, Uruguay built up its offshore banking system beginning in 1989. A negative outgrowth of this was the nation's growing reputation as a center for money laundering; such activity increased dramatically in Uruguay after Colombian drug traffickers abandoned Panama following the United States military intervention in December 1989. According to a document issued by the United States Department of State in April 1991, Uruguay continued to be a "significant" center for money laundering because of its free-trade system, the large number of currency exchange houses (more than seventy in Montevideo), and the absence of government regulation of the operation and movement of funds. In May 1991, Uruguay and the United States signed an agreement, which was similar to one signed between Switzerland and the United States that year, to facilitate joint action against money laundering operations by drug smugglers. The accord had not yet gone into effect as of mid-July 1991, pending ratification by the legislatures of both countries.

Most Uruguayans were more concerned with their own bank accounts than with those of foreign drug traffickers. Lacalle did not improve his standing in the popularity polls by introducing "unpleasant" economic measures in his speech on his first anniversary in office. He also warned the General Assembly that unless it reformed the social security system by curbing its generous benefits (already cut by 17.4 percent in 1990), his savings in controlling public expenditures would be lost. Although Uruguay supported the world embargo against Iraq, its effects were, in Lacalle's words, "particularly painful" for Uruguay because of lost mutton exports to Iraq and higher oil import costs.

On March 26, 1991, Uruguay sought to revive its export sector by signing, along with Argentina, Brazil, and Paraguay, the Treaty of Asunción, a pact that created the Southern Cone Common Market (Mercado Común del Sur—Mercosur). Mercosur, which was scheduled to go into effect on January 1, 1995 (a member, however, could decide to drop out before then), was the goal of various regional integration agreements, such as the River Transport System, consisting of the Río Paraguay-Río Paraná-Río Uruguay waterway.

Mercosur was formed in part in response to President George H.W. Bush's June 1990 Enterprise for the Americas Initiative (see Glossary). The Mercosur nations and the United States signed a letter of intent on June 19, 1991, that could eventually lead to a free-trade pact modeled on the Mexico-United States accord. However, serious obstacles to a free-trade pact between the United States and the Mercosur nations remained, such as a collective US$200 billion foreign debt and persistent regional trade barriers.

Although Uruguay's Senate ratified the country's participation in Mercosur, the nation's initial enthusiasm soon waned. Uruguayan business and agricultural organizations were concerned that neighboring giants, particularly Brazil, would only take advantage of lower Uruguayan tariffs to increase competition. In an interview with the Buenos Aires daily *El Clarín* in late June 1991, Lacalle said, somewhat optimistically, that Uruguayan businessmen were viewing Mercosur not with resistance but with feelings of "caution, a reasonable expectation, a desire for a smooth transition period."

Of course, the emergence of Mercosur and the prospect of a free-trade agreement with the United States were anathema to the Uruguayan left. The Broad Front also feared proposed military cooperation within Mercosur, arguing that Uruguay could become a pawn of Argentina and Brazil. In any event, Montevideo, in its growing capacity as a regional financial and banking services center and potential hub of free trade—despite its Marxist mayor—seemed in July 1991 to be moving closer, if reluctantly, to becoming what Lacalle envisioned as the "gateway" to Mercosur.

July 16, 1991

* * *

In 1992 Mercosur continued to be President Lacalle's main instrument for ensuring that competition came to his country. Aided by events in Eastern Europe, Lacalle's tariff-free trading vision of Uruguay's future found greater receptivity among Uruguayans to free-market reforms and smaller government. Nevertheless, resistance to the Lacalle government's attempts to restructure the state sector remained substantial. Uruguayan businessmen worried that Argentine and Brazilian industries would devour them. According to a poll taken in February 1992, about 54 percent of the Uruguayans who were queried opposed the privatization policy.

With only thirty-nine seats in the Chamber of Representatives, the Lacalle government was forced to negotiate support for each of its initiatives with the Colorado Party (thirty seats), Broad Front (twenty-one seats), and New Sector (Nuevo Espacio; nine seats). Consequently, it was not until September 1991, by which time Lacalle's popularity had fallen to 11 percent, that the General Assembly narrowly approved his privatization law (the Public Companies Law), after eighteen months of drafting it and four months of debating it. This law allowed private entrepreneurs to compete in a bidding system for the right to privatize public services.

Reflecting growing opposition to his economic policy of austerity and privatization, Lacalle's National Coincidence alliance and his narrow parliamentary majority collapsed by early 1992. At the end of January 1992, Lacalle had to call for the resignation of his cabinet ministers, who were then "provisionally ratified." By that April, dissent had emerged even within the ruling National Party, with two factions opposing the strong tightening of workers' salaries, which had particularly affected state workers. One of these factions, calling itself the Progressive Pole (Polo Progresista) and supported by several prominent Blancos, including Senator Alberto Sáenz de Zumarán, launched itself as a new party on May 10. Opposition to Lacalle's new law focused on the major privatizations planned for Uruguayan National Airlines (Primeras Líneas Uruguayas de Navegación Aérea—PLUNA), the National Administration for the Generation and Transmission of Electricity (Administración Nacional de Usinas y Transmisiones Eléctricas—UTE), and the National Administration of Fuels, Alcohol, and Portland Cement (Administración Nacional de Combustibles, Alcohol, y Portland—ANCAP). So-called peripheral divestments included the National Printing Press (Imprensa Nacional), hospital services, administration of air terminals and three port terminals, and agricultural development facilities. Confrontations were imminent within these and other state enterprises, which operated as autonomous entities (autonomous agencies or state enterprises; see Glossary) run by five-member executive boards in which three were progovernment party members and two were opposition party members. The opposition Colorado Party members were expected to ally themselves with the National Party members opposed to the government's economic policy.

The government's salary measure, which prompted the sixth general strike against the government, was implemented as a result of an agreement with the International Monetary Fund (IMF—see Glossary) to unfreeze some US$300 million in credits to be used for repaying the US$7.4 billion foreign debt, which grew by US$405 million in the Lacalle administration's first two years.

In a few other areas, Uruguay made some good economic progress in 1991. Buoyed by 850,000 tourists plus internal demand (both consumption and investment), the country enjoyed robust growth during the year. Inflation was at least 90 percent, as compared with 129 percent in 1990.

However, other economic and social problems worsened. In addition to the increase in trade union conflicts, unemployment rose from 8.4 percent in January 1991 to 9.2 percent at the end of 1991, and GDP grew by at best 0.5 percent in 1991, as compared with 0.9 percent in 1990. Moreover, according to a report by the General Directorate of Statistics and Census based on a household survey, 15.8 percent of all Uruguayan families were living in a state of "critical poverty" in 1991 (as compared with 11 percent in 1981), while 22.3 percent lacked one or more basic needs, such as housing, water supply, sanitation, education, or a living wage.

Meanwhile, middle-class Uruguayans and the political system were resisting Lacalle's proposals to restructure the old welfare system, such as a proposal to raise the qualifying age for retirement pensions—fifty-five years of age for women and sixty for men—by five years. In his speech to the nation on May 26, 1992, Lacalle pointed out that the country's social security bill had risen from US$718 million in 1985 to US$1.1 billion in 1991, creating an ever-widening deficit.

Ironically, the country was enjoying a bout of euphoria over the startling discovery of a gold-laden Spanish galleon, *El Preciado,* that sank eight kilometers from the Montevideo harbor in June 1792. Many Uruguayans, including some politicians and government officials, anticipated a windfall that could be used for social services from the treasure and from as many as seven other sunken ships known to be in the area with large amounts of gold. Based on the amount of gold already recovered, the *El Preciado* booty was estimated to be worth from US$300 million to US$3 billion.

In contrast to the plunging popularity of Lacalle and his National Party, the popularity rating of Montevideo's leftist mayor, Tabaré Vázquez, soared to 53 percent in September 1991, increasing the Broad Front's confidence of victory in the 1994 elections. By November 1991, the Broad Front's popularity had risen to 24 percent, making it the second most popular party after the Colorado Party, which had a 41 percent popularity rating (the National Party was supported by only 19 percent of those surveyed in an April 1992 poll). Taking a cue from events in the former Soviet Union, the Broad Front officially abandoned its commitment to Marxist-Leninist principles.

In April 1992, however, the Broad Front's most radical member, the Uruguayan Revolutionary Movement (Movimiento Revolucionario Oriental—MRO), stepped back into an earlier, dark era by endorsing "an armed struggle strategy." That approach was also adopted by a self-styled right-wing paramilitary group linked to military officers and called the Juan Antonio Lavalleja Command (Comando Juan Antonio Lavalleja), which launched a series of bombings, including one against Sanguinetti's office, and bomb threats in May. The resulting climate of fear and restlessness, which had characterized the early 1970s, seemed anachronistic in the Uruguay of the 1990s, where democracy supposedly had been consolidated. The military-linked terrorism and the public remarks made by some retired military officers revealing sentiment in favor of a coup also seemed to reflect growing military uneasiness over the prospects of a Broad Front electoral victory in 1994.

June 4, 1992   Rex A. Hudson

Chapter 1. Historical Setting

José Gervasio Artigas, leader of the independence movement

WHEN SPANIARDS DISCOVERED the territory of present-day Uruguay in 1516, they found only a rolling prairie populated by groups of Indians living in primitive conditions. When confronted by the Spaniards, the Indians fiercely defended their freedom and their independent way of life. Their continued ferocious resistance to Spanish conquest, combined with the absence of gold and silver, discouraged settlement in this region during the sixteenth and early seventeenth centuries. Colonization by Spain began to increase, however, when Portugal showed an interest in expanding Brazil's frontiers to the Río de la Plata Estuary in the late seventeenth century (see fig. 1). Indeed, the early history of Uruguay is dominated by the struggle between Spain and Portugal and then between Brazil and Argentina for control of the Banda Oriental (as Uruguay was then known), the eastern side, or bank, so called because the territory lies to the east of the Río Uruguay, which forms the border with Argentina and flows into the Río de la Plata.

The conquistadors imported cattle, which were well suited to the region, with its abundant pastureland, temperate climate, and ample water supply. Cattle soon became the main source of wealth and consequently the main attraction of the region, and the territory was opened up by hardy pioneers and gauchos, or cowboys, whose wide-ranging way of life contributed in no small part to the spirit of independence that has long characterized Uruguay. Montevideo was founded by the Spanish in the early eighteenth century as a military stronghold. The Spanish fleet used its natural harbor, which soon developed into a commercial center competing with Buenos Aires, the Argentine capital established on the opposite shore of the Río de la Plata.

The move to independence began, as elsewhere in Latin America, in the early nineteenth century. Uruguay's revolt against Spain was initiated in 1811 by José Gervasio Artigas, a gaucho chieftain who became a hero of the independence movement. Artigas is known to Uruguayans as the father of Uruguayan independence, although his attempt to gain autonomy for the country within the boundaries of a regional federation was unsuccessful. Independence was not finally and formally achieved until 1828, following a war between Brazil and Uruguayan patriots supported by Argentina. British diplomatic mediation ended the conflict and resulted in the recognition of the Oriental Republic of Uruguay (República Oriental del Uruguay) as an independent state. Nevertheless, civil wars, invasions, and foreign intervention continued to disrupt the nation's development until the end of the nineteenth century.

The two political parties that have dominated Uruguayan political life since independence were born in these early years of instability, although at that time they were little more than feuding bands of gauchos. The issue that provoked the initial major confrontation was federalism versus unitary rule. In 1838 the federalist sympathies of General Manuel Oribe (president, 1835–38) led to a revolt by the forces of General José Fructoso Rivera (president, 1830–35), who again became president following the defeat of Oribe and his followers. Oribe's forces, supported by merchants, landowners, and the high clergy, became known as Blancos in reference to the white (*blanco*) hatbands they wore to distinguish their own men from the enemy on the field of battle. Rivera's forces, representing more liberal urban elements, were distinguished by red (*colorado*) hatbands and thus were designated Colorados. The political lines drawn in the 1830s evolved into two rival parties: the Colorado Party (Partido Colorado), which identified itself as the defender of Uruguayan sovereignty and as the champion of the common man and liberalism, and the National Party (Partido Nacional, usually referred to as the Blancos), which stood for order and conservatism and declared itself protector of the faith.

During the last three decades of the nineteenth century, a period that included fifteen years of military rule, there were frequent confrontations and clashes between the Colorados and the Blancos and among competing rival factions of the Colorados. A growing gulf between the capital city and the interior contributed to a solidification of the previously somewhat amorphous ideologies of the two parties as the Colorados recruited urban immigrant groups, especially laborers, and the Blancos represented more conservative rural elements.

Political stability came about in the first two decades of the twentieth century largely through the efforts of the dominant figure in the Colorado Party. José Batlle y Ordóñez (president, 1903–07, 1911–15) brilliantly promoted the social, economic, and political modernization of the country until his death in 1929, guiding a social transformation that reordered virtually every aspect of national life. His programs included the establishment of a comprehensive social welfare program, the encouragement of domestic industry, the improvement of working conditions, the expansion of education, and the separation of church and state.

Batlle y Ordóñez's Colorado successors did not uniformly or consistently share his commitment to economic and social reform, but progress toward political, social, and economic modernization nevertheless continued. Between 1946 and 1956, Luis Batlle Berres (president, 1947–51), a nephew of Batlle y Ordóñez, was the leading political figure. Espousing neo-Batllism, he attempted to further industrialize the economy, develop its agricultural sector, and expand the state apparatus, as well as to renew social progress. But the process came to a halt in the mid-1950s as a result of economic difficulties and ended with the triumph of the National Party (the Blancos) in 1958, after more than ninety years of Colorado government.

During the eight Blanco administrations (1958–67), instruments of state-directed economic policy were dismantled, relations with the International Monetary Fund (IMF—see Glossary) became closer, and the livestock sector became increasingly important. Nevertheless, the economic crisis continued, and political and social turbulence increased. Unions formed a centralized organization in which the left had a dominant influence, and an urban guerrilla group, the National Liberation Movement-Tupamaros (Movimiento de Liberación Nacional-Tupamaros—MLN–T) was formed.

In 1967 the Colorados regained power, but President Jorge Pacheco Areco (1967–72) enforced a limited state of siege throughout most of his tenure. He applied a price- and wage-freeze policy to fight inflation, banned leftist groups, and called in the military to repress the Tupamaros, whose acts of urban terrorism posed a major national security threat. In 1972 Pacheco's successor, President Juan María Bordaberry Arocena (1972–76), supported by the military, declared a state of "internal war," closed the General Assembly, persecuted the opposition, banned unions and leftist parties, and curtailed civil liberties. The military dictatorship that he instituted also implemented a neoliberal, monetarist, economic policy that sought to reverse years of capital flight and economic stagnation by increasing exports and controlling inflation. Although it scored some economic successes, the military suffered a defeat in 1980 after submitting an authoritarian constitution to a plebiscite. From then on, civilian political leaders returned to the political scene, and in 1984 the majority of the political parties and the military agreed to call for elections in November 1985, thus allowing for a transition to democracy.

From Pre-Columbian Times to the Conquest

In contrast to most Latin American countries, no significant vestiges of civilizations existing prior to the arrival of European settlers were found in the territory of present-day Uruguay. Lithic remains dating back 10,000 years have been found in the north

5

of the country. They belonged to the Catalan and Cuareim cultures, whose members were presumably hunters and gatherers. Other peoples arrived in the region 4,000 years ago. They belonged to two groups, the Charrúa and the Tupí-Guaraní, classified according to the linguistic family to which they belonged. Neither group evolved past the middle or upper Paleolithic level, which is characterized by an economy based on hunting, fishing, and gathering. Other, lesser indigenous groups in Uruguay included the Yaro, Chaná, and Bohane. Presumably, the Chaná reached lower Neolithic levels with agriculture and ceramics.

In the early sixteenth century, Spanish seamen searched for the strait linking the Atlantic and the Pacific oceans. Juan Díaz de Solís entered the Río de la Plata by mistake in 1516 and thus discovered the region. Charrúa Indians allegedly attacked the ship as soon as it arrived and killed everyone in the party except for one boy (who was rescued a dozen years later by Sebastian Cabot, an Englishman in the service of Spain). Although historians currently believe that Díaz de Solís was actually killed by the Guaraní, the "Charrúa legend" has survived, and Uruguay has found in it a mythical past of bravery and rebellion in the face of oppression. The fierce Charrúa would plague the Spanish settlers for the next 300 years.

In 1520 the Portuguese captain Ferdinand Magellan cast anchor in a bay of the Río de la Plata at the site that would become Montevideo. Other expeditions reconnoitered the territory and its rivers. It was not until 1603 that Hernando Arias de Saavedra, the first Spanish governor of the Río de la Plata region, discovered the rich pastures and introduced the first cattle and horses. Early colonizers were disappointed to find no gold or silver, but well-irrigated pastures in the area contributed to the quick reproduction of cattle—a different kind of wealth. English and Portuguese inhabitants of the region, however, initiated an indiscriminate slaughter of cattle to obtain leather.

During the sixteenth and early seventeenth centuries, the Charrúa learned the art of horsemanship from the Spaniards in adjacent areas, strengthening their ability to resist subjugation. The Indians were eventually subdued by the large influx of Argentines and Brazilians pursuing the herds of cattle and horses. Never exceeding 10,000 in number in eighteenth-century Uruguay, the Indians also lacked any economic significance to the Europeans because they usually did not produce for trade. As a result of genocide, imported disease, and even intermarriage, the number of Indians rapidly diminished, and by 1850 the pureblooded Indian had virtually ceased to exist.

Two gauchos in Tacuarembó Department
Courtesy Inter-American Development Bank

In 1680 the Portuguese, seeking to expand Brazil's frontier, founded Colonia del Sacramento on the Río de la Plata, across from Buenos Aires. Forty years later, the Spanish monarch ordered the construction of Fuerte de San José, a military fort at present-day Montevideo, to resist this expansion. With the founding of San Felipe de Montevideo at this site in 1726, Montevideo became the port and station of the Spanish fleet in the South Atlantic. The new settlement included families from Buenos Aires and the Canary Islands to whom the Spanish crown distributed plots and farms and subsequently large haciendas in the interior. Authorities were appointed, and a *cabildo* (town council) was formed.

Montevideo was on a bay with a natural harbor suitable for large oceangoing vessels, and this geographic advantage over Buenos Aires was at the base of the future rivalry between the two cities. The establishment of the Viceroyalty of the Río de la Plata in 1776, with Buenos Aires as its capital, aggravated this rivalry (see fig. 2). Montevideo was authorized to trade directly with Spain instead of through Buenos Aires.

Montevideo's role as a commercial center was bolstered when salted beef began to be used to feed ship crews and later slaves in Cuba. The city's commercial activity was expanded by the introduction of the slave trade to the southern part of the continent because

7

Montevideo was a major port of entry for slaves. Thousands of slaves were brought into Uruguay between the mid-eighteenth and the early nineteenth century, but the number was relatively low because the major economic activity—livestock raising—was not labor intensive and because labor requirements were met by increasing immigration from Europe.

Throughout the eighteenth century, new settlements were established to consolidate the occupation of the territory, which constituted a natural buffer region separating Spanish from Portuguese possessions. To combat smuggling, protect ranchers, and contain Indians, the Spanish formed a rural patrol force called the Blandengues Corps.

In late 1806, Britain, at war with Spain, invaded the Río de la Plata Estuary to avenge Spain's recapture of Buenos Aires from the British. The 10,000-member British force captured Montevideo in early 1807 and occupied it until that July, when it left and moved against Buenos Aires, where it was soundly defeated.

In 1808 Spanish prestige was weakened when Napoleon invaded Spain and installed his brother Joseph on the throne. The *cabildo* of Montevideo, however, created an autonomous junta that remained nominally loyal to Ferdinand VII as the king of Spain. Montevideo's military commander, Javier Elío, eventually persuaded the Spanish central junta to accept his control at Montevideo as independent of Buenos Aires. In 1810 criollos (those born in America of Spanish parents) from Buenos Aires took the reins of government in that city and unseated the Spanish viceroy. The population of the Banda Oriental was politically divided. The countryside favored recognizing Elío's junta in Buenos Aires; the authorities in Montevideo wanted to retain a nominal allegiance to the Spanish king.

The Struggle for Independence, 1811–30
Artigas's Revolution, 1811–20

In February 1811, when Elío prepared to take the offensive against Buenos Aires, the interior of the Banda Oriental, led by José Gervasio Artigas, captain of the Blandengues Corps, rose in opposition to Elío, and Artigas offered his services to Buenos Aires. Artigas, then forty-six years old, was the scion of a family that had settled in Montevideo in 1726. Influenced by federalism, Artigas had been dissatisfied with the administration of the former colonial government in Buenos Aires, particularly with its discrimination against Montevideo in commercial affairs. Artigas's army won its most important victory against the Spaniards in the Battle of

Las Piedras on May 18, 1811. He then besieged Montevideo from May to October 1811. Elío saved Montevideo only by inviting in the Portuguese forces from Brazil, which poured into Uruguay and dominated most of the country by July 1811. That October Elío concluded a peace treaty with Buenos Aires that provided for the lifting of the siege of Montevideo and the withdrawal of all the troops of Artigas, Portugal, and Spain from Uruguay. Artigas, his 3,000 troops, and 13,000 civilians evacuated Salto, on the Río Uruguay, and crossed the river to the Argentine town of Ayuí, where they camped for several months. This trek is considered the first step in the formation of the Uruguayan nation. The Portuguese and Spanish troops did not withdraw until 1812.

At the beginning of 1813, after Artigas had returned to the Banda Oriental, having emerged as a champion of federalism against the unitary centralism of Buenos Aires, the new government in Buenos Aires convened a constituent assembly. The Banda Oriental's delegates to elect assembly representatives gathered and, under instructions issued by Artigas, proposed a series of political directives. Later known as the "Instructions of the Year Thirteen," these directives included the declaration of the colonies' independence and the formation of a confederation of the provinces (the United Provinces of the Río de la Plata) from the former Viceroyalty of the Río de la Plata (dissolved in 1810 when independence was declared). This formula, inspired by the Constitution of the United States, would have guaranteed political and economic autonomy for each area, particularly that of the Banda Oriental with respect to Buenos Aires. However, the assembly refused to seat the delegates from the Banda Oriental, and Buenos Aires pursued a system based on unitary centralism. Consequently, Artigas broke with Buenos Aires and again besieged Montevideo.

Artigas lifted his siege of Montevideo at the beginning of 1814, but warfare continued among the Uruguayans, Spaniards, and Argentines. In June 1814, Montevideo surrendered to the troops of Buenos Aires. Artigas controlled the countryside, however, and his army retook the city in early 1815. Once the troops from Buenos Aires had withdrawn, the Banda Oriental appointed its first autonomous government. Artigas established the administrative center in the northwest of the country, where in 1815 he organized the Federal League under his protection. It consisted of six provinces— including four present-day Argentine provinces—demarcated by the Río Paraná, Río Uruguay, and Río de la Plata—with Montevideo as the overseas port. The basis for political union was customs unification and free internal trade. To regulate external trade,

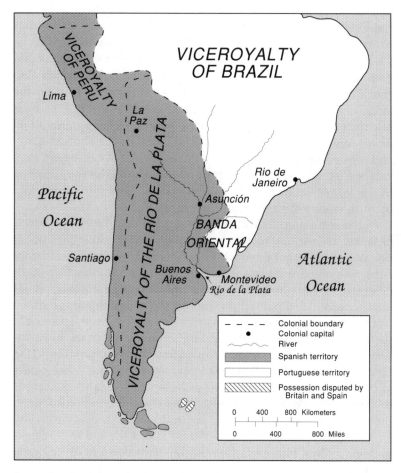

Source: Based on information from A. Curtis Wilgus, *Historical Atlas of Latin America,* New York, 1967, 112.

Figure 2. Three South American Viceroyalties, ca. 1800

the protectionist Customs Regulations Act (1815) was adopted. That same year, Artigas also attempted to implement agrarian reform in the Banda Oriental by distributing land confiscated from his enemies to supporters of the revolution, including Indians and mestizos (people of mixed Indian and European ancestry).

In 1816 a force of 10,000 Portuguese troops invaded the Banda Oriental from Brazil and took Montevideo in January 1817. After nearly four more years of struggle, a defeated Artigas fled into exile in Paraguay in September 1820 and remained there until his death in 1850. After routing Artigas, Portuguese Brazil annexed the Banda Oriental as its southernmost Cisplatine Province.

From Insurrection to State Organization, 1820–30

Following its independence from Portugal in 1822, Brazil was confronted by unrest in the Banda Oriental. On April 19, 1825, a group of Uruguayan revolutionaries (the famous Thirty-Three Heroes) led by Juan Antonio Lavalleja, reinforced by Argentine troops, crossed the Río de la Plata from Buenos Aires and organized an insurrection that succeeded in gaining control over the countryside. On August 25, 1825, in a town in the liberated area, representatives from the Banda Oriental declared the territory's independence from Brazil and its incorporation into the United Provinces of the Río de la Plata. Brazil declared war on them. The ensuing conflict lasted from December 1825 to August 1828.

In 1828 Lord John Ponsonby, envoy of the British Foreign Office, proposed making the Banda Oriental an independent state. Britain was anxious to create a buffer state between Argentina and Brazil to ensure its trade interests in the region. With British mediation, Brazil and Argentina signed the Treaty of Montevideo at Rio de Janeiro on August 27, 1828, whereby Argentina and Brazil renounced their claims to the territories that would become integral parts of the newly independent state on October 3. However, Argentina and Brazil retained the right to intervene in the event of a civil war and to approve the constitution of the new nation.

Argentine and Brazilian troops began their withdrawal, while a constituent assembly drew up the constitution of the new country, created its flag and coat of arms, and enacted legislation. The constitution was approved officially on July 18, 1830, after having been ratified by Argentina and Brazil. It established a representative unitary republic—the República Oriental del Uruguay (Oriental Republic of Uruguay), the word *oriental* (eastern) representing the legacy of the original designation of the territory as the Banda Oriental. The constitution restricted voting, made Roman Catholicism the official religion, and divided the territory into nine administrative jurisdictions known as departments (see Constitutional Background, ch. 4).

Beginnings of Independent Life, 1830–52

The First Presidents, 1830–38

At the time of independence, Uruguay had an estimated population of just under 75,000, of which less than 20 percent resided in Montevideo, the capital. Indeed, the new nation was born with most of its population scattered throughout the countryside. Political power centered on local leaders, or caudillos, who attracted followers because of their power, bravery, or wealth. There were three major caudillos at the time of independence: Rivera, Oribe, and Lavalleja. The first two were later elected presidents, Rivera from 1830 to 1835 and from 1838 to 1843 and Oribe from 1835 to 1838. Their rivalry, which turned violent, led to the formation of the first political groups, known as Colorados and Blancos because of the red and white hatbands, respectively, worn during armed clashes beginning in 1836. The groups would subsequently become the Colorado Party and the National Party (the Blancos).

During the 1830–38 period, the economy came to depend increasingly on cattle, on the proliferation of *saladeros* (meat-salting establishments), and on the export of salted beef and leather. But political instability was the most significant feature of this period. Caudillos and their followers were mobilized because of disputes arising from deficient land demarcation between absentee landowners and squatters and between rightful owners and Artigas's followers who were granted land seized by Artigas. Rivera remained in the countryside for most of his presidency, during which Lavalleja organized three unsuccessful rebellions. Rivera was followed as president by Oribe, one of the Thirty-Three Heroes, but they began to quarrel after Oribe permitted Lavalleja and his followers to return from Brazil. Rivera initiated a revolutionary movement against President Oribe, who, aided by Argentine troops, defeated Rivera's forces at the Battle of Carpintería on September 19, 1836. In June 1838, however, the Colorados, led by Rivera, defeated Oribe's Blanco forces; Oribe then went into exile in Buenos Aires.

Internationally, the new territory was at the mercy of the influence of its neighbors. This resulted from its lack of clearly defined borders, as well as from Rivera's ties with Brazil and Oribe's with Argentina.

Rivera again became the elected president in March 1838. In 1839 President Rivera, with the support of the French and of Argentine émigrés, issued a declaration of war against Argentina's dictator, Juan Manuel de Rosas, and drove Rosas's forces from Uruguay. The French, however, reached an agreement with Rosas and withdrew their troops from the Río de la Plata region in 1840, leaving Montevideo vulnerable to Oribe's Argentine-backed forces. For three years, the locus of the struggle was on Argentine territory. Oribe and the Blancos allied themselves with Argentina's federalists, while Rivera and the Colorados sided with Argentina's rival unitary forces, who favored the centralization of the Argentine state. In 1842 Oribe defeated Rivera and later, on

Montevideo's Thirty-Three Heroes Obelisk
Courtesy Inter-American Development Bank

February 16, 1843, laid siege to Montevideo, then governed by the Colorados.

The Great War, 1843-52

Oribe's siege of Montevideo marked the beginning of the Great War (Guerra Grande, 1843-52). The Great War centered on the nine-year-long siege of Montevideo, described by Alexandre Dumas as a "new Troy," although the city itself suffered relatively little from the war. Britain had saved Montevideo at the outset by allowing the city to receive supplies. During the Great War, there were two governments in Uruguay: the Colorados at Montevideo (the so-called government of the "defense") and the Blancos at Cerrito (Little Hill), a promontory near Montevideo.

The intervention first of France (1838-42) and then of Britain and France (1843-50) transformed the conflict into an international war. First, British and French naval forces temporarily blockaded the port of Buenos Aires in December 1845. Then, the British and French fleets protected Montevideo at sea. French and Italian legionnaires (the latter led by Giuseppe Garibaldi) participated, along with the Colorados, in the defense of the city.

Historians believe that the reason for the French and British intervention in the conflict was to restore normalcy to commerce in the

13

region and to ensure free navigation along the Río Paraná and Río Uruguay, thus guaranteeing access to provincial markets without Buenos Aires's interference. Their efforts were ineffective, however, and by 1849 the two European powers had tired of the war. In 1850 both withdrew after signing a treaty that represented a triumph for Rosas of Argentina. It appeared that Montevideo would finally fall. But an uprising against Rosas led by Justo José de Urquiza, governor of Argentina's Entre Ríos Province, with the assistance of a small Uruguayan force, changed the situation. They defeated Oribe in 1851, thereby ending the armed conflict in Uruguayan territory and leaving the Colorados in full control of the country. Brazil then intervened in Uruguay in May 1851 on behalf of the besieged Colorados, supporting them with money and naval forces. With Rosas's fall from power in Argentina in February 1852, the siege of Montevideo was lifted by Urquiza's pro-Colorado forces.

Montevideo rewarded Brazil's vital financial and military support by signing five treaties in 1851 that provided for perpetual alliance between the two countries, confirming Brazil's right to intervene in Uruguay's internal affairs; extradition of runaway slaves and criminals from Uruguay (during the war, both the Blancos and the Colorados had abolished slavery in Uruguay in order to mobilize the former slaves to reinforce their respective military forces); joint navigation on the Río Uruguay and its tributaries; tax exemption on cattle and salted meat exports (the cattle industry was devastated by the war); acknowledgment of debt to Brazil for aid against the Blancos; and Brazil's commitment to granting an additional loan. Borders were also recognized, whereby Uruguay renounced its territorial claims north of the Río Cuareim (thereby reducing its boundaries to about 176,000 kilometers) and recognized Brazil's exclusive right of navigation in the Laguna Merín and the Río Yaguarón, the natural border between the countries.

The Struggle for Survival, 1852–75

Intervention by Neighboring Countries

After Rosas went into exile in Britain in 1852, internal strife in Argentina continued until 1861, when the country was finally unified. Uruguay was affected because each Uruguayan faction expressed solidarity with various contenders in Argentina or was, in turn, supported by them.

Brazil's intervention in Uruguay was intensified both because of Argentina's temporary weakness and because of Brazil's desire to expand its frontiers to the Río de la Plata. Brazil intervened

militarily in Uruguay as often as it deemed necessary, in accordance with the 1851 treaties. In 1865 the Triple Alliance—formed by the emperor of Brazil, the president of Argentina, and General Venancio Flores (1854-55, 1865-66), the Uruguayan head of government whom they both had helped to gain power—declared war on Paraguay. Francisco Solano López, Paraguay's megalomaniac dictator, had been verbally rattling his saber against Argentina and Brazil. The conflict lasted five years (1865-70) and ended with the invasion of Paraguay and its defeat by the armies of the three countries. Montevideo, which was used as a supply station by the Brazilian navy, experienced a period of prosperity and relative calm during the war.

After the war with Paraguay, the balance of power was restored between Argentina and Brazil, the guarantors of Uruguayan independence. Thus, Uruguay was able to internalize its political struggles, an indispensable condition for consolidation of its independence.

Evolution of the Economy and Society

After the Great War, immigration increased, primarily from Spain and Italy. Brazilians and Britons also flocked to Uruguay to snap up hundreds of *estancias* (ranches). The proportion of the immigrant population in Uruguay rose from 48 percent in 1860 to 68 percent in 1868. Many were Basques of Spanish or French nationality. In the 1870s, another 100,000 Europeans settled in Uruguay. By 1879 the total population of the country was over 438,000. Montevideo, where approximately one-fourth of the population lived, expanded and improved its services. Gas services were initiated in 1853, the first bank in 1857, sewage works in 1860, a telegraph in 1866, railroads to the interior in 1869, and running water in 1871. The creation in 1870 of the typographers' union, the first permanent workers' organization, was soon followed by the establishment of other unions. Montevideo remained mainly a commercial center. Thanks to its natural harbor, it was able to serve as a trade center for goods moving to and from Argentina, Brazil, and Paraguay. The cities of Paysandú and Salto, on the Río Uruguay, complemented this role.

After the Great War, livestock raising recovered and prospered. Improvements in breeding techniques and fencing were introduced, and between 1860 and 1868 sheep breeding, stimulated by European demand, expanded from 3 million head to 17 million head. A group of modernizing hacendados (landowners), a large number of whom were foreigners, was responsible for this change. In 1871 they established the Rural Association (Asociación Rural) to improve livestock-raising techniques. The association developed a reputation for defending rural traditions and exerting considerable influence on policy makers.

Meat-salting enterprises were the main stimulus for the industrialization of livestock products. In 1865 the Liebig Meat Extract Company of London opened a meat-extract factory at Fray Bentos on the Río Uruguay to supply the European armies, thus initiating diversification in the sector. This type of meat processing, however, was dependent on cheap cattle. As the price of cattle increased, the meat-extract industry declined, along with the *saladeros,* which prepared salted and sun-dried meat. Cuba and Brazil were the main purchasers of salted meat; Europe, of meat extract; and the United States and Europe, of leather and wool.

Caudillos and Political Stability

Until 1865 the prevailing political idea was fusion (*fusión*), meaning unity among Uruguayans, the putting aside of the colors and banners that divided them in the past. This idea inspired the administrations of Juan Francisco Giró (1852–53), Gabriel Pereira (1856–60), and Bernardo Berro (1860–64). Hatred and rivalry flared up, however, preventing harmony. Giró was forced to resign. Pereira suppressed almost six coup attempts, and Berro, the last

Blanco president until 1958, confronted a revolution led by Colorado Venancio Flores, who took power with the support of Brazil and Buenos Aires. However, General Flores, who had been commanding the armed forces instead of governing the country since that March, was assassinated in Montevideo in 1868, on the same day that Berro was assassinated. During the period preceding the Great War, the long conflict between church and state also began. It involved Freemasons in government circles and resulted in the expulsion of the Jesuits in 1859 (they were allowed to return in 1865) and the secularization of cemeteries in 1861. Until then the church had almost exclusive control over the cemeteries.

The constitutional government of General Lorenzo Batlle y Grau (1868-72) was forced to suppress an insurrection led by the National Party. After two years of struggle, a peace agreement was signed in 1872 that gave the Blancos a share in the emoluments and functions of government, through control of four of the country's departments. This establishment of the policy of coparticipation (*coparticipación*) represented the search for a new formula of compromise, based on the coexistence of the party in power and the party in opposition.

A permanent break in the cycle of near anarchy and repression was anticipated when José Ellauri (1872-75) was elected president. His administration was characterized by the predominance of university men over caudillos. A number of them, known as the "Girondists of 73," were sent to the General Assembly. Unfortunately, however, the ensuing economic crisis and the weakness of civil power paved the way for a period of militarism.

Modern Uruguay, 1875-1903

Militarism, 1875-90

Between 1875 and 1886, political parties headed by caudillos or university men declined, and the military became the center of power. A transition period (1886-90) followed, during which politicians began recovering lost ground, and there was some civilian participation in government. Nevertheless, political parties during this period were not parties in the modern sense of the term. Nor, however, was the army a professional institution despite its successful foreign and domestic campaigns.

Because of serious disturbances, Ellauri was forced to resign in 1875. His successor, José Pedro Varela (1875-76), curtailed liberties, arrested opposition leaders and deported the most notable among them to Cuba, and successfully quelled an armed rebellion. At the beginning of 1876, Colonel Lorenzo Latorre (1876–80) assumed power; he was appointed constitutional president in 1879, but the following year he resigned, after declaring that Uruguayans were "ungovernable," and moved to Argentina.

Colonel Máximo Santos (1882–86) was appointed president in 1882 by a General Assembly elected under his pressure, and his political entourage named him leader of the Colorado Party. In 1886 Santos, who had been promoted to general, suppressed an insurrection led by the opposition. After an attempt against his life, however, he too resigned and went to live in Europe.

During this authoritarian period (1875–86), the government took steps toward the organization of the country as a modern state and encouraged its economic and social transformation. Pressure groups, particularly businessmen, hacendados, and industrialists, were organized and had a strong influence on government, as demonstrated by their support of numerous measures taken by the state.

In the international realm, the country improved its ties with Britain. Loans increased significantly after the 1870s, when the first one was granted. In 1876 British investors acquired the national railroad company, the North Tramway and Railway Company. They later dominated construction of railroads and continued their policy of ensuring control over, and concessions to, some essential services in Montevideo, such as gas (1872) and running water (1879). Uruguay's adoption of the gold standard facilitated commercial transactions between the two countries.

Under Latorre's administration, order was restored in the countryside. His government vigorously repressed delinquency and unemployment (those without jobs were considered "vagrants") to protect farmers and ranchers. Fencing of the countryside stimulated modernization of the system. Barbed wired was such an indispensable element for livestock improvement and for the establishment of accurate property boundaries that an 1875 law exempted imports of barbed wire from customs duties. This measure was accompanied by the approval of the Rural Code (1875), drawn up with the participation of the Rural Association. The code ensured land and livestock ownership and thus social order.

The government adopted a number of measures to promote national industrial development. Most important was a series of customs laws in 1875, 1886, and 1888 raising import duties on products that could be manufactured in the country, thus protecting indigenous industry. The Latorre government also improved the means of transportation and communications, giving tax and other concessions for the construction of railroads, whose network doubled in size in ten years. The state also reorganized and took over the postal service and connected all departmental capitals by telegraph. Education reform authored by Varela and implemented in 1877 under the Latorre administration established free compulsory primary education. Reform also reached the University of the Republic (also known as the University of Montevideo—established in 1849 and the country's only university until 1984), where the medical and the mathematics faculties were created in 1876 and 1877, respectively.

The secularization process also continued during this period. Under the pretext of needing to deal with the chaos in parochial archives, Latorre created the Civil Register (1876), which transferred to the state the registration of births, deaths, and marriages. Under the Santos administration, the Law of Mandatory Civil Marriage (1885) established that only marriages performed in accordance with this law would be considered valid.

The Return of Civilians

General Máximo Tajes (1886-90), who was appointed president by the General Assembly, tried to restore the constitution and remove the military chiefs who had supported Santos. During the Tajes administration, civilian political activity resumed. At the end of the Tajes term, Julio Herrera y Obes was elected president (1890-94). Herrera y Obes belonged to the Colorado Party, had been an adviser to his predecessor, and was instrumental in the transition process that displaced the military from power. He selected his aides from among a small group of friends and was convinced that the executive had to play a leading role in elections and the makeup of the General Assembly. This policy, called the "directing influence," was resisted by a sector of the Colorado Party led by José Batlle y Ordóñez, son of the former president, Lorenzo Batlle y Grau.

In 1894, after much internal debate, the General Assembly appointed Juan Idiarte Borda (1894-97), a member of the inner circle of the departing administration, as the new president. But Herrera y Obes and Borda had succeeded in irritating the National Party, when the latter was granted control of only three of the four departments agreed on in the 1872 pact between the two rival parties.

In 1897 discontent led to an armed uprising by Blanco forces. The insurrection was led by Aparicio Saravia, a caudillo from a ranching family originally from the Brazilian state of Rio Grande do Sul who was involved in military and political affairs on both sides of the border. The Saravia revolution raised the flag of electoral guarantees, the secret ballot, and proportional representation. Military action had not yet decided the situation when President Borda was assassinated. The president of the Senate (the upper house of the General Assembly), Juan Lindolfo Cuestas (1897–1903), served as provisional president until 1899, when he was elected constitutional president. Cuestas quickly signed a peace agreement with the National Party, giving it control over six of Uruguay's departments and promising all citizens their political rights. An anticlericalist, Cuestas placed restrictions on the exercise of Roman Catholicism and tried to prevent admission to the country of friars and priests.

A majority of the members of the General Assembly, who had ties to the Herrera y Obes faction, submitted another presidential candidate in 1898 for the scheduled election. Cuestas, unwilling to give up power, led a coup d'état. He included members of the opposition in his government in a rudimentary attempt at proportional representation. Late that same year, the Cuestas regime promulgated the Permanent Civil Register Law, dealing with electoral matters, and the Elections Law, formally establishing the principle of minority representation. Through this legislation, the opposition gained access to one-third of the seats if it obtained one-fourth of the total votes.

The political consensus achieved by Cuestas resulted in the unanimous support by the General Assembly for his candidacy and appointment as constitutional president in 1899. In fact, however, political peace was an illusion. There were, in effect, two countries, one Blanco and one Colorado. President Cuestas had to send an envoy to caudillo Saravia, near the border with Brazil, in order to coordinate government action. This precarious balance would break down in 1903 when Batlle y Ordóñez took power.

In spite of political and economic fluctuations, the flow of immigrants continued. From the 1870s to the 1910s, Uruguay's population doubled to just over 1 million inhabitants, 30 percent of whom lived in Montevideo. Montevideo also continued to experience modernization, including the installation of a telephone system (1878) and public lighting (1886). At the same time, the euphoria and speculation of the 1870s and 1880s saw a proliferation of banks and corporations and a stimulation of land sales, as well as the construction of multifamily dwellings.

The economic crisis of 1890 was a traumatic event for Uruguayan society. Bankruptcies followed one after another, and the banking system saw the collapse of a key banking institution, created by a Spanish financier, which had served the needs of the state and promoted production and construction. The ruling elite felt the impact, and some of its more progressive sectors directed their efforts to the creation of a development model for the country. They were aware of both the need to encourage agricultural and industrial development and the need to redefine the limits of the state. The growing importance of British investment had stimulated the rise of economic nationalism and had, by 1898, provoked more active state intervention.

State intervention in the economy continued in 1896 when the electric utility company was transferred to the municipality of Montevideo and the Bank of Uruguay (Banco de la República Oriental del Uruguay—BROU) was created as an autonomous entity (autonomous agency or state enterprise; see Glossary). Moreover, under Cuestas's administration, the state undertook construction of the modern harbor of Montevideo, in reaction to the new facility in Buenos Aires, which had absorbed part of the river traffic with Paraguay and the Argentine littoral. Nevertheless, the nationalization of economic activities and the creation of state enterprises did not fully gather momentum until the administration of Batlle y Ordóñez.

The New Country, 1903-33

Batlle y Ordóñez and the Modern State

The election of José Batlle y Ordóñez as the first Uruguayan president in the twentieth century (1903-07, 1911-15) marked the beginning of a period of extraordinary change in the country. The son of former President Lorenzo Batlle y Grau, Batlle y Ordóñez was a member of the Colorado Party, founder of the newspaper *El Día* (in 1886), and an active opponent of militarism.

The dominant political event during the first administration of Batlle y Ordóñez was another National Party insurrection in 1904, led by Saravia. After nine months of fierce fighting and Saravia's death, it ended with the Treaty of Aceguá (1904). The civil war triumph of Batlle y Ordóñez and the Colorados meant the end of the coparticipation politics that began in 1872, the political and administrative unification of the country, the consolidation of the state, and, most profoundly, the end of the cycle of civil wars that had persisted throughout the nineteenth century.

The period's most significant economic change occurred in meat processing. In 1905 the first shipment of frozen beef, produced by a refrigeration plant (*frigorífico*) established by local investors two years before, was exported to London in a refrigerated ship.

Uruguay now entered the age of refrigeration, making possible the diversification of one of its main export items and giving the country access to new markets. With the inauguration of the modernized port of Montevideo in 1909, Uruguay could compete with Buenos Aires as a regional trade center.

Claudio Williman (1907–11), the president's handpicked candidate, succeeded Batlle y Ordóñez, who sailed for Europe, where he spent the next four years studying governmental systems. In some respects, Williman's administration was considered more conservative than that of Batlle y Ordóñez, although Batllists maintained their political influence. Williman tried to ensure political peace by enacting electoral laws in 1907 and 1910 that increased political representation of minority opposition parties. Williman also ensured peace with Uruguay's northern neighbor by signing a border treaty with Brazil, thereby putting an end to pending litigation and disputes dating back half a century.

The National Party, disappointed with Williman's electoral laws and with the announcement that Batlle y Ordóñez would once again run for president, did not participate in the elections held in 1910. This helped foster the emergence of two new political parties: the Catholic-oriented Civic Union of Uruguay (Unión Cívica del Uruguay—UCU) and the Marxist-inspired Socialist Party of Uruguay (Partido Socialista del Uruguay—PSU). Church and state relations also underwent changes. The government passed a divorce law in 1907, and in 1909 it eliminated religious education in public schools.

In 1911 Batlle y Ordóñez reassumed the presidency. A non-Marxist social democrat, he set about modernizing the country, taking into account the aspirations of emerging social groups, including industrialists, workers, and the middle class. Writing and promoting progressive social legislation, Batlle y Ordóñez fought for the eight-hour workday (enacted in 1915 under the administration of his successor), unemployment compensation (1914), and numerous pieces of social legislation. Some of these would be approved years later, such as retirement pensions (1919) and occupational safety (1920) (see Batllism, ch. 3).

Batlle y Ordóñez firmly believed that the principal public services had to be in the hands of the state to avoid foreign remittances that weakened the balance of payments and to facilitate domestic capital accumulation. In a relatively short period of time, his administration established a significant number of autonomous entities. In 1911 it nationalized BROU, a savings and loan institution that monopolized the printing of money. In 1912 the government created the State Electric Power Company, monopolizing

Contrasting buildings in Montevideo's Old City
Courtesy Edmundo Flores

23

electric power generation and distribution in the country; it nationalized the Mortgage Bank of Uruguay; and it founded three industrial institutes for geology and drilling (coal and hydrocarbon explorations), industrial chemistry, and fisheries. In 1914 it purchased the North Tramway and Railway Company, later to become the State Railways Administration.

Attempts to change the agrarian productive structure were not as successful. Influenced by United States economist Henry George, Batlle y Ordóñez thought that he could combat extensive landholdings by applying a progressive tax on land use and a surcharge on inheritance taxes. The agrarian reform plan also contemplated promoting colonization and farming. Very little was accomplished in this regard, however, partly because of the opposition of large landowners who created a pressure group, the Rural Federation (Federación Rural), to fight Batlle y Ordóñez's policies. The government did make one important accomplishment with regard to agriculture, namely, the creation of a series of government institutes dedicated to technological research and development in the fields of livestock raising, dairying, horticulture, forestation, seeds, and fodder.

The government adopted a protectionist policy for industry, imposing tariffs on foreign products, favoring machinery and raw materials imports, and granting exclusive licensing privileges to those who started a new industry. Indigenous companies sprang up, but foreign capital—especially from the United States and Britain—also took advantage of the legislation and came to control the meat industry. The growth of the *frigorífico* meat-processing industry also stimulated the interbreeding of livestock, Uruguay's main source of wealth.

Education policy was designed to take into account the continuous inflow of European migrants. Although it fluctuated, immigration was significant until 1930. Furthermore, education was a key to mobility for the middle classes. The state actively sought to expand education to the greatest number of people by approving free high school education in 1916 and creating departmental high schools throughout the country in 1912. A "feminine section" was created to foster mass attendance of women at the University of the Republic, where the number of departments continued to expand.

The secularization process, initiated during the second half of the nineteenth century, was accelerated by Batlle y Ordóñez's anticlericalism. Uruguay banned crucifixes in state hospitals by 1906 and eliminated references to God and the Gospel in public oaths in 1907. Divorce laws caused a confrontation between church and state. In addition to the 1907 and 1910 laws (divorce with cause and by mutual agreement), a law was passed in 1912 allowing women to file for divorce without a specific cause, simply because they wanted to.

Batlle y Ordóñez also proposed the institutional reorganization of government in 1913. Essentially, he wanted to replace the presidency with a nine-member collegial executive (*colegiado*) inspired by the Swiss model (see Constitutional Background, ch. 4). This proposal caused an immediate split in the Colorado Party. One sector opposed the political reform and also feared some of Batlle y Ordóñez's economic and social changes. Subsequently, these dissidents, led by Carlos Manini Ríos, founded a faction known as the Colorado Party-General Rivera (Riverism). The National Party, under Luis Alberto de Herrera, the leading opposition figure from 1920 to his death in 1959, did not back Batlle y Ordóñez's proposal either.

Feliciano Viera (1915–19), a Colorado who was more conservative than Batlle y Ordóñez, became president at the time of the debate between "collegialists" and "anticollegialists." During his mandate, elections were held for a constituent assembly (July 30, 1916). The rules for this election enabled the National Party to ensure incorporation of many of the principles it advocated, such as the secret ballot, partial proportional representation, and universal male suffrage.

Batlle y Ordóñez and his political faction of the Colorados lost these first popular elections, but the Colorados continued to be the majority party, and the 1917 constitution, the country's second, reflected many of the changes that had taken place under Batlle y Ordóñez. It separated church and state, expanded citizens' rights, established the secret ballot and proportional representation, and banned the death penalty. It also created autonomous state enterprises in the areas of industry, education, and health. But in a bitter compromise for Batlle y Ordóñez, the executive was divided between the president, who appointed the ministers of foreign affairs, war, and interior, and the nine-member *colegiado,* the National Council of Administration (Consejo Nacional de Administración). The latter, which included representatives from the party that received the second highest number of votes, the Blancos, was placed in charge of the ministries dealing with economic, educational, and social policy.

President Viera, like many of Batlle y Ordóñez's followers, interpreted the 1916 electoral defeat as a direct consequence of previous policy. He thus announced a halt to economic and social reforms. Some of the old projects as well as some new proposals were approved, however, such as restrictions on night work in 1918 and the creation in 1916 of a new autonomous entity, the Montevideo Port Authority, also known as the National Administration of Ports (Administración Nacional de Puertos—ANP). Workers' strikes, however, were repressed severely. Finally, in 1919 Viera, in disagreement with Batlle y Ordóñez, founded a dissident Colorado Party faction known as Vierism.

The Consolidation of Political Democracy

The 1920s witnessed electoral struggles in which the various parties sought to consolidate the political peace achieved in 1904. The National Party participated actively in political life, and although the Colorado Party was dominant, its electoral advantage was slight. Relative electoral parity and the still recent memory of the last armed uprising compelled participants to preserve electoral purity and to improve the corresponding legislation. In 1924 the Electoral Court was created to prepare and control national elections. The 1917 constitution eliminated restrictions on male suffrage and required elections almost every year to renew the various governmental bodies.

Each political party was internally divided because of ideological, economic, and social differences. To the existing Colorado factions—Riverism and Vierism—were added the Colorado Party for Tradition (also known as Sosism), founded by Julio María Sosa in 1925, and the Advance Grouping (Agrupación Avanzar), founded by Julio César Grauert in 1929. Splinter groups of the National Party included the Radical Blanco Party, founded by Lorenzo Carnelli in 1924, and Social Democracy, founded by Carlos Quijano in 1928. The small PSU also split in 1920, and one of its factions formed the Communist Party of Uruguay (Partido Comunista del Uruguay—PCU). The parties were divided into "traditional" (Colorado Party and National Party) and "minor," or "ideological," parties (UCU, PSU, and PCU). The former, by means of a 1910 law that allowed a double simultaneous vote for a party and a faction of the party (*sub-lema*), became "federations" of parties with different agendas and were thus able to attract followers from all sectors of society.

These contradictions forced Batlle y Ordóñez to make electoral arrangements with his opponents within the Colorado Party to prevent the victory of the National Party. The resultant "politics of compromise" diluted his reformist agenda. Baltasar Brum (1919–23), one of Batlle y Ordóñez's followers and a former foreign minister, was succeeded as president by a "neutral" Colorado, José Serrato (1923–27), who turned over the office to a Riverist, Juan Campisteguy (1927–31).

It was difficult for adherents of Batllism to implement their agenda despite having the occasional support of other political sectors. Nevertheless, additional social reforms were enacted. In 1920 compensation for accidents in the workplace and a six-day work week were made law. In 1923 a minimum rural wage was passed, although it was never enforced. A social security system was created in 1919 for public-sector employees, and the program was extended to the private sector in 1928. Despite the reforms, a union movement, weak in numbers, was organized in several umbrella organizations: the Uruguayan Syndicalist Union, encompassing anarcho-syndicalists and communists, in 1923; and the communist General Confederation of Uruguayan Workers, in 1929.

The only state enterprise created during these years reflected the difficulties in expanding state control over industry because of opposition from the conservatives. Ranchers complained that foreign refrigeration plants, which had established quotas for shipments and for access of meat to the London market, did not pay a fair price for cattle. In 1928 the government created National Refrigerating (Frigorífico Nacional—Frigonal) as a ranchers' cooperative supported by the state and governed by a board made up of representatives from the government, the Rural Association, and the Rural Federation.

Although the country had suffered the immediate consequences of the post-World War I crisis, a period of recovery had quickly followed. It was characterized by growing prosperity sustained mainly by United States loans. A continued increase in population accompanied economic prosperity. The 1920s saw the arrival of the last great wave of immigrants, consisting mainly of Syrians, Lebanese, and East Europeans. Between 1908 and 1930, Montevideo's population doubled.

In 1930 Uruguay celebrated the centennial of the promulgation of its first constitution and won its first World Cup in soccer. Elections were held that year, the results of which were to presage difficulties, however. Batlle y Ordóñez died in 1929, leaving no successor for his political group. The Blanco leader, Herrera, was defeated by a wide margin of votes for the first time. The electoral balance between the parties had been broken. By a few votes, the conservative Colorado Manini, a Riverist leader and newspaper publisher, failed to become president.

The Conservative Adjustment, 1931–43
The Terra Era, 1931–38

Gabriel Terra (1931–38), a "heterodox" Batllist who had differed with Batlle y Ordóñez and who would soon distance himself from the latter's sons and followers, became president in March 1931. For the first time, the Batllist wing of the Colorados had a strong representation in the *colegiado.*

Terra's inauguration coincided with the effects of the Great Depression and a worsening of Uruguay's economic and social situation. Prices of agricultural products plunged. In 1932 Britain, traditionally the major purchaser of Uruguayan exports, began restricting purchases of meat. Uruguay's currency was devalued, and unemployment grew rapidly.

Batllists tried to implement their program from the *colegiado.* In 1931 BROU was authorized to control purchases and sales of foreign exchange and to set exchange rates, a measure that initially jeopardized cattle ranchers, exporters, and private banks. In the face of foreign-exchange scarcity, foreign companies were forced to suspend remittances abroad. Limits on imports were imposed to try to reduce the balance of payments deficit and to stimulate industrialization. Furthermore, attempts were made to reduce the fiscal deficit. At the same time, a political agreement known as the Pork Barrel Pact (Pacto del Chinchulín) between the Batllists and an emerging sector of the National Party opposing Herrera made possible the expansion of state control over industry. The pact resulted in the creation of the National Administration of Fuels, Alcohol, and Portland Cement (Administración Nacional de Combustibles, Alcohol, y Portland—ANCAP), a state enterprise with a monopoly over oil refining and alcohol production, and the power to begin producing portland cement. Unfortunately, it quickly became a source of patronage for the party faithful. The State Electric Power Company was granted a monopoly over the telephone system, becoming the State Electric Power and Telephone Company (Usinas Eléctricas y Teléfonos del Estado).

Social reform measures, such as the adoption of the forty-four-hour work week, and the growing economic crisis alarmed the most conservative sectors and affected the interests of large cattle ranchers, import merchants, foreign capital, and the population at large. The social climate became tense as a result of the lack of jobs. There were confrontations in which police and leftists died.

Terra distanced himself from his followers and began a campaign to reform the constitution and eliminate the *colegiado,* which was responsible for making economic and social policy and which Terra accused of inefficiency and lack of vision to overcome the crisis. He was supported by the National Economic Inspection Committee, which was created in 1929 and encompassed most business organizations. This committee proposed restricting statism, ending implementation of social legislation, and suspending the application of new taxes.

During the first months of 1933, when it became evident that Uruguay would have serious difficulties in paying the interest on its foreign debt, Terra obtained the support of Herrera and of Manini to organize a coup d'état. On March 31, 1933, Terra dissolved the General Assembly and the *colegiado* and governed by decree. Former President Brum (a Batllist) committed suicide one day after the fall of the liberal democratic regime. Another Batllist leader, Grauert, was assassinated. The Terra regime deported numerous opposition leaders and imposed press censorship.

In June 1933, elections were held for a constituent assembly that would be responsible for reforming the constitution. In 1934 the new constitution was submitted to a plebiscite, and although re-election of the president was unconstitutional, Terra was elected to a new term. More than half of the electorate participated in these elections, distributing their preferences between parties supporting the coup and those opposing it. The constitution promulgated in 1934 formally eliminated the *colegiado* and transferred its powers to the president. The new constitution restricted the creation of autonomous entities by requiring approval by a two-thirds majority in each chamber of the General Assembly. It banned usury, recognized certain social rights (e.g., housing and the right to work), and established women's suffrage. The cabinet ministers and heads of autonomous enterprises were to be distributed between the two parties obtaining the most votes, in a two-thirds to one-third ratio. The Senate was to be divided in half between the two parties winning the most votes, thus ensuring control by the coup factions. The Chamber of Representatives was to be elected by proportional representation.

In the mid-1930s, the opposition tried, unsuccessfully, to organize itself and resist the regime in the face of persecution. Military and armed civil uprisings were suppressed. In 1935 a political opponent unsuccessfully tried to assassinate Terra. An attempt to form a "popular front," including the left and dissident Colorados and Blancos, was also unsuccessful. To prevent this coalition, as well as a coalition of sectors from the traditional parties, from opposing the regime's social and economic policies, a series of electoral laws was promulgated beginning in 1934. The new Political Parties Law granted control of the Colorado and Blanco slogans, or party titles, to those who had participated in the elections and therefore supported the dictatorship.

Support from ranchers, one of the sectors most affected by the crisis, seemed to indicate a return to the traditional agro-exporting model. However, neither the "machete dictatorship" (an ironic name given to the regime by the socialist leader and writer Emilio Frugoni, referring to Terra's use of the police during the coup) nor the "March Revolution" (as it was solemnly called by its organizers) stressed an agrarian alternative because unemployment seemed to call for a diversification of the job market. Moreover, Uruguay was already an urban country with budding industrialization.

Terra's economic policies supported both livestock raising and industry, if unevenly. Livestock had stagnated—the 1930 livestock census showed fewer animals than the 1908 census. The problem of increasing livestock productivity remained unsolved, despite advances in breeding. Cattle ranchers were granted premiums in order to improve the quality of herds. Other benefits accorded them included tax rebates, debt-servicing alternatives, preferential exchange privileges, and the effects of the 1935 devaluation. At the same time, import limitations adopted in 1931 continued in effect, and in 1935 an industrial franchise law was passed. Industrial activities were further protected by currency depreciation and the fall in salaries caused by an abundance of labor.

The Terra government also attempted to regulate foreign trade. BROU maintained control over the price and sale of foreign currency. In 1934 the government created the Honorary Commission for Imports and Exchange to control the allotment of import quotas and foreign exchange. The government used pesos (for value of the peso—see Glossary) to pay the reduced interest rates on the foreign debt. It also carried out, in 1937, satisfactory negotiations for a new payment schedule with the United States and, in 1939, with Britain.

In general, the Terra government weakened or neutralized economic nationalism and social reform, the most controversial facets of the Batllist model. British public-service industries (railroads, water, gas, and tramways) and United States industries (oil, cement, refrigeration plants, and automobiles) that were established in the early 1900s received additional concessions. The government did not privatize existing state enterprises, as would have been expected from the antistatism espoused by Herrerists and Riverists. State enterprises were, however, affected in 1936 by a law that eliminated provisions granting some autonomous state enterprises the power to establish monopolies. ANCAP began constructing an oil refinery, and in 1938 it guaranteed private oil companies participation in Uruguay's market.

Nevertheless, although the government abolished certain redistributive policies fostered by social legislation, it reinforced the public assistance role of the state. It created "emergency jobs" for the unemployed through the National Affordable Housing Institute (1937) and the Institute for the Scientific Nutrition of the People (1937). In 1934 legislation was passed that regulated child labor for minors over twelve years of age, allowed maternity leave, and extended pensions to all commercial and industrial sectors, including employers.

The government also revamped the education system. The University of the Republic, whose structure had been transformed by the creation of new faculties (for example, engineering and architecture in 1915, chemistry and dentistry in 1929, and economics in 1932), no longer administered secondary education, which in 1935 was handed over to an autonomous agency.

The foreign policy of the regime resulted in a substantial improvement of relations with the United States (Franklin D. Roosevelt visited Uruguay in 1936) and with Britain. Under a 1935 pact with Britain, Uruguay agreed to pay its foreign debt, to purchase British coal, and to treat British companies generously in exchange for ensuring placement of Uruguayan products. In 1935 Uruguay severed relations with the Soviet Union and in the next year, with Republican Spain. At the same time, however, it established closer relations with Benito Mussolini's Italy and Adolf Hitler's Germany. Construction of a hydroelectric dam at Paso de los Toros on the Río Negro was begun in 1937 with German capital, creating the Embalse del Río Negro, the largest artificial lake in South America.

In 1938 general elections were held—the first in which women were allowed to vote. Terra divided his support between his son-in-law's father, Eduardo Blanco Acevedo, and his brother-in-law, General Alfredo Baldomir. These candidacies reflected a split in Terra's political faction within the Colorado Party. The PSU and PCU joined forces to vote for a common candidate, but the Colorado Party won. Baldomir (1938–43) was elected president. Once again, Batllists, Independent Nationalists, and Radical Blancos abstained from voting.

Baldomir and the End of Dictatorship

After his inauguration, and after suppressing a coup attempt, Baldomir announced his intention to reform the 1934 constitution but then procrastinated on carrying out the project. Several months later, the opposition led one of the most important political demonstrations in the history of the country, demanding a new constitution and a return to democracy. Under pressure from organized labor and the National Party, Baldomir advocated free elections, freedom of the press, and a new constitution.

Baldomir's administration could not avoid the consequences of World War II or the pressures and interests of the Allied forces. Although he declared Uruguay's neutrality in 1939, that December the Battle of the Río de la Plata took place. The badly damaged German battleship *Graf Spee*, cornered by a British naval force and required by the Uruguayan government to leave its refuge in the port of Montevideo, was blown up and scuttled by its own crew just outside the harbor. After this, Uruguay assumed a pro-Allied stance. In 1940 it began an investigation of Nazi sympathizers and finally, in 1942, broke relations with the Axis.

The Blancos persistently attempted to obstruct legislation introduced by Baldomir and criticized the Colorados' policy of cooperation with the United States in hemispheric defense. Baldomir's Blanco ally, Herrera, fought for neutrality, and in 1940 Herrera opposed the installation of United States bases in Uruguay. In 1941 Baldomir forced his three Herrerist ministers to resign; they had been appointed to his cabinet in accordance with provisions of the 1934 constitution. Baldomir subsequently appointed a board, without the participation of Herrerists, to study a constitutional reform. Finally, in February 1942 Baldomir dissolved the General Assembly and replaced it with the Council of State (Consejo de Estado), composed of Batllists and other Colorados. This quasi-coup was carried out without arrests, deportations, or the closing of newspapers. It was an in-house agreement to overcome the institutional crisis initiated on March 31, 1933, and to avoid enforcement of the existing constitution. Batllists and Communists welcomed the new situation, but the Socialists argued that Baldomir had been one of the protagonists of the 1933 coup. Independent Nationalists remained on the sidelines. Herrerism, freely accused of being pro-Nazi, pro-Franco, and pro-Argentine, was the big loser.

In November 1942, national elections were held. Although an electoral law had been passed in 1939 to avoid the formation of coalitions that would endanger the two-party system (Blancos and Colorados), Independent Nationalists were allowed to participate as a new political party, separate from Herrerism. Thus, the National Party divided into two splinter parties and continued as such until 1958. Socialists and Communists were also split, a situation that continued until 1971, when the Broad Front (Frente Amplio) coalition was created. Batllists supported the Colorado candidate, Juan José Amézaga (1943–47), who won the election.

At the same time, a new constitution was submitted to plebiscite and was approved by 77 percent of the electorate. As amended

on November 19, 1942, the constitution retained the presidency, restored the General Assembly, implemented strict proportional representation in the Senate, and abolished the mandatory co-participation imposed by the 1934 constitution for ministries and boards of autonomous entities.

"There's No Place Like Uruguay," 1943–58
The Administration of Amézaga, 1943–47

After Amézaga reinstitutionalized and restored civil liberties, Uruguay entered a new historical era, characterized by the increasing importance of industrialization and significant gains for virtually all sectors of society. No other phrase expresses as eloquently perceptions about this period by the average citizen as the slogan proclaimed by a politician: "Como el Uruguay no hay" (There's no place like Uruguay). During the Amézaga administration, the state reorganized its interventionist and welfare role and strongly pushed social legislation. In 1943 the government implemented a system of wage councils (including representatives from the state, workers, and employers) to set salaries, and it established a family assistance program. In 1945 the General Assembly passed legislation requiring paid leave for all work activities, as well as other legislation that addressed the needs of rural workers, one of

Uruguay's poorest sectors. In 1943 the rural workers were incorporated into the pension system, and in 1946 the Rural Worker Statute set forth their rights and also put women's civil rights on a par with men's.

Neo-Batllism, 1947-51

From the beginning of the 1940s, and especially after creation of the wage councils, real wages increased, which meant an improvement in the living standards of the working class and dynamism in the internal market. The period of increased industrial development lasted from 1945 to 1955; total production practically doubled during this time. Agriculture also experienced a boom. Social legislation was improved, the pension system was expanded, and the state bureaucracy grew. Resorts near Montevideo were developed through the sale of lots on the installment plan, and Punta del Este became an international tourist attraction. Gold reserves in BROU reached their highest level ever. In 1950, when Uruguay again won the World Cup in soccer, it was already known as the "Switzerland of South America."

Batllism returned to power with the victory of the presidential ticket of Tomás Berreta (1947) and Luis Batlle Berres (1947-51) in the 1946 elections. Berreta's administration was brief; he died six months after taking office and was succeeded by his vice president, Batlle Berres.

Batlle Berres, a nephew of José Batlle y Ordóñez, represented the most popular faction of Batllism, later to be known as Unity and Reform (Unidad y Reforma), or List 15 because of the list number under which it would participate in successive elections. He gradually became estranged from his cousins—Lorenzo and César, Batlle y Ordóñez's sons—who promoted a more conservative vision from their newspaper, *El Día,* and who would later form a new Colorado Party faction, List 14. Batlle Berres founded his own newspaper (*Acción*) in 1948, bought a radio station, and surrounded himself with young politicians. His ideological-political agenda, adapted to the changes in his country and the world, became known as neo-Batllism. He rejected the communist and populist-authoritarian experiences of other Latin American countries, especially that of Juan Domingo Perón in Argentina. Batlle Berres formed a multiclass movement that promoted compromise and conciliation. He believed the state's role was to safeguard social peace and to correct, through adequate measures, the "unfair differences" created by the socioeconomic structure. In contrast to Peronism, neo-Batllism respected the political autonomy of the workers' movement, accepted social cooperation, and rejected the kind of corporative structure that characterized Mexico's governing party.

Batlle Berres was an enthusiastic supporter of economic development based on import-substitution industrialization (see Glossary) and agricultural expansion. He applied interventionist and statist economic measures to promote such development and did not abide by the IMF's austerity recommendations. He supported agriculture and industry through credits and subsidies, as well as control over the nation's currency, a fact that brought him into conflict with ranchers. BROU, which controlled sales of foreign currency, paid less for foreign currency earned from livestock raising to favor industrial requirements for raw materials and machinery. This differential exchange-rate policy stimulated the development of light industry, more than 90 percent of which was directed toward the internal market. Nevertheless, the state guaranteed profitable prices for agriculture and stimulated imports of agricultural machinery. New crops were developed to supply industry with raw materials, and surpluses were exported. By contrast, livestock raising continued to stagnate.

An earlier agreement with Britain obliged the government to acquire some British enterprises to cancel its outstanding debt to Britain. The state's economic role was thus increased through the creation of new public service enterprises, including Montevideo's tramways, railroads, and water system.

Another potentially significant event in the socioeconomic realm was the creation of the National Land Settlement Institute in 1948. It was designed to stimulate land subdivision and agricultural and livestock settlements and was authorized to purchase and expropriate land. But action was limited because of a lack of funds, and significant agrarian reform never took place. However, in order to favor lower-income groups, subsidies were set for various basic food items, and in 1947 the National Subsistence Council was created to control the price of basic items.

The traditional parties maintained their differences, which were reflected in the significant variations in their platforms. The Political Parties Law, which allowed party factions to accumulate votes, guaranteed the predominance of the Colorado Party. Together, the Colorados and Blancos continued to capture almost 90 percent of the votes. But because of the splits in his own party, Batlle Berres was forced to seek political support from other factions. Paradoxically, he sought a "patriotic coincidence" with Herrera and gave cabinet posts to some leading figures of Terrism, past enemies within his own party.

Conservative sectors, particularly landowners, opposed or distrusted the growing bureaucracy, the expansion of social legislation, and the policy of income redistribution that favored the industrial sector to the detriment of the rural sector. In 1950 Benito Nardone—an anticommunist radio personality supported by Juan Domingo R. Bordaberry, one of the directors of the Rural Federation (and father of Juan María Bordaberry Arocena; president, 1972–76)—created the Federal League for Rural Action (Liga Federal de Acción Rural—LFAR). The Ruralist faction thus created attempted to unite the disenchanted rural middle-class constituencies, especially wool producers, from both traditional parties. He proposed a free-market economic model in contrast to Luis Batlle Berres's statist model.

Unity and Reform won the 1950 elections. Its presidential candidate was a Batllist, Andrés Martínez Trueba (1951–55), who quickly put forward a new constitutional amendment, this time to make good on Batlle y Ordóñez's dream of a purely plural executive, the *colegiado*. He was supported by Herrera, who was seeking to enhance both his personal power and Blanco political power and to recover the ground lost in the 1942 coup. He was also supported by conservative Colorado factions who feared Batlle Berres's becoming president again.

The new constitution was approved by plebiscite in 1951 and went into effect in 1952. It reestablished the *colegiado* as the National Council of Government (Consejo Nacional de Gobierno). The council had nine members, six from the dominant faction of the majority party and three from the party receiving the second highest number of votes (two from its leading faction and one from its second-ranking faction). The presidency was to rotate each year among the six members of the majority party. The constitution mandated coparticipation in directing autonomous entities and ministries, using a three-and-two system (three members appointed by the majority party on the council and two by the minority party). Uruguay enjoyed unprecedented prosperity at this time, and the establishment of a purely collegial, Swiss-style executive reinforced the country's title as the "Switzerland of South America."

Decline of the Economy and the Colorado Party, 1951–58

The Martínez administration in the first half of the 1950s, however, was one of economic decline. At the end of the Korean War (1950–53), during which Uruguay had exported wool for cold-weather uniforms, Uruguay experienced a reduction in exports, a drop in the price of agricultural and livestock products, labor unrest, and unemployment. Livestock production, which had basically stagnated since the 1920s, was not capable of providing the foreign exchange needed to further implement the import-substitution industrialization model. Starting in 1955, the industrial sector stagnated and inflation rose. At the same time, Uruguay had difficulties with the United States regarding wool exports and suffered the negative effects of both restrictive United States trade policies and competition from the foreign sales of United States agricultural surpluses.

In 1951 a faction opposing the more radical leadership of the General Union of Workers (Unión General de Trabajadores—UGT; established in 1942) founded the General Confederation of Labor. Nevertheless, strikes and stoppages continued. In 1952, in the face of labor unrest, the National Council of Government invoked the emergency provision of the constitution known as the *medidas prontas de seguridad* (prompt security measures). From 1956 to 1972, the gross national product (GNP—see Glossary) fell 12 percent, and in the decade from 1957 to 1967 real wages for public employees fell 40 percent. In 1958 the General Assembly approved strike insurance and maternity leave. In addition, worker and student mobilization pressured the General Assembly into approving the Organic University Law, whereby the government recognized the autonomy of the University of the Republic and the right of professors, alumni, and students to govern it. Nevertheless, labor unrest increased.

At first, dramatic political events masked the economic crisis. In the 1958 elections, the Independent Nationalists, who had joined the Democratic Blanco Union (Unión Blanca Democrática—UBD), agreed to include their votes under the traditional National Party of the Herrerists. Thus, for the first time in decades, the National Party voted as one party. In addition, Herrera joined forces with Nardone and his LFAR, transforming it from a union into a political movement. Aided by the LFAR and a weakening economy, the National Party won, and the Colorado Party lost control of the executive for the first time in ninety-four years.

Economic Crisis and Decline
The Blanco Administrations, 1959–67

From March 1959 to February 1967, eight National Party governments ruled Uruguay. The death of Herrera (1959) aggravated divisions in the National Party and demonstrated the fragility of the electoral accords that had led to its victory. The economic crisis and social unrest that had beset Uruguay from the mid-1950s continued, and the 1960s opened with gloom and sadness for the country. At the time of the 1962 elections, inflation was running at a historically high 35 percent. The Colorado Party was defeated once again, although by a much smaller margin of votes (24,000 as compared with 120,000 in 1958). The National Party split. The UBD joined a splinter faction of Herrerism, the Orthodox faction, led by Eduardo Víctor Haedo. Another faction of Herrerism, led by Martín R. Echegoyen (1959–60), kept its alliance with Nardone's Ruralists. At the same time, divisions between the List 14 faction and Unity and Reform were intensified in the Colorado Party. Important changes also took place in the minor parties. Catholics formed the Christian Democratic Party (Partido Demócrata Cristiano—PDC). Communists formed a coalition with other minor parties, the Leftist Liberty Front (Frente Izquierda de Libertad—Fidel). The PSU joined with intellectuals and dissidents from traditional parties and formed the Popular Union (Unión Popular).

The thin majority of the governing party, as well as its internal divisions, hindered the administration of the National Council of Government during the 1963–67 period. In 1964 the political scene was further affected by the death of two important leaders: Batlle Berres and Nardone. That same year, the workers' movement formed a single centralized union, the National Convention of Workers (Convención Nacional de Trabajadores—CNT). In addition, a new political protagonist appeared. In 1962 Raúl Antonaccio Sendic, head of the sugarcane workers from the north of the country, formed, together with other leftist leaders, the National Liberation Movement-Tupamaros (Movimiento de Liberación Nacional-Tupamaros—MLN–T), a clandestine urban guerrilla movement.

Economically, the 1958 Blanco victory brought ranching and agricultural forces to power. This led to the implementation of liberal (free-market) economic policies aimed at eliminating the protectionist-interventionist model that had fostered industrial development. In 1960 Uruguay agreed to sign its first letter of intent with the IMF. The Blanco government devalued the currency and established a single, free monetary exchange market (while maintaining the interventionist role of BROU), as well as the free import and export of goods and services. The reorientation of economic policy tended to favor the agro-exporting sector. However, the model could not be applied fully, nor in an orthodox manner. Inflation increased to more than 50 percent per year between 1963 and 1967, and in 1965 an overstretched financial system and massive speculation produced a banking crisis. Labor and social conflict increased as well, and a state of siege was imposed in 1965.

To try to solve the problem of economic stagnation, the government complied with one of the principal recommendations of the

Alliance for Progress (a United States program to help develop and modernize Latin American states) by preparing a ten-year development plan. However, virtually none of the plan's recommendations were ever put into practice.

During the Blanco era, sectors from both traditional parties had begun blaming the country's difficulties on the collegial constitutional arrangement of executive power. In the 1966 elections, three constitutional amendments were submitted. The approved changes, supported by Blancos and Colorados, were incorporated in the 1967 constitution, which put an end to the collegial executive, thereby returning the country to a presidential regime; granted increased powers to the executive; and extended the presidential term to five years. They also eliminated the three-and-two (coparticipation) system for appointing heads of autonomous entities and ministries and created new state agencies to modernize government: the Office of Planning and Budget, the Social Welfare Bank, and the Central Bank of Uruguay. High school education became compulsory.

Pachequism, 1967–72

Given the growing economic and social crisis, it was not surprising that the Colorado Party won the November 1966 elections. In March 1967, General Oscar Gestido (1967), a retired army general who had earned a reputation as an able and honest administrator when he ran the State Railways Administration, became president. He was supported by the Colorado and Batllist Union (Unión Colorada y Batllista—UCB), comprising List 14 and other conservative Colorados.

Between June and November of 1967, the government, with the influence of some Batllists, attempted to reverse economic and social policies implemented since 1959 and to return to the old developmentalist model. But in November, César Charlone, responsible for economic policies under Terra, became head of the Ministry of Economy and Finance. He agreed to the IMF's suggestions, again establishing a unified exchange market and drastically devaluing the currency. Inflation exceeded 100 percent in 1967, the highest in the country's history.

In December President Gestido died and was succeeded by his vice president, Jorge Pacheco Areco (1967–72). A little-known politician and former director of the newspaper *El Día*, Pacheco would leave an indelible mark on Uruguay. Within one week of taking office, Pacheco issued a decree banning the PSU and other leftist groups and their press, which he accused of subverting the constitutional order and advocating armed struggle. To implement the new monetarist policy adopted in 1968, Pacheco appointed Alejandro

Végh Villegas as director of the Office of Planning and Budget. In a sharp policy change, Pacheco decreed a wage and price freeze in June 1968 to try to control inflation. He also created the Productivity, Prices, and Income Commission (Comisión de Productividad, Precios, e Ingresos—Coprin) to control the price of basic food items. In 1968 real wages were the lowest in the decade, and inflation reached a maximum annual rate of 183 percent that June.

The newly created umbrella labor organization, the CNT, resisted these economic policies, and student and other social conflict intensified. The government responded by repressing strikes, work stoppages, and student demonstrations. The death of a student, Líber Arce, during a protest paralyzed Montevideo, and relations between the University of the Republic and the government further deteriorated. "Prompt security measures," a limited form of a state of siege, which had been included in the constitution to deal with extraordinary disturbances of domestic order and applied in 1952 and 1965, were enforced during almost all of Pacheco's time in office. He justified his actions, which included drafting striking bank and government employees to active military service, on the basis of the growing urban guerrilla threat from the Tupamaros.

During this period, the Tupamaros had grown in strength, and their actions—robberies, denunciations, kidnappings, and, eventually, killings—shook the country and became known worldwide. The General Assembly acquiesced twice in the suspension of all civil liberties, once for twenty days following the assassination in August 1970 of Dan A. Mitrione, a United States security official, and then for forty days following the kidnapping of British ambassador Geoffrey Jackson in January 1971—both by the Tupamaros. On September 9, 1971, after the escape from prison of more than 100 Tupamaros, Pacheco put the army in charge of all counterguerrilla activity.

The November 1971 national elections were held in a relatively quiet atmosphere because of a truce declared by the Tupamaros. Uruguayan society had become polarized. Political sectors supporting Pacheco promoted his reelection to a new presidential term, as well as the corresponding constitutional amendment to legitimize it. The left was able to unite and draw supporters from traditional parties, such as the Colorado Party's List 99. The new coalition was named the Broad Front (Frente Amplio). In the National Party, a faction of Herrerists chose General Mario Aguerrondo, considered a hard-liner, as its presidential candidate. Liberal Blancos supported the reformist program of a new movement, For the Fatherland (Por la Patria—PLP), led by Senator Wilson Ferreira Aldunate.

The constitutional amendment did not succeed, but Pacheco's handpicked successor, Juan María Bordaberry Arocena of the Colorado Party, won the controversial elections by some 10,000 votes, after a mysterious halt in the vote count. It was noteworthy, however, that Ferreira obtained a large number of votes (he was actually the candidate receiving the most votes—26 percent of the total to Bordaberry's 24 percent), and the left increased its following, receiving about 18 percent of the votes. Bipartisan politics had come to an end, replaced by a multiparty system bitterly divided by political, social, economic, and ideological differences. In economic terms, the stabilization measures taken between 1969 and 1971 by the Pacheco administration to increase wages and reduce inflation had been moderately successful. But by 1972, the situation was out of control again. Another free-market, monetarist experiment would have to await the imposition of an authoritarian regime.

The Emergence of Militarism, 1972-73

In March 1972, Bordaberry was sworn in as president (1972-76). He ran as a Colorado, but he had been active in Nardone's Ruralist movement and had been elected to the Senate as a representative of the National Party. Bordaberry's narrow victory forced him to seek the support of other political parties. He found it in Mario Aguerrondo's Herrerist faction of the National Party and in the Colorado Party's Unity and Reform, led by Jorge Batlle Ibáñez, a son of Luis Batlle Berres, who had founded the faction.

Bordaberry appointed Julio María Sanguinetti Cairolo, who headed a faction of Unity and Reform, as minister of education and culture. Sanguinetti promoted education reform that brought together primary, secondary, and vocational education under the National Council for Education (Consejo Nacional de Educación—Conae) and established secret and mandatory voting for the election of university authorities. Unity and Reform also took charge of economic policy by implementing a five-year development plan inspired by neoliberal (free-market) and monetarist principles, which would slowly open the economy to greater influence from financial and commercial groups, as well as to foreign investment.

The Bordaberry administration, however, continued its predecessor's policies, giving greater budgetary priority to the military than to education and other social areas. Bordaberry also proposed legislation to eliminate university autonomy and enhance the powers of the army and police.

When the Tupamaros finally renewed their armed activities following their six-month electoral truce from October 1971 to April

1972, they faced a firmly entrenched administration backed by an increasingly well-equipped and adequately prepared military, which had a blank check to defeat them. In April 1972, after a bloody shoot-out with the Tupamaros, Bordaberry declared a state of "internal war." All civil liberties were suspended, initially for thirty days but later extended by the General Assembly until 1973. On July 10, 1972, the government enacted the draconian State Security Law. By the end of the year, the army had decisively defeated the Tupamaros, whose surviving members either were imprisoned or fled into exile. Despite their victory over the Tupamaros, the military had grown impatient with civilian rule. It was now time for the armed forces' final assault on the Uruguayan polity.

The Military Government, 1973–85

The New Situation, 1973–80

In February 1973, a deep conflict emerged among the president, the General Assembly, and the armed forces. The army and air force rebelled against Bordaberry's selection of a civilian as minister of national defense. On February 9 and 10, the army issued two communiqués proposing a series of political, social, and economic measures. Initially, the navy maintained its loyalty to the president but subsequently joined the other military services. Bordaberry made an agreement with the military, known as the Boisso Lanza Pact, that guaranteed their advisory role and their participation in political decision making. In effect, the pact constituted a quasi-coup. The National Security Council (Consejo de Seguridad Nacional—Cosena) was created as an advisory body to the executive. Its members included the commanders of the army, navy, and air force, plus an additional senior military officer, and the ministers of national defense, interior, and foreign affairs.

The military then pushed for the final approval and implementation of the State Security Law. However, differences with the General Assembly, which was investigating charges of torture committed by the military and felt that the military had exceeded its powers, continued until June 27, 1973. On that date, with the backing of the armed forces, Bordaberry dissolved the General Assembly and replaced it with the Council of State, and he empowered the armed forces and police to take whatever measures were necessary to ensure normal public services. In essence, a de facto dictatorship had been announced. The new situation was supported by some Colorados (the Pachequist faction) and some Blancos (Aguerrondo's Herrerists). But the CNT called for the occupation of factories and a general strike that lasted almost two weeks. When the civil-military dictatorship was consolidated, it banned the CNT, the PCU, and other existing and alleged Marxist-Leninist organizations, and it intervened in the university to quell dissident activities by the students. The military's "Doctrine of National Security" was a pseudo-scientific analysis of society grounded in geopolitics. It posited that sovereignty no longer resided in the people but derived instead from the requirements of state survival. This was basically the same ideology made famous by the Brazilian generals after their takeover in 1964. The core of the doctrine was articulated by Brazil's General Artur Golbery do Couto e Silva in his book *Geopolítica do Brasil.* Essentially, the book described a world divided into two opposing blocs—the capitalist and Christian West and the communist and "atheistic" East—each with its own values that were considered irreconcilable. The Brazilian and Uruguayan generals saw themselves as part of the Western bloc and were therefore engaged in an unrelenting global struggle with the opposition. This struggle called for a war in which there was no room for hesitation or uncertainty against a cunning and ruthless enemy. Thus, it was necessary to sacrifice some secular freedoms in order to protect and preserve the state.

"Preventive" repression by the Uruguayan military regime was intense. To the dead and disappeared were added thousands of persons who went to jail because they were accused of politically motivated crimes. Many were tortured. Others were fired from their government jobs for political reasons. The regime restricted freedom of the press and association, as well as party political activity. Amnesty International calculated that in 1976 Uruguay had more political prisoners per capita than any other nation on earth. During these years, approximately 10 percent of Uruguay's population emigrated for political or economic reasons.

In June 1976, Bordaberry was forced to resign after submitting a proposal to the military calling for the elimination of political parties and the creation of a permanent dictatorship with himself as president. National elections were to be held that year, although politicians could hardly be sanguine after the assassinations in Argentina of Uruguayan political leaders Héctor Gutiérrez Ruiz (National Party) and Zelmar Michelini (Broad Front). Bordaberry was replaced by Alberto Demichelli Lizaso, president of the Council of State, who, through Institutional Act No. 1, decreed the suspension of elections. Three months later, Demichelli was succeeded by Aparicio Méndez (1976–81), who essentially decreed the political prohibition of all individuals who had participated in the 1966 and 1971 elections. Political life thus came to a halt.

In 1977 the military government made public its political plans. Over the next few years, the National Party and the Colorado Party would be purged, a new constitution would be submitted to a plebiscite, and national elections would be held with a single candidate agreed on by both parties. A charter that gave the military virtual veto power over all government policy was drawn up. In 1980 the armed forces decided to legitimize themselves by submitting this constitution to a plebiscite.

Opposing the constitutional project were Batlle Ibáñez, Ferreira, Carlos Julio Pereyra, a Herrerist faction led by Luis Alberto Lacalle de Herrera, Pachequist dissidents, and the Broad Front, who considered it authoritarian and in conflict with Uruguay's democratic tradition. When Uruguay's citizens went to the polls, they dealt the military regime a tremendous blow and rejected the proposed new constitution by 57 to 43 percent.

The Military's Economic Record

When the military took power in 1973, they did so in the face of a decade and a half of economic stagnation, high inflation, and increased social unrest. Massive repression brought the social unrest under control and eliminated the urban guerrilla threat. Economic policy and performance soon became the regime's ultimate claim to legitimacy and justification for its harsh rule. The military and their civilian technocrats hoped to reverse Uruguay's economic stagnation, which had led to an absence of capital accumulation and investment, as well as to capital flight. The dissolution of the General Assembly and the banning of union organizations eliminated any possibilities for action by the opposition and thus made possible a new economic model. The long-term model sought by the military involved a profound change in the traditional roles of the public and private sectors and the response of the public sector to the influence of the external market.

The military's economic program sought to transform Uruguay into an international financial center by lifting restrictions on the exchange rate; ensuring the free convertibility of the peso and foreign remittances, thus further ''dollarizing'' the economy; facilitating the opening of branches of foreign banks; and enacting a law to promote foreign investment. More attention was paid to the international market. The reduction of import duties, promotion of nontraditional exports, integration of trade with Argentina and Brazil, and liberalization of the agricultural and livestock markets were key goals. Although proposals were made to reduce state interventionism, the state participated actively in the preparation of the new program.

The principal architect of the program was Harvard-trained Alejandro Végh Villegas, who had served as minister of economy and finance from 1974 to 1976. Végh hoped to dismantle the protectionist structure of the economy; free the banking and financial communities from the restraints under which they operated; cut the budget, especially social spending; reduce state employment; and sell off most of the state enterprises. However, some of the nationalist and populist military leaders opposed his plan for mass reductions in government employment and divestiture of state enterprises such as ANCAP. Végh succeeded somewhat in his budgetary and monetary objectives and managed to reduce some tariffs. Between 1975 and 1980, his strict monetary policy reduced inflation from 100 percent in 1972 to 40 to 67 percent in 1980, and by 1982 it was only 20 percent. He managed this by strict control of the social service side of the budget and by a policy of depressed real wages, which fell by 50 percent during the 1970s.

Between 1974 and 1980, the gross domestic product (GDP—see Glossary) grew, although unevenly. Beginning in 1980, however, the situation changed as the military's economic program began to unravel. High interest rates and recession in the United States did not help matters. Between 1981 and 1983, GDP fell some 20 percent, and unemployment rose to 17 percent. The foreign debt burden, exacerbated by the quadrupling of oil prices in 1974, grew exponentially and stood at about US$3 billion by 1984.

Industry and agriculture, whose accumulation of debt in dollars had been encouraged by official policies, were adversely affected by the government's elimination in November 1982 of its "crawling peg" system (a minidevaluation monetary policy) in effect since 1978. The progressively overvalued currency had limited the ability of domestic producers to raise prices to compete with cheaper imports. The resulting collapse of the Uruguayan new peso (for value of the Uruguayan new peso—see Glossary) bankrupted thousands of individuals and businesses. Industry was in better shape, although it had unused capacity and no substantial diversification had taken place. The financial sector, which was largely foreign owned, was consolidated and expanded at the same time. As the situation deteriorated, the state, in order to save the banking system, purchased noncollectible debt portfolios of ranchers, industrialists, and importers, which were held by private banks. This adversely affected the fiscal deficit and increased the foreign debt, which grew sevenfold between 1973 and 1984 (see Restructuring under the Military Regime, 1973–85, ch. 3).

The failure of the regime's economic model, combined with its stifling of political opposition, prompted thousands of Uruguay's best professionals to go into exile. By late 1983, Végh returned from an ambassadorship in the United States to once again become minister of economy and finance. As the most important technocrat to serve the military regime, he had returned to help smooth out the expected transition to civilian rule. He failed, however, to turn over a revived economy to a democratic government. The lack of success of the military's economic policies and their failure to achieve legitimacy or consensus led to a watering down of their own plan to reinstitute a civilian government under military tutelage.

The Opposition and the Reemergence of Parties, 1980-84

After the electoral defeat of the military's constitution, retired Lieutenant General Gregorio Alvarez Armelino (1981-85), one of the leaders of the coup, became president, and political dialogue was slowly restored. The 1982 Political Parties Law was enacted to regulate the election of political leaders, the functioning of political conventions, and the preparation of political platforms. Its aim was the controlled regeneration and democratization of the political system, but it excluded the left to avoid a return to the situation prior to 1973. In 1982 the officials of the National Party, the Colorado Party, and the Civic Union (Unión Cívica—UC; created in 1971), a small conservative Catholic party, were elected. Once again, election results were a blow to the military. Sectors opposing the dictatorship won overwhelmingly in both traditional parties. A divided left, although officially banned, also participated: some cast blank ballots, while others believed it would be more useful to back the democratic sectors of traditional parties.

The dialogue between politicians and the military gathered momentum but was marked by advances and setbacks and accompanied by increasing civil resistance. Uruguay was now experiencing its worst economic crisis since the Great Depression. In 1983 the Interunion Workers' Assembly (or Plenum) (Plenario Intersindical de Trabajadores—PIT) reclaimed the banner of the CNT and was authorized to hold a public demonstration on May 1; it later assumed the name PIT-CNT to show its link with the earlier organization. Students—united under the Students' Social and Cultural Association for Public Education (Asociación Social y Cultural de Estudiantes de la Enseñanza Pública—ASCEEP), heir to the banned student organizations—were allowed to march through the streets of Montevideo. In November all opposition parties including the left staged a massive political rally, demanding elections with full restoration of democratic norms and without political proscriptions.

The Transition to Democracy, 1984-85

In March 1984, the PIT-CNT organized a civil strike and freed General Líber Seregni Mosquera, leader of the Broad Front, whom the military had imprisoned since January 11, 1976. By mid-1984 yet another civil strike took place, this time organized by political parties and social groups. Blanco Senator Ferreira returned from exile. His subsequent imprisonment essentially deprived the National Party of the opportunity to participate in the meetings between politicians and the military that ended with the Naval Club Pact. Signed by the armed forces and representatives from the Colorado Party, UC, and Broad Front, this pact called for national elections to be held that same year on the traditional last Sunday in November.

The discussions at the Naval Club saw the military give up its long-sought goal of a Cosena dominated by the military and with virtual veto power over all civilian government decisions. The military now settled for an advisory board that would be controlled by the president and the cabinet. Some transitional features were agreed to by the civilian leadership, mostly relating to the ability of the armed forces to maintain its seniority system in the naming of the commanders of the various military services. The military also agreed to review the cases of all political prisoners who had served at least half of their sentences. Moreover, the military acquiesced to the relegalization of the left, although the PCU remained officially banned (until March 1985). The Communists were nonetheless able to run stand-in candidates under their own list within the leftist coalition. Nothing was said about the question of human rights violations by the dictatorship.

The election results were no great surprise. With Ferreira prohibited from heading the Blanco ticket and a similar fate for Seregni of the Broad Front, and with effective use of young newcomers and a savvy media campaign, the Colorado Party won. The Colorados received 41 percent of the vote; the Blancos, 34 percent; and the Broad Front, 21 percent. The UC received 2.5 percent of the vote. Within the Broad Front's leftist coalition, social democratic Senator Hugo Batalla, who headed List 99, a faction started by Zelmar Michelini in 1971, was the big winner, garnering over 40 percent of the alliance's vote. For the victorious Colorados, former President Pacheco brought the party 25 percent of its vote. However, the Colorado presidential ticket receiving the most votes (in a system that allowed multiple candidacies for president in each party) was headed by Sanguinetti. After being sworn in as president on March 1, 1985, Sanguinetti led the transition to democracy.

He did so with dignity and fairness, although the legacy of human rights violations under the dictatorship proved a troublesome problem (see Democratic Consolidation, 1985–90, ch. 4).

* * *

Eduardo Acevedo's voluminous work *Anales históricos del Uruguay*, which starts in the sixteenth century and ends in 1930, provides a solid bibliographical background for both political and socioeconomic changes. A more modern version, restricted to the 1851–1914 period, may be found in José Pedro Barrán and Benjamín Nahum's *Historia rural del Uruguay moderno*. This seven-volume work contains an analysis of Uruguay's main sources of wealth, as well as a review of political events and social change.

Historiographical production on Uruguay slowed down beginning in 1930, a fact demonstrated by a decrease in contemporary historical research. There are, however, short works covering the period from 1930 to the present: Raúl Jacob's *El Uruguay de Terra, 1931–1938;* Ana Frega, Mónica Maronna, and Yvette Trochon's *Baldomir y la restauración democrática, 1938–1946;* Germán D'Elía's *El Uruguay neo-Batllista, 1946–1958;* Rosa Alonso Eloy and Carlos Demassi's *Uruguay, 1958–1968;* Oscar Bruschera's *Las décadas infames, 1967–1985;* and Gerardo Caetano and José Pedro Rilla's *Breve historia de la dictadura, 1973–1985.* An excellent economic history of Uruguay is M.H.J. Finch's *A Political Economy of Uruguay since 1870.* Useful English-language sources on contemporary Uruguay include Martin Weinstein's *Uruguay: The Politics of Failure* and *Uruguay: Democracy at the Crossroads.* Although somewhat dated, Marvin Alisky's *Uruguay: A Contemporary Survey* and Russell H. Fitzgibbon's *Uruguay: Portrait of a Democracy* also contain useful background information. (For further information and complete citations, see Bibliography.)

Chapter 2. The Society and Its Environment

Street of Sighs, a seventeenth-century historical site in Colonia del Sacramento

URUGUAY WAS ONCE KNOWN as the "Switzerland of South America" as a result of its relative governmental stability, advanced level of economic development, and social peace. Indeed, in the creation of a welfare state, it was far ahead of Switzerland during the first half of the twentieth century. Starting in the 1950s, however, Uruguay's economy began to stagnate, and the once-vaunted welfare state became increasingly poor. Commentators talked of the "Latin Americanization" of Uruguay as it descended from the ranks of the developed nations to the level of the developing nations. Political and social unrest eventually culminated in the military coup of 1973; by then the case for seeing Uruguay as very different from the rest of Latin America was largely undermined.

During the sixty-year period from 1870 to 1930, foreign immigrants flooded into Uruguay, mainly from Spain and Italy, to improve their standard of living. A historical study of social and economic development ranked Uruguay fourth among all independent nations in the world in the 1880s. In 1990 Uruguay's levels of education and nutrition were still among the highest in Latin America, as well as its per capita ownership of radios, televisions, and telephones and its newspaper readership.

However, four decades of economic stagnation had seriously eroded Uruguay's lead in terms of per capita gross domestic product (GDP—see Glossary). Historically, only Argentina rivaled it in Latin America in terms of this crucial economic indicator. By the middle of the twentieth century, Uruguay had been overtaken by Venezuela in terms of per capita GDP, and in 1970 Chile had almost caught up. By 1980 so had Brazil, Costa Rica, Panama, and Mexico.

A study published by the United Nations Development Programme (UNDP) in 1990 attempted to rank 130 countries of the world by their level of social (rather than purely economic) development. Switzerland was the richest nation as measured by per capita GDP, adjusted for purchasing power parities. Using the same indicator, Uruguay was ranked forty-fifth, underlining how far it had fallen economically. Nevertheless, Uruguay ranked far higher on a composite indicator of social progress dubbed by the UNDP the "Human Development Index." The index took into account life expectancy and level of literacy, as well as adjusted per capita GDP. By this measure, Uruguay ranked twenty-ninth, immediately above Hungary. Only two Latin American countries scored higher on this index: Costa Rica (ranking twenty-eighth) and Chile (ranking twenty-fourth). In comparison, the United States ranked nineteenth. Japan had the highest Human Development Index of all.

In sum, Uruguayan society in 1990 presented a contradictory picture of advanced social indicators and declining economic status. In many ways, it remained unlike other Latin American and developing countries.

Geography

Uruguay is located in the Southern Hemisphere on the Atlantic seaboard of South America between 53° and 58° west longitude and 30° and 35° south latitude (see fig. 1). It is bounded on the west by Argentina, on the north and northeast by Brazil, and on the southeast by the Atlantic Ocean. To the south, it fronts the Río de la Plata, a broad estuary that opens out into the South Atlantic. Montevideo, the capital and major port, sits on the banks of the Río de la Plata and is on approximately the same latitude as Capetown and Sydney. Uruguay is the smallest Spanish-speaking nation in South America with a land area of 176,220 square kilometers, slightly smaller than North Dakota.

Topography and Hydrography

Most of Uruguay is a gently rolling plain that represents a transition from the almost featureless Argentine pampas to the hilly uplands of southern Brazil. The country itself has flat plains on its eastern, southern, and western edges. The narrow Atlantic coastal plain is sandy and marshy, occasionally broken by shallow lagoons. The littorals of the Río de la Plata and the Río Uruguay are somewhat broader and merge more gradually into the hilly interior (see fig. 3).

The remaining three-quarters of the country is a rolling plateau marked by ranges of low hills that become more prominent in the north as they merge into the highlands of southern Brazil. Even these hilly areas are remarkably featureless, however, and elevations seldom exceed 200 meters.

Uruguay is a water-rich land. Prominent bodies of water mark its limits on the east, south, and west, and even most of the boundary with Brazil follows small rivers. Lakes and lagoons are numerous, and a high water table makes digging wells easy.

Three systems of rivers drain the land: rivers flow westward to the Río Uruguay, eastward to the Atlantic or tidal lagoons bordering the ocean, and south to the Río de la Plata. The Río Uruguay, which forms the border with Argentina, is flanked by low

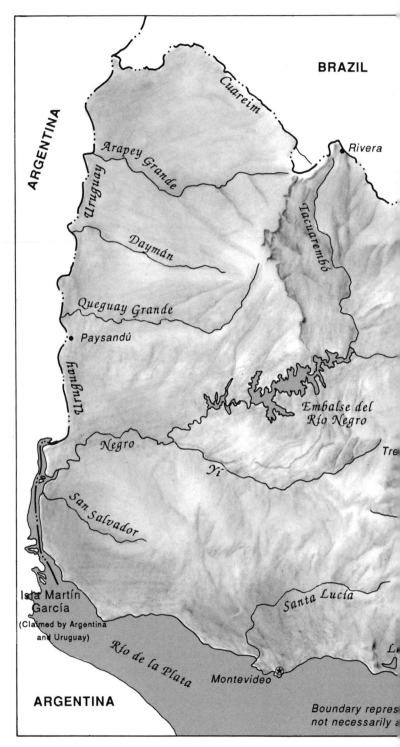

Figure 3. Topography and Drainage

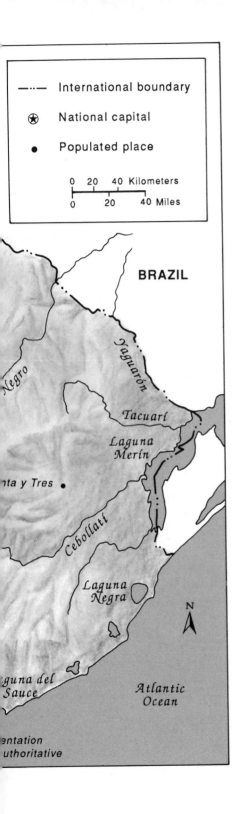

BRAZIL

Yaguarón

Tacuarí

Laguna
Merín

ta y Tres

Cebollatí

Laguna
Negra

N

guna del
Sauce

Atlantic
Ocean

Negro

ntation
uthoritative

banks, and disastrous floods sometimes inundate large areas. The longest and most important of the rivers draining westward is the Río Negro, which crosses the entire country from northeast to west before emptying into the Río Uruguay. A dam on the Río Negro at Paso de los Toros has created a reservoir—the Embalse del Río Negro—that is the largest artificial lake in South America. The Río Negro's principal tributary and the country's second most important river is the Río Yí.

The rivers flowing east to the Atlantic are generally shallower and have more variable flow than the other rivers. Many empty into lagoons in the coastal plain. The largest coastal lagoon, Laguna Merín, forms part of the border with Brazil. A half-dozen smaller lagoons, some freshwater and some brackish, line the coast farther south.

Climate

Located entirely within the temperate zone, Uruguay has a climate that is fairly uniform nationwide. Seasonal variations are pronounced, but extremes in temperature are rare. As would be expected by its abundance of water, high humidity and fog are common. The absence of mountains, which act as weather barriers, makes all locations vulnerable to high winds and rapid changes in weather as fronts or storms sweep across the country.

Seasons are fairly well defined, and in most of Uruguay spring is usually damp, cool, and windy; summers are warm; autumns are mild; and winters are chilly and uncomfortably damp. Northwestern Uruguay, however, is farther from large bodies of water and therefore has warmer summers and milder and drier winters than the rest of the country. Average highs and lows in summer (January) in Montevideo are 28°C and 17°C, respectively, with an absolute maximum of 43°C; comparable numbers for Artigas in the northwest are 33°C and 18°C, with the highest temperature ever recorded 42°C. Winter (July) average highs and lows in Montevideo are 14°C and 6°C, respectively, although the high humidity makes the temperatures feel colder; the lowest temperature registered in Montevideo is -4°C. Averages in July of a high of 18°C and a low of 7°C in Artigas confirm the milder winters in northwestern Uruguay, but even here temperatures have dropped to a subfreezing -4°C.

Rainfall is fairly evenly distributed throughout the year, and annual amounts increase from southeast to northwest. Montevideo averages 950 millimeters annually, and Artigas receives 1,235 millimeters in an average year. As in most temperate climates, rainfall results from the passage of cold fronts in winter, falling in overcast drizzly spells, and summer thunderstorms are frequent.

High winds are a disagreeable characteristic of the weather, particularly during the winter and spring, and wind shifts are sudden and pronounced. A winter warm spell can be abruptly broken by a strong *pampero,* a chilly and occasionally violent wind blowing north from the Argentine pampas. Summer winds off the ocean, however, have the salutary effect of tempering warm daytime temperatures.

Land Use and Settlement Patterns

Uruguay may be divided into four regions, based on social, economic, and geographical factors. The regions include the interior, the littoral, Greater Montevideo, and the coast.

The Interior

This largest region includes the departments of Artigas, Cerro Largo, Durazno, Flores, Florida, Lavalleja, Rivera, Salto, Tacuarembó, and Treinta y Tres and the eastern halves of Paysandú, Río Negro, and Soriano. The topsoil is thin and unsuited to intensive agriculture, but it nourishes abundant natural pasture.

Only 2 to 3 percent of Uruguay's land is forested. An estimated 3 to 4 million hectares (17 to 23 percent of the total land) are arable, but only one-third of this (about 7 percent of the total productive land) was cultivated in 1990. Almost all of the interior consisted of cattle and sheep ranches; pasture accounted for 89 percent of the country's productive land.

Sheep rearing was typically undertaken on medium-sized farms concentrated in the west and south. It began to boom as an export industry in the last quarter of the nineteenth century, particularly following the invention of barbed wire, which allowed the easy enclosure of properties. Uruguayan wool is of moderate quality, not quite up to Australian standards (see Livestock Ranching, ch. 3).

Cattle ranches, or *estancias,* for beef and hides were typically quite large (over 1,000 hectares) and were concentrated in the north and east. (Dairying was concentrated in the department of Colonia.) Because ranching required little labor, merely a few gauchos, the interior lacked a peasantry and large towns. Despite being sparsely populated, however, the interior was relatively urbanized in that the capital of each department usually contained about half the inhabitants. Social and economic development indicators were lowest for the departments along the Brazilian border to the northeast. Government attempts to encourage agricultural colonization by means of land reform in the interior had largely failed in economic terms, as had the promotion of wheat production. One exception, rice, most of which was produced in the east, had become a major nontraditional export in recent years (see Crop Production, ch. 3).

The Littoral

Stretching west along the Río de la Plata from Montevideo are the agricultural and dairying departments of San José and Colonia. To the north along the Río Uruguay lie the departments of Soriano, Río Negro, and Paysandú. Their western halves form part of the littoral, a region that is somewhat more developed than the interior. Here soils are alluvial and more fertile, favoring crop production and farms of more modest size than in the interior. Citrus cultivation for export has increased in the departments along the Río Uruguay. The department of Colonia, some of which was settled by the Swiss, was famous for the production of milk, butter, cheese, and *dulce de leche* (a dessert made from concentrated milk and sugar). Most wheat (in which Uruguay was self-sufficient) also was produced in this region.

Construction with Argentina of the Salto Grande Dam across the Río Uruguay north of Salto was a major boost to the development of the northern littoral in the 1970s. By contrast, the closure of the famous meat-packing plant at Fray Bentos in the department of Río Negro transformed it into a virtual ghost town. Farther south, the littoral economy had benefited from completion of the General Artigas Bridge across the Río Uruguay from Paysandú to the Argentine province of Entre Ríos. However, the advent of a convenient (if circuitous) land route from Montevideo to Buenos Aires via the new bridge reduced freight and passenger traffic through the small port of Colonia on the Río de la Plata just opposite the Argentine capital. To compensate, the Uruguayan government encouraged the architectural restoration of Colonia, which was originally built by the Portuguese in colonial times. By 1990 Colonia had became one of Uruguay's most historic tourist attractions, and many of its houses had been bought by vacationers from Buenos Aires.

Greater Montevideo

According to the 1985 census, the population of the department of Montevideo was 1,311,976, and that of the neighboring department of Canelones was 364,248, out of a total population of 2,955,241. Thus, these departments and the eastern portion of San José, which together constituted the Greater Montevideo region, held over one-half of Uruguay's population. This monocephalic pattern of settlement was more pronounced in Uruguay than in any other nation of the world, barring city-states. The 1985 census

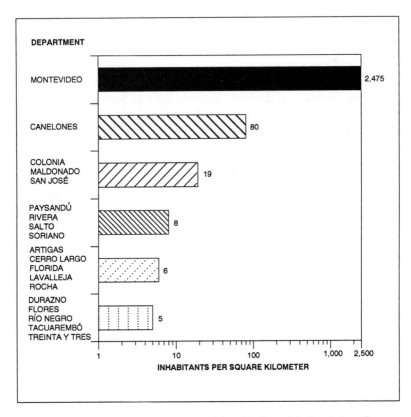

Source: Based on information from Uruguay, Dirección General de Estadística y Censos, *Anuario estadístico, 1988,* Montevideo, 1989.

Figure 4. Average Population Density by Department, 1985

indicated a population density of about 2,475 inhabitants per square kilometer in the department of Montevideo and about 80 inhabitants per square kilometer in the department of Canelones. Densities elsewhere in the country were dramatically lower (see fig. 4; table 2, Appendix).

Montevideo was originally founded on a promontory beside a large bay that forms a perfect natural harbor. In the nineteenth century, the British promoted it as a rival port to Buenos Aires. The city has expanded to such an extent that by 1990 it covered most of the department. The original area of settlement, known as the Old City, lies adjacent to the port, but the central business district and the middle-class residential areas have moved eastward. The only exception to this pattern of eastward expansion is that banking and finance continued to cluster in the Old City around the Stock Exchange, the Bank of Uruguay (Banco de la República Oriental del Uruguay—BROU), and the Central Bank of Uruguay.

Since the 1950s, Montevideo's prosperous middle classes have tended to abandon the formerly fashionable downtown areas for the more modern high-rise apartment buildings of Pocitos, a beach-front neighborhood east of the center. Still farther east lies the expensive area of Carrasco, a zone of modern luxury villas that has come to replace the old neighborhood of El Prado in the north of the city as home to the country's wealthy elite. Its beaches were less polluted than those closer to the center. Montevideo's Carrasco International Airport is located there. The capital's principal artery, 18th of July Avenue, was long the principal shopping street of Montevideo, but it has been hurt since the mid-1980s by the construction of a modern shopping mall strategically located between Pocitos and Carrasco.

Montevideo's poorer neighborhoods tended to be located in the north of the city and around the bay in the areas of industrial activity. However, the degree of spatial separation of social classes was moderate by the standards of other cities in South America. Starting in the 1970s, the city began to acquire a belt of shantytowns around its outskirts, but in 1990 these remained small compared with Rio de Janeiro or Guayaquil, for example. About 60,000 families lived in such shantytowns, known in Uruguay as *cantegriles*. An intensive program of public housing construction was undertaken in the 1970s and 1980s, but it had not solved the problem by 1990.

In 1990 Greater Montevideo was by far the most developed region of Uruguay and dominated the nation economically and culturally. It was home to the country's two universities, its principal hospitals, and most of its communications media (television stations, radio stations, newspapers, and magazines). Attempts by the military governments from 1973 to 1985 to promote the development of the north of the country (partly for strategic reasons) failed to change this pattern of extreme centralization. In one way, however, they achieved a major success: the introduction of direct dialing revolutionized the country's long-distance telephone system. By contrast, the local telephone network in Montevideo remained so hopelessly antiquated and unreliable that many firms relied on courier services to get messages to other downtown businesses.

Until the construction boom of the late 1970s, relatively few modern buildings had been constructed. In many parts of the center, elegant nineteenth-century houses built around a central patio were still to be seen in 1990. In some cases, the patio was open to the air, but in most cases it was covered by a skylight, some of which were made of elaborate stained glass. Few of these houses were used for single-family occupancy, however, and many had been converted into low-cost apartments.

The middle classes preferred to live in more modern apartments near the city center or the University of the Republic. Alternatively, they might purchase a single-family villa with a small yard at the back. Many of these were close to the beaches running east from the downtown along the avenue known as the Rambla. In Pocitos, however, high-rise apartments had replaced the single-family homes on those streets closest to the beach.

The Coast

Stretching east from Montevideo along the Río de la Plata are the departments of Canelones, Maldonado, and Rocha. The inland portion of Canelones is an area of small farms and truck gardens, which produce vegetables for the capital. It was relatively poor in 1990. Many inhabitants of the department's small towns also commuted to jobs in Montevideo by express bus. Along the coast lie a string of small seaside towns (*balnearios*), from which more prosperous employees had also begun to commute. Farther east in the highly developed department of Maldonado lies the major resort of Punta del Este. This has been developed as a fashionable playground more for Argentines than for average Uruguayans, who found it too expensive. With its hotels, restaurants, casino, and nightclubs, Punta del Este was a major export earner, and it dominated Uruguay's tourism industry (see Tourism, ch. 3).

Vacationing Uruguayans of more modest means were concentrated in smaller resorts such as Piriápolis and Atlántida, which are closer to Montevideo. Beyond Punta del Este in the still mostly undeveloped department of Rocha, a number of communities had sprouted along the unspoiled Atlantic coast with its miles of sandy beaches and huge breakers. These small vacation communities—such as Aguas Dulces and Cabo Polonio, both in Rocha Department—were entirely unplanned and lacked essential services. In many cases, simple holiday chalets had been built on public property adjoining the seashore without any legal title to the land. In 1990 the authorities in Rocha Department announced plans to regulate and improve this development in hopes of encouraging visits by higher-spending tourists.

Regional Development

Uruguay's regions differed markedly not only in population size and density but also in their indexes of social and economic development, including education, health care, communications,

Dairy farm families near
Treinta y Tres
Courtesy Inter-American
Development Bank

energy consumption, and industrialization. Least developed were the northern ranching departments along the Brazilian border— Artigas, Rivera, and Cerro Largo—and also Tacuarembó. Somewhat more developed was a band of six departments stretching across the center of the country, from west to east: Río Negro, Flores, Florida, Durazno, Treinta y Tres, and Rocha. More industrialized and urbanized, but still quite poor, were the departments of Soriano and Salto, which, as noted previously, benefited from the construction of a bridge and a dam, respectively, across the Río Uruguay in the late 1970s and early 1980s. The two remaining western departments—Colonia and Paysandú—were the most developed of the littoral.

Three departments close to Montevideo—San José, Canelones, and Lavalleja—presented a contradictory picture of relatively advanced economic development combined with low indexes of social modernization. Finally, Montevideo and the department of Maldonado (which is strongly affected by the tourism industry in Punta del Este) had the highest indexes of social and economic development in the country (see table 3, Appendix).

Population

In 1988 Uruguay's population was estimated at 3,081,000, up somewhat from the 2,955,241 inhabitants recorded in the 1985 census. From 1981 to 1988, the population growth rate averaged about 0.7 percent per year. In South America, only Guyana and Suriname had a lower growth rate. According to projections, the growth rate would continue in the 0.6 to 0.7 range through the year 2020, resulting in an estimated total population of 3,152,000 in 1995, 3,264,000 in 2000, and 3,679,000 in 2020 (see table 4, Appendix).

A major factor in Uruguay's low population growth rate was its relatively low birth rate. The average birth rate for 1990 was the lowest in Latin America at just 17 per 1,000 inhabitants. Significant levels of emigration also inhibited the growth of the population. At the same time, the average life expectancy of Uruguayans (seventy years for men and seventy-six years for women in 1990) was relatively high. Together, the comparatively low birth rate, net emigration, and long life expectancy gave Uruguay an aging population with a pyramidal structure more typical of a developed country than of a developing country (see fig. 5).

In addition to its remarkably low population growth rate, low birth rate, high life expectancy, and aging population, Uruguay also was notable for its extremely high level of urbanization. According to the 1985 census, 87 percent of Uruguay's population could be classified as urban. Moreover, this trend was expected to continue because the urban population was continuing to grow at a faster rate than the population as a whole, while the rural population growth rate was well under that for the total population. In the 1981–88 period, Uruguay's urban population grew at a rate of 0.9 percent, while its rural population grew at a rate of only 0.3 percent (as compared with a total population growth rate of 0.7 percent).

Ethnically, Uruguay enjoyed a high level of homogeneity. Its population was estimated to be nearly 90 percent white, having descended from the original Spanish colonists as well as from the many European immigrants, chiefly from Spain and Italy, who flocked to Uruguay in the late nineteenth and early twentieth centuries. (The remainder were primarily black and mestizo, or people of mixed Indian and European ancestry.)

Historical Patterns of Settlement

First administered from Buenos Aires, Uruguay came into being as an independent nation in 1828 when the British intervened to create a buffer (and client) state between Argentina and Brazil. The fact that Uruguay was scarcely settled beyond a thin coastal strip during the colonial period meant that unlike many other areas of Latin America, little of its colonial heritage survived. The British dominated the country's economic and commercial development until World War I. In marked distinction to Chile's or Peru's minerals, however, Uruguay's prime productive asset (land) remained in the hands of Uruguayans, or at least settlers who wanted to become Uruguayans.

Shortly after independence, civil war broke out between the two political factions that came to form Uruguay's traditional parties, the Colorado Party (Partido Colorado) and the National Party (Partido Nacional, usually referred to as the Blancos). Military conflicts between caudillos on both sides were to recur frequently until 1904. The main cause of conflict was the rivalry between center and periphery: in Montevideo the Colorados predominated, but in the interior the Blancos wished to preserve their control. A dictatorship by a Colorado caudillo, Lorenzo Latorre (1876–80), imposed strict order in the countryside. Concurrently, Uruguay's exports of beef products and wool to Europe began to boom.

After 1911 massive growth of frozen meat exports revived the profitability of the large cattle ranches that had been somewhat eclipsed after the 1860s by medium-sized sheep farms. By World War I, two-fifths of the nation's farmland was in the hands of large landowners (the 3 to 4 percent of proprietors who had over 2,000

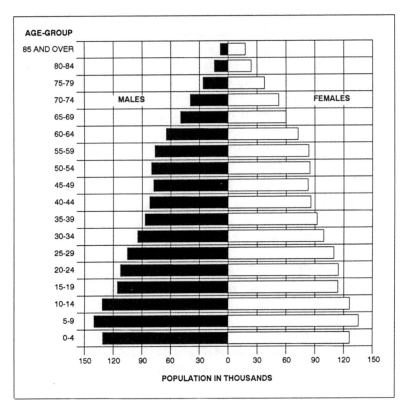

Source: Based on information from Uruguay, Dirección General de Estadística y Censos, *Anuario estadístico, 1988,* Montevideo, 1989.

Figure 5. Population by Age and Sex, 1985

hectares). However, historians have argued that Uruguay's rural society was "pluralist" in character. Thus, along with the big land-owners (*latifundistas*) and smallholders (*minifundistas*), a middle sector had arisen, constituting 40 percent of the proprietors and accounting for 55 percent of the land.

Contemporary Ethnic Composition

In 1990 about 88 percent of Uruguay's population was white and descended from Europeans, and the nation has always looked to Europe for its cultural cues. Eight percent of the population was mestizo, and 4 percent was black. Although in 1990 Uruguay had an aging population, it was once a young nation of immigrants. According to the 1908 census, over two-fifths of the population was foreign born. While the descendants of the original Spanish colonists (known as criollos) predominated in the interior, the origins of the population were varied in the densely populated areas of Montevideo and the coast. In these areas, citizens of Italian descent were particularly numerous, constituting as much as one-third of the population.

In 1990 estimates of the number of Uruguayans of African descent ranged from as low as 40,000 to as high as 130,000 (about 4 percent). In Montevideo, many of them traditionally made a living as musicians or entertainers. Few had been allowed to achieve high social status. As many as three-quarters of black women aged eighteen to forty were employed in domestic service. In the interior, citizens of African or mixed descent were concentrated along the Brazilian border. Early in the twentieth century, the traditional folkways of Afro-Uruguayans were captured in the impressionist paintings of Pedro Figari. Although vestiges of African culture survived in the annual carnival celebrations known as the Llamadas, Uruguay's black population was relatively assimilated in 1990.

Uruguay's Indian population had virtually disappeared and was no longer in evidence in 1990. Even the mestizo, or mixed-race, population was small—8 percent—by Latin American standards. In 1990 signs of intermarriage between whites and Indians were common only in the interior. The slightly derogatory term *chino* was still applied by the inhabitants of Montevideo to the somewhat darker-skinned migrants from the interior.

Montevideo also had a highly assimilated Jewish population of some importance. Estimated at 40,000 in 1970, the Jewish community had fallen to about 25,000 by the late 1980s as a result of emigration, particularly to Israel. Anti-Semitism was not uncommon, but it was less virulent than, for example, in Argentina.

Fertility, Mortality, and Population Growth

Uruguay's population has grown slowly throughout its history, reaching the 1 million mark early in the twentieth century. In the twentieth century, the rate of population growth declined steadily, however, despite significant amounts of immigration and virtually halted in the 1950s. Registered at over 2 percent in 1916, the annual growth rate had dropped to 1.4 percent by 1937. It continued in the 1.2 to 1.5 percent range until 1960, but in the 1960s population growth averaged only 1 percent annually. In the 1970s, the average annual growth rate was even lower, at 0.4 percent. In the 1981–88 period, annual population growth was 0.7 percent, but in 1990 it was 0.6 percent.

A major contributor to the slow population growth rate was Uruguay's low, and declining, crude birth rate. It fell steadily throughout the first half of the twentieth century, from 38.9 per 1,000 population in the 1900–04 period to 21.1 per 1,000 in the 1945–49 period, where it more or less stabilized through the mid-1960s. In the 1980–85 period, the birth rate was 19.5 per 1,000. In 1987 it was estimated at 17.5, and in 1990 it was estimated at 17 per 1,000. (In comparison, the birth rates for Argentina, Brazil, and the United States in 1990 were 20 per 1,000, 26 per 1,000, and 15 per 1,000, respectively.) This relatively low birth rate was usually ascribed to Uruguay's prosperity and the widespread availability of contraception. Given the secularization of Uruguayan society at the beginning of the twentieth century, the influence of the Roman Catholic Church was minor (see Religion, this ch.). The total fertility rate in 1990 was 2.4 children born per woman.

The crude death rate, which had averaged 14 to 15 per 1,000 since the 1895–99 period, began to decline significantly starting in the 1920s. In the 1940s, it reached 10 per 1,000, and it has stayed at approximately this level ever since. In 1987 the crude death rate was estimated at 9.5 per 1,000 and in 1990 at 10 per 1,000.

Advances in medicine resulted in longer life expectancy. Uruguay's General Directorate of Statistics and Census noted that overall life expectancy in the 1984–86 period was 71.6 years (68.4 years for men and 74.9 years for women). Estimates in 1990 placed life expectancy for males at seventy years and that for females at seventy-six years. Because Uruguayans were living longer, the population began to age. By the census year of 1963, demographers already were beginning to worry that the rising proportion of the population in retirement might overstrain the country's social security system (see Social Security Pensions, this ch.). The 1975 and 1985 censuses confirmed the acceleration of this aging trend. The trend was aggravated as net immigration, which had characterized Uruguay in the early twentieth century, gave way to net emigration and the exodus in particular of young, well-educated Uruguayans.

Urbanization

In the nineteenth century, Uruguay was already highly urbanized. But in the twentieth century, it has been one of the world's most urbanized states. According to the 1985 census, 87 percent of Uruguayans lived in urban areas, the highest percentage in Latin America. The department of Montevideo alone accounted for 44 percent of the country's population; the department of Canelones accounted for another 12 percent. Furthermore, the interior of Uruguay, although sparsely populated, was also quite urban. Census figures from 1985 indicate that even outside Montevideo over 80

A flea market in Montevideo
Courtesy Edmundo Flores

percent of the country's inhabitants could be classified as "urban," i.e., living in towns of 2,000 inhabitants or more. Most of these townspeople lived in the departmental capitals.

Uruguay's level of urbanization seemed likely to continue to rise, based on estimates of the growth rate of the urban population vis-à-vis that of the population as a whole and that of the rural population. During the 1960s, the urban population grew at an annual rate of 1.7 percent, while the overall population growth rate was only 1.0 percent. In the 1970s, the growth rates were 0.6 and 0.4 percent, respectively. For the 1981–88 period, the overall population growth rate was 0.7 percent, while the urban population grew by 0.9 percent and the rural population by only 0.3 percent.

Migration

Rural depopulation has been a striking trend in Uruguay during the twentieth century. According to the 1975 census, one-fifth of those citizens born in the eighteen interior, littoral, and coastal departments lived in Montevideo. The departments that produced the highest flow of outward migration between the 1963 and 1975 censuses were in the interior of the country. In the littoral and coastal departments (except the department of Rocha), the greater net retention of population correlated with the growth of the local

67

urban population. This showed that people tended to stay in the department where they were born if there were local towns to which they could move. Otherwise, they moved farther afield.

Migration in Uruguay thus appeared to follow the classic pattern by which those born in isolated rural areas moved to the nearest towns, whereas those born in interior towns headed for Montevideo. Montevideans, in turn, sought to migrate to large cities in Latin America, notably Buenos Aires, where their accents and customs blended successfully and where wages were much higher on average.

Emigration

Since the 1950s, Uruguay's traditional pattern of net immigration has given way to a severe pattern of emigration, which has been of concern to the authorities. This was particularly worrisome because those most likely to leave were the youngest and best-educated citizens. The emigration of youth and the country's aging population had created a very high dependency ratio and serious difficulties for Uruguay's social security system. A famous piece of black-humored graffiti in the port of Montevideo in the early 1970s read: "Last one to leave, please turn off the lights!" Estimates of emigration as high as one-third of the population have, however, been wildly exaggerated.

Economics motivated emigration in the 1960s, but political repression became a major factor during the 1973–85 military regime. Official figures suggest that 180,000 people left Uruguay from 1963 to 1975. In 1973 about 30,000 left, in 1974 nearly 60,000, and in 1975 nearly 40,000. According to the General Directorate of Statistics and Census, 150,000 Uruguayans left the country between 1975 and 1985. By 1989 only 16,500 of them had returned. If the 180,000 who left between 1963 and 1975 are added, the proportion of the population that emigrated from 1963 to 1985 can be estimated at about one-tenth. Along with the low birth rate, this is the major explanation for the country's low population growth rate.

Most of the emigrants were young. Of those who emigrated between 1963 and 1975, 17.7 percent were aged fourteen or younger, 68 percent were between the ages of fifteen and thirty-nine, and only 14.3 percent were forty years or older. Those leaving were on average also better educated than the total population. Only 1.5 percent were uneducated, 52.1 percent had completed primary school, 33.6 percent had attended secondary school or teachers' training colleges, and 12.8 percent had attended university or technical college.

In the late 1980s, the lack of jobs for young people was again a fundamental factor contributing to emigration. Those people leaving Uruguay were not only younger and better educated than the population as a whole but also tended to have more job skills. Among those aged fourteen and older who emigrated from 1963 to 1975 and who were economically active, the relative proportions of different occupations were as follows: professionals, technicians, managers, and administrators made up 12.8 percent, 2.9 percentage points higher than in the economically active population (EAP) as a whole in 1975; office employees constituted 16 percent of those emigrating, 4.3 points above their share of the EAP; salespeople made up 12.4 percent of emigrants, 2 points above the EAP; and drivers, skilled and unskilled workers, and day laborers constituted 34.2 percent of the EAP in 1975, but 47.6 percent of those emigrating.

On the one hand, the proportion of emigrants who had worked as domestic servants was 10.4 percent, close to their share of the EAP. On the other hand, whereas 18.2 percent of the EAP was classified as farmers and fishermen in 1975, these made up only 0.8 percent of those leaving the country in the previous twelve years.

By far the most popular destination for Uruguayan emigrants was Argentina, which in the first half of the 1970s took over one-half of the emigrants. Also important were the United States and Australia, followed by Spain, Brazil, and Venezuela. Small numbers of artists, intellectuals, and politicians experiencing persecution emigrated to Western Europe, notably to the Netherlands and Spain. Many of these political exiles, however, chose to return to Uruguay after 1984.

The Uruguayan community in Argentina was officially given as 58,000 in 1970 but was actually much larger. Many Uruguayans in Argentina returned to Montevideo at election time to vote. Political exiles were allowed to return to Uruguay after 1984, but many of them found it difficult to make a living. This was even true in those cases where they had the right to return to former government posts, for example in education. Often they expressed shock at the decay of public services and the dilapidated state of buildings compared with their memories of Montevideo.

Social Classes

By Latin American standards, Uruguay is a relatively egalitarian society with a large middle class. One factor that historically helped the country avoid social polarization was the broad provision of free public education by the state starting in the 1870s. Economic stagnation since the 1950s has reduced the opportunities for upward social mobility, but the incidence of extreme wealth and poverty still approximated the pattern of developed countries rather than that of developing countries.

Uruguay's upper classes consisted of ranchers, businessmen, and politicians. The middle classes included professionals, white-collar workers, small businessmen, and medium-sized farmers. The lower classes consisted of blue-collar workers, domestic workers, a small number of peasants, and those forced to survive precariously in the informal sector of the economy.

Estimates of the proportion of different sectors of the population in each class are by definition arbitrary. The upper classes are conventionally held to constitute 5 percent of the citizenry, but the relative sizes of the middle and lower classes have been much debated. In the 1950s, mainstream sociologists estimated that the middle classes constituted as much as two-thirds of the population. More radical writers in the 1960s suggested a figure as low as one-third. A reasonable figure, however, would be 45 percent, a proportion broadly consistent with the occupational structure revealed by census data. This left half the population in the lower-class category, although it must be stressed that class differences in Uruguay were far less pronounced than in much of Latin America.

The Ranching Elite

Compared with their counterparts on the Argentine pampas, Uruguay's *latifundistas* (large landholders) never achieved the same level of social and political preeminence. Constituting a tiny fraction of the population, they nevertheless controlled the bulk of the nation's land, which they typically used for cattle and sheep ranching (see Land Use and Tenure, ch. 3). Intermarriage with newer urban commercial elites was common, but many of the ranchers descended from colonial Spanish settlers. Those who could afford it ran their ranches as absentee landlords, spending as much of the year as possible in Montevideo. Their children were traditionally educated in private schools, which were either Roman Catholic or English-speaking schools. Originally founded for the children of expatriates, the latter institutions continued to model themselves on Britain's elite private schools.

For the ranchers, the social event of the year was the annual agricultural show at the Prado, a park in Montevideo, where prizes were awarded for the best breeds of cattle and sheep and where the latest farm machinery was displayed. Politically, the ranchers were organized in the Rural Federation (Federación Rural), which acted as a pressure group for their interests. Because the incomes of the ranchers varied with the profitability of beef and wool exports, they were constantly lobbying the government for favorable tax and exchange-rate policies. Under military rule from 1973 to 1985, they were deprived of much of their influence, and thus many of them turned against the government. Historically, the majority of ranchers voted for the National Party rather than the Colorado Party. However, the distinction has tended to break down. One factor in this breakdown was the emergence in the 1950s of a nonparty Ruralist movement called the Federal League for Rural Action (Liga Federal de Acción Rural—LFAR), which allied with different parties in successive elections.

Uruguay's rural society remained much more rigidly hierarchical than its urban society, and status differences were pronounced. This was also true of towns outside the Montevideo region, where the majority of the interior population lived.

Business Elites

Uruguay's commercial, financial, and industrial elites were more cosmopolitan than the big ranchers. However, the high number of basic industries and utilities run by the state meant that large private entrepreneurs were less numerous than would otherwise be the case. The urban-rural divide was no longer very pronounced: traditional landowning families had diversified into food processing and other businesses, while the sons and daughters of businessmen were ensured a private education. Until 1984 there was only one university in the country, the University of the Republic (also known as the University of Montevideo); it served as a major force for miscegenation among elites and even among the middle classes.

Foreign multinational corporations were less active in Uruguay than in many other Latin American countries because of the small size of its domestic market. One exception to this, however, was the banking system, which was heavily taken over by European and North American conglomerates in the 1970s and 1980s. A pattern of close cooperation between domestic and foreign business interests had emerged on the basis of joint ventures and licensing agreements.

Urban business interests were organized in two rival associations: the Chamber of Industry, which was dominated by industrial manufacturers, and the Chamber of Commerce, which was more oriented toward services and retail trades. The Chamber of Commerce was enthusiastic about the liberalization of imports and the maintenance of a strong currency from 1977 to 1982. By contrast, foreign competition hit industry hard, accustomed as it was to the high rates of protection given by the previous model of import-substitution industrialization (see Glossary).

Political Elites

Uruguay's party leaders were sometimes viewed as forming a "political class." Many of the surnames of those active in politics in the 1980s would have been familiar to Uruguayans a century earlier. Blanco leaders were more likely than Colorados to have attended private secondary schools and to describe themselves as practicing Catholics, although this distinction was breaking down. With the exception of an apparent increase in the late 1960s, these politicians only rarely had business careers, apart from ranchers in the National Party. Rather, most made their living as lawyers and as public servants.

The leaders of Uruguay's leftist parties were drawn from a somewhat wider spectrum of backgrounds than the Colorados and Blancos. Among the leaders of the former were many white-collar workers, especially educators, and a few labor union leaders.

The power of traditional political bosses, or caudillos, has resided in their ability to mobilize voters by means of patronage machines. This system of doling out favors, such as public-sector jobs and pensions, through local political clubs had, nevertheless, declined by 1990. Young voters were more motivated by ideology than their parents, which is one reason that the membership of Uruguay's leftist parties was growing, whereas that of the traditional National and Colorado parties was declining.

The Middle Class

Uruguay has often been described as the most middle-class nation in Latin America. In this social category were to be found civil servants, teachers, white-collar workers, small businessmen, officers in the military, and medium-sized farmers. Economic crises since the 1960s have, nevertheless, squeezed this sector of the population hard. One reason for the rise of women in the labor force was the struggle of middle-class families to maintain their standard of living. Moreover, it was very common for middle-class Uruguayans to have two (or even more) jobs.

For much of the twentieth century, Uruguay's middle classes benefited from the provision of excellent public education at no cost up through university. Public schools began to decline in quality in the 1970s, however, and few members of the middle class could afford the requisite fees to have their children educated privately. A similar pattern of deterioration in public health care and the value of state pensions occurred, adding to the difficulties of the middle classes. Public-sector wages were severely squeezed under military rule (from 1973 to 1985), as were private-sector wages, but to a slightly lesser degree. A major factor was the virtual suspension of wage bargaining under a climate of systematic repression of labor unions. Previously, white-collar unionization had been high (see The Labor Movement, ch. 3).

The middle classes were typically employed as civil servants or white-collar workers. Many worked in small businesses, but some of these businesses were hurt by the market-oriented economic reforms of the 1970s, which led to the liberalization of manufactured imports (see Restructuring under the Military Regime, 1973–85, ch. 3). From 1978 until 1982, the middle classes benefited from a boom in imported durable consumer goods, such as automobiles, appliances, and electronics. The subsequent economic slump left many families heavily in debt and unable to meet their obligations. Particularly hard hit were individuals who had taken out mortgages denominated in dollars. When the Uruguayan new peso (for value of the Uruguayan new peso—see Glossary) collapsed in 1982, many of them found their house and apartment payments had tripled overnight. A similar debt crunch hit many medium-sized firms that had expanded by borrowing.

The Uruguayan middle classes were avid joiners of interest groups and professional associations. Among these were the professional associations of lawyers, civil servants, notaries, accountants, bankers, and physicians. Some white-collar labor unions, although less prestigious than the professional associations, were home to the middle classes. For instance, workers in health care had the Federation of Uruguayan Sanitation Workers, with 13,400 members.

High school teachers (*profesores*) were organized in the National Federation of Secondary Teachers, which had nearly 2,400 members. Grade school teachers (*maestros*) had the Uruguayan Federation of Elementary Teachers, with nearly 7,100 members. University professors (*docentes*) belonged to the Association of Professors of the University of the Republic, which had 2,000 affiliates. The Uruguayan Association of Bank Employees (Asociación de Empleados Bancarios del Uruguay—AEBU) was much larger, with 15,344 members, as was the Confederation of State Civil Service Organizations, with 25,508 members. Many of these associations ran cooperative stores and social clubs. For example, the AEBU had a large modern headquarters in downtown Montevideo containing meeting rooms and a theater.

The importance of education to the middle classes was underlined by the widespread use of professional titles. Lawyers were formally addressed as *doctor,* accountants as *contador,* engineers as *ingeniero,* and so forth. However, the rapid expansion of higher education began to lead to graduate unemployment and underemployment in the 1960s, a further source of strain on the middle classes.

Small Farmers and Rural Workers

Although they accounted for only about 5 percent of Uruguay's total land, small farms were common in the littoral and the south. Owners of medium-sized farms were able to approximate the living standards of the urban middle class, but for tenant farmers and proprietors of smaller areas, life was a constant struggle. Particularly poor were the small producers of Canelones Department who grew vegetables for the capital.

Because the rural economy was not at all labor intensive, Uruguay had very few rural workers. One exception was the department of Artigas, where large sugarcane plantations had grown up. The very low wages of the cane cutters caused them to form a union in the 1960s and to bring their protests to the streets of the capital. Apart from this, however, Uruguay's few rural workers and small farmers had not managed to form organizations to defend their economic interests. In particular, the Ruralist movement of the 1950s and 1960s, which began as a protest by the small farmers against government taxes, soon fell under the leadership of large landowners. In the late 1980s, a rural workers' union claimed a membership of only 4,000 (see The Labor Movement; Land Use and Tenure, ch. 3).

Blue-Collar Workers

Uruguay lacked a large industrial labor force by the standards of the developed world. Indeed, urban employment was dominated by the service industries. Only 23 percent of the total labor force was employed in industry in 1988. Skilled manual workers nevertheless had tended to form unions quite successfully and hence maintained a relatively comfortable standard of living, at least until the military takeover in 1973. Since 1985 they have fought to restore the former level of their wages in real terms, but statistics suggest that in 1990 these were still lower than in 1980.

Many workers made only the official minimum wage, which fluctuated according to inflation, the exchange rate, and government policy. In the 1980s, it was under the equivalent of US$100 per month. As of June 1990, it stood at US$76, although it must be remembered that the cost of living in Uruguay was on the whole much lower than in the United States. Overall, the economic position of urban blue-collar workers was far superior to, and much more stable than, that of workers in the informal sector, which was variously defined to include domestic service, street vending (particularly of contraband goods from Brazil), home-based piecework, sewing, laundering, recycling, begging, and even prostitution and crime.

Plowing in Los Arenales, Canelones Department
Courtesy Inter-American Development Bank

In 1964 Uruguay's labor unions came together to form a single federation known as the National Convention of Workers (Convención Nacional de Trabajadores—CNT). In 1973 the military declared the CNT illegal; labor union activity virtually ceased during the following decade. In 1983, however, a new labor federation, known as the Interunion Workers' Assembly (or Plenum) (Plenario Intersindical de Trabajadores—PIT), was formed. The PIT later changed its name to PIT–CNT to emphasize its historical links to the pre-1973 labor movement (see Political Forces and Interest Groups, ch. 4).

About 15 percent of the economically active population was employed as domestic servants, most of them women. In terms of status and income, their class position was between that of blue-collar workers and the poor.

The Urban Poor

The urban poor were concentrated among the unemployed, those working in the informal sector of the economy, unskilled laborers, and retired persons. Official unemployment figures for Montevideo fluctuated from around 8 percent to 15 percent in the 1980s. Estimates of the proportion of the labor force in the informal sector were, by definition, hard to find. But the proportion has certainly been rising since the 1960s. At the height of the building boom of the late 1970s and early 1980s, about 6 percent of the labor force was employed in construction, a highly cyclical (and thus unstable) source of jobs. In addition, the real value of state pensions was severely eroded in the 1960s and 1970s, leading to widespread misery among the elderly.

Since 1985 the level of unemployment has remained below 10 percent in Montevideo, and the government has made modest efforts to restore some of the erosion in the real value of pensions (see The Sanguinetti Government, ch. 3). However, the informal sector of the economy has continued to grow.

Income Distribution and Living Standards

Uruguay's pattern of income distribution remained the most egalitarian in Latin America, although it apparently worsened under military rule from 1973 to 1985. In 1976 the poorest fifth of Uruguayan households received 4.8 percent of total household income, the top 10 percent of households took in 30.1 percent of total household income, and the top 20 percent of households took in 46.4 percent of income. Although unequal, this pattern was closer to that of the developed world than to the rest of Latin America.

Despite erosion of the minimum wage, the net impact of the recovery of real wages and pensions in the first year after the return to democracy in March 1985 appears to have slightly improved the distribution of incomes. Both in Montevideo and elsewhere in Uruguay, the highest 10 percent of households were reported to take in just under 30 percent of household income in 1986, while the lowest 20 percent of households garnered just under 6 percent of income (see table 5, Appendix).

During the first half of the twentieth century, living standards in Uruguay approximated those of the developed world. Since the 1950s, however, economic stagnation and even decline have meant severe falls in real wages (see table 6, Appendix). This process became particularly marked starting in 1968, the year in which the government imposed a wage and price freeze and abolished the so-called wage councils, in which government representatives, employers, and unions negotiated salaries. (The councils were revived in 1985.)

Real wages grew particularly fast from 1985 to 1987 (see table 7, Appendix). However, this was less true in the public sector, where in 1989 they remained below their 1980 level. The Colorado government also allowed the real value of the legal minimum wage to continue to fall (see table 8, Appendix).

Although the Colorado government made only cautious attempts to redistribute income to the most needy, the revival of economic growth helped to produce some improvement in various indicators of income distribution. The wage share of national income grew from 30.3 percent to 31.4 percent between 1985 and 1987, while the income share of the self-employed grew from 10 percent to 12.7 percent. According to the household survey of the General Directorate of Statistics and Census, the proportion of families below the poverty line in Montevideo fell from 27 percent in 1984 to 16 percent in 1987.

Reliable data on rural wages were hard to collect. Clearly, they were much lower than in interior towns or Montevideo, but official statistics suggested that they did not fall as far or as fast as wages in the rest of the economy in the 1970s.

Family Life

By the beginning of the twentieth century, the traditional pattern of patriarchy was breaking down in Uruguay. The relative emancipation of women put Uruguay far ahead of the rest of Latin America in terms of legal rights and social custom. Civil marriage became legally required in 1885, and the influence of the church declined. Divorce on the grounds of cruelty by the husband was legalized in 1907, and in 1912 women were given the right to file for divorce without a specific cause. Married women were allowed to maintain separate bank accounts as early as 1919. Women also were provided with equal access to educational opportunities at all levels early in the twentieth century, and they began to enter the professions in increasing numbers. In 1938 women voted for the first time in national elections. Nevertheless, there was a paternalistic flavor to many of the reforms, which were often seen as protecting women rather than guaranteeing their inalienable rights.

One factor that made it easier for middle-class women to go out of the home to work was the widespread availability of domestic servants willing to undertake cooking, cleaning, and taking care of children for comparatively low wages. By the 1960s, one-quarter of all adult women worked. This proportion continued to rise steadily, reaching over 45 percent in Montevideo by 1985. In 1975 one-fifth of all households were headed by women. Nuclear families made up 61.2 percent of all households, while there were almost as many single-person households (14.6 percent) as traditional extended families (17.6 percent). The average number of persons in each household was 3.4.

The small size of Uruguayan families by Latin American standards was related to the widespread practice of birth control and the middle-class aspiration to provide the best possible education for children. Families tended to be larger in rural areas, where the birth rate was much higher. In rural areas, however, there was an imbalance in the sex ratio because women had a much higher propensity to migrate to the towns in search of work, particularly as domestic servants. Poor families in rural areas were often unstable; common-law marriage and illegitimacy were widespread. Although abortion was illegal, there was no legal distinction between children born in and out of wedlock.

In rural areas, the maintenance of symbolic kinship ties remained common. When babies were baptized, they often were given a godfather (*compadre*) chosen from among the members of the local elite. This practice, known as *compadrazgo,* was intended to provide the children with useful connections in later life. It formed an important link in the pattern of interaction between rural elites and subordinate classes. Reciprocal obligations ranged from help from the godparent in finding employment to the requirement of loyalty in voting on the part of the godchild.

Relations between husbands and wives in Uruguay were relatively equal by Latin American standards. The divorce rate had grown steadily from 1 per 10,000 population in 1915 to 14 per 1,000 in 1985. In 1927 the compulsory civil marriage ceremony was amended so that the bride no longer promised obedience, but both man and woman vowed to treat each other with respect. It was not uncommon for women to keep their surnames after marriage. Often, they simply added the husband's name to theirs. Children had their father's surname followed by their mother's.

Uruguayan children, and especially girls, had a relatively high degree of freedom compared with their counterparts in many other Latin American countries. Chaperonage was rare. It was expected that women would have careers, and by 1970 almost half the total school population was female.

During the 1960s, the phenomenon known as the "generation gap" began to be acutely felt in Uruguay. Young people rebelled against their parents and adopted permissive life-styles. In many cases, they were drawn into radical politics; in fact, in 1990 youth was still one of the strongest predictors of left-voting in Uruguay.

Family ties remained strong in Uruguay despite the rebelliousness of youth. Children frequently lived in the parental home well into their thirties, in some cases even after marriage. The usual reason for staying at home was economic necessity; many couples found affordable housing hard to come by.

Despite the relative freedom of women, attitudes toward gender roles and sexuality remained traditionally stereotypical. The pattern of machismo was less pronounced than in much of Latin America, but males were expected to show "masculine" traits; "feminine" characteristics were seen as inferior. At social gatherings, women tended to congregate with other women, and men with men.

Upper-middle-class Uruguayans usually tried to escape Montevideo for the beach resorts on weekends and during the long December to January summer holidays. Family gatherings typically centered on outdoor barbecues (*asados*), in which large quantities of meat were consumed. Another typical custom, symbolic of family and friendship ties, was the sharing of yerba maté, a form of green tea. A hollowed-out gourd (the maté) or sometimes a china cup is packed almost full with the green tea. A metal straw (*bombilla*) is then inserted into the tea, and boiling water is poured on top. The maté is then passed around in a circle, each person adding a little more hot water. This custom was particularly significant under the military regime of 1973 to 1985, when citizens were often afraid to congregate in public squares for fear their gossip might be seen as political. An innocent maté ceremony could hardly arouse suspicions.

As in other countries, the advent of television has reduced movie and theater attendance precipitously, causing more leisure hours

79

to be spent in the home. Uruguayans remained enthusiastic in their participation in competitive sports, however. Amateur soccer continued to thrive among the middle and lower classes, whereas the upper-middle classes preferred tennis, golf, and sailing. For the elite, membership in a country club was an important focus of leisure activity and a symbol of social status.

Health and Welfare

Uruguay has been described as South America's "first welfare state" as a result of its pioneering efforts in the fields of public education, health care, and social security. The steady rise in public employment, often by the creation of jobs that fulfilled no particular function, served to keep the unemployment level down, particularly in election years. However, the stagnation of the economy starting in the 1950s put increasing strains on this system. In particular, declining tax revenues and increased spending produced large government deficits and accelerating rates of inflation. Foreign advisers began to recommend severe budget cuts as the only solution to the chronic fiscal crisis.

During the first half of the twentieth century, Uruguay, along with Argentina, led Latin America in its advanced standards of medical care. Even in 1990, the University of the Republic's medical school had a high international reputation and continued to attract students from other countries in South America. Starting with the progressive reforms of the early part of the twentieth century, the state has taken a leading role in the provision of health care, particularly for the lower classes. Private medicine remained the preferred option of the middle and upper classes, however. Under military rule from 1973 to 1985, standards of care in public hospitals and clinics were adversely affected by budget restrictions.

By the 1970s, Uruguay's welfare state had declined sharply in the standards of protection that it afforded to the mass of the population. The government bureaucracy, however, continued to swell. Total health care spending in 1984 represented 8.1 percent of GDP, a proportion similar to that of the developed world. In the same year, about 7.5 percent of household spending went to health care, but 400,000 Uruguayans were without state or private health care coverage.

Under the civilian administration inaugurated in 1985, progress was made in redirecting the budget away from spending on the military and toward social welfare. Defense spending fell from 13.0 percent of government outlays in 1984 to 11.8 percent in 1986. Over the same period, social security decreased from 31.5 percent to 27.6 percent, but education grew from 7.4 percent to 10.1 percent

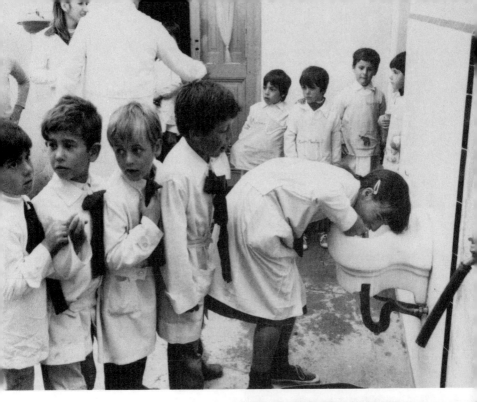

Water line at an elementary school in a barrio of Colonia
Courtesy Inter-American Development Bank

Children playing in a barrio of Artigas
Courtesy Charles Guy Gillespie

and sanitation from 4.3 percent to 6.7 percent of public expenditure.

In 1987 Montevideo had over sixty public health facilities, including seven major public hospitals. About half the interior departments had their own hospital; the rest had only a *centro auxiliar* (auxiliary center). Altogether, Uruguay's public health system had about 9,505 hospital rooms available.

In 1985 the number of inhabitants per physician was 466, about the same rate as in the developed world. However, the distribution of health care services was highly skewed. Outside Montevideo the ratio was a much less favorable 1,234 citizens per physician; by contrast, there were only 262 inhabitants of Montevideo for every doctor.

Infant Mortality and Life Expectancy

The infant mortality rate was 48.6 per 1,000 live births in 1975. In the first half of the 1980s, it fell to 37.6 per 1,000—low by Latin American standards but still almost twice the rate of Chile and Costa Rica. In the second half of the decade, however, infant mortality began to decline to levels close to those of the latter two countries: in 1986 it was 27.7; in 1987, 23.8; in 1988, 20.3; and in 1990, 22. The increasing share of government spending devoted to infant health care and nutrition programs appeared to have been one reason for this sharp improvement.

The average life expectancy at birth in 1990 was seventy years for men and seventy-six years for women, only slightly behind Chile, Costa Rica, and Argentina. The mortality rate remained just below 10 per 1,000 population in the 1980s. The leading causes of death in 1985 included circulatory disease (40.2 percent), tumors (22.6 percent), trauma (4.1 percent), respiratory disorders and infections (3.8 percent), perinatal complications (2.4 percent), infectious diseases and parasites (2.4 percent), suicide (1.0 percent), and cirrhosis of the liver (0.9 percent).

In the late 1980s, Uruguay did not remain exempt from the worldwide epidemics of acquired immune deficiency syndrome (AIDS) and drug addiction among youth. Although the total number of cases of AIDS has not reached the numbers recorded in the United States, Europe, or Brazil, AIDS has become a greater concern. According to the Ministry of Public Health, by the end of June 1990 there had been 129 cases of AIDS in Uruguay since 1983, when it was first detected. Of those cases, 100 were from Montevideo and 29 from the rest of the country. Fifty-nine of the cases were contracted inside Uruguay, whereas seventy of the victims caught the virus outside the country. One hundred and seventeen of the cases were men; twelve were women. An additional 627 individuals were found to be carrying the virus, without having yet shown symptoms of the disease. In the 1983–89 period, sixty-five people were known to have died of complications resulting from the human immunodeficiency virus (HIV).

In 1990 Uruguay still enjoyed the image of a "clean" country insofar as drugs were concerned. In response to some significant negative signs, however, the government formed the National Board for the Control of Drug Trafficking and Narcotics Abuse in January 1988. The board included representatives from the office of the president and the ministries of public health, education and culture, and interior. It found that drug addiction grew continuously in Uruguay in 1988. The number of adult drug addicts had more than doubled from 321 in 1983 to 697 in 1987; the number of children addicted to drugs had quintupled from 62 in 1983 to 292 in 1987. According to the Ministry of Public Health, the drug consumer was predominantly single, with good family relations, and the majority had attended secondary school; half of the total were employed. The most commonly abused drug was marijuana, followed by amphetamines and industrial-use inhalants; cocaine and lysergic acid diethylamide (LSD) were also included on the list, but to a lesser extent.

State and Private Health Care

In 1971 about 82 percent of hospital beds were provided in establishments run by the Ministry of Public Health. The same public hospitals accounted for 69.5 percent of hospitalizations. About 61 percent of visits to general practitioners were covered by private health plans known as *mutuales* (mutuals). In the same year, 58.9 percent of the inhabitants of Montevideo were covered by these private associations. About 11.8 percent had the official health card of the Ministry of Public Health, entitling them to free health care. A further 6.8 percent had other health plans, usually through their place of work. This left 5.8 percent with multiple forms of coverage and 16.6 percent with no coverage at all.

In 1980 there were 9,089 public hospital beds, about three-fifths in the capital and the remainder in the rest of the country. During the period of military rule from 1973 to 1985, the government had shifted health care spending toward military hospitals, which were, however, open only to relatives of the members of the armed forces. After 1985 the government made a sustained effort to increase health care coverage. From 1985 to 1988, public health cardholders increased from 566,000 to 692,000 in the interior but decreased slightly from 323,000 to 310,000 in Montevideo.

At the end of 1984, there were 918,000 members of private health plans in Montevideo and 325,000 in the rest of the country. By 1988 the numbers had risen to 963,000 and 488,000, respectively. Overall, this represented a 17 percent increase in the membership of the *mutuales* from 1984 to 1988. As with the state health provision, the greatest increase in coverage occurred in the interior, where it was most needed.

A concurrent effort was made to increase the proportion of infants receiving inoculations. In 1985 there were 503 cases of whooping cough, and in 1986 there were 1,117; but in the first nine months of 1988, there were only 21. Over the same period, the number of cases of measles first rose from 160 in 1985 to 1,190 in 1987 but then fell sharply to just 73 in the first nine months of 1988. The proportion of infants immunized before age one rose from 61 to 79 percent in 1985 to 80 to 88 percent in 1987, depending on the particular vaccination.

Government investment in health care equipment rose dramatically after the return to democracy, climbing from US$564,000 in 1985 to US$2.2 million in 1987. Over the same period, expenditures on construction of health care facilities rose from US$772,000 to US$2.7 million. Total spending by the Ministry of Public Health rose 34 percent in real terms, while spending on medications doubled. Grandiose plans for new hospitals to be financed by foreign development loans were announced in 1989, but their realization remained a distant prospect.

Social Security Pensions

Uruguay pioneered social security pension programs, starting as early as 1896 with a fund for teachers. The plans were subsequently extended piecemeal to different sectors of the labor force and soon grew extremely complex and bureaucratic. A system of family allowances (based on the number of dependent children) was introduced in 1943 and consolidated in 1950. Unfortunately, the provision of welfare benefits became politicized as politicians from rival parties would intercede on behalf of voters to speed up the endless delays.

Ultimately, the system of benefits began to be abused by politicians in order to "buy" votes. The most notorious example was the case of the seamstresses: far more pensions were handed out to alleged garment workers than there were garment workers. Criticism of the various programs became vociferous by the 1960s, and the programs were reorganized in the single Social Welfare Bank

Delivering milk in Treinta y Tres
Courtesy Inter-American Development Bank

under the 1967 constitution. During the military regime of 1973–85, further efforts at rationalization were undertaken, including the consolidation of most funds under the General Directorate of Social Security (Dirección General de Seguridad Social—DGSS). The number of claimants continued to rise rapidly, however, reaching 629,077 in July 1984.

Social security transfers were not all paid out in the form of pensions, although in 1983 these accounted for 78.3 percent of total outlays. Other categories included family allowances for households with young children (6.4 percent in 1983) and benefits for sickness (4.8 percent) and for unemployment (3.0 percent). However, these had suffered similar declines. In 1983 the total outlays of the DGSS were financed as follows: employers' contributions, 28.1 percent; workers' contributions, 28.1 percent; and state contributions, 43.8 percent.

Uruguay's population has continued to age since 1963, as the censuses of 1963, 1975, and 1985 show. In 1985 the average age of the population was 30.3 years. The percentage of the population over age sixty rose from 11.6 in 1963, to 14.3 in 1975, and to 15.7 in 1985. Those over age sixty-five accounted for 7.6 percent, 9.8 percent, and 11.1 percent, respectively, in the same years. This long-term aging trend, similar to that of developed countries, worried social planners because of the projected strain on social security programs. It was compounded by the high life expectancy of Uruguayans after retirement: ten years for men and twenty-one years for women.

The population's aging trend also made the impact of the decline in the real value of pensions even more serious because it affected an increasingly large share of the population. However, with the return to democracy in 1985, efforts were made by the Colorado administration of Julio María Sanguinetti Cairolo (1985–90) to restore some of their real value. Although the opposition parties severely criticized the Colorados for not increasing social security payments faster, these at least grew 20 percent from 1984 to 1987 in real terms. The greatest increases were awarded to those receiving the smallest pensions.

Education

Uruguay had the highest literacy rate in Latin America, at 96 percent in 1985. There was no appreciable difference in literacy rates between males and females, but there were discrepancies between urban and rural rates (rural rates being demonstrably lower). Uruguay's system of universal, free, and secular education required a total of nine years of compulsory school attendance, from ages six to fourteen. The proportion of children of primary school age enrolled in school had long been virtually 100 percent. Furthermore, from 1965 to 1985 the proportion of children of secondary school age enrolled in some form of secondary school grew from 44 to 70 percent, also the highest rate in Latin America. The postsecondary education enrollment rate was about 20 percent. Coeducation was the norm, and females and males attended school in near-equal numbers at all levels. As is typical of any country, however, rates of schooling were higher in urban areas than in rural areas.

The quality of education in Uruguay was rated as high. Teaching was a socially respected profession and one that paid relatively well. Most teachers, trained in teachers' training colleges, were deemed well qualified. The main problem confronting the education system was the inadequacy of facilities, instructional materials, and teachers' aides. Rural areas often suffered from woefully insufficient facilities and supplies. Urban schools often were seriously overcrowded and were forced to resort to holding classes in multiple shifts. In addition, drop-out and repetition rates, although moderate by Latin American standards, were still considered high.

The Education System

Primary education in Uruguay was free and compulsory; it encompassed six years of instruction. The number of primary schools in 1987 was 2,382, including 240 private schools. There were 16,568 primary school teachers and 354,177 primary school students. This resulted in a pupil-teacher ratio of approximately twenty-one to one in 1987, compared with about thirty to one in 1970. Boys and girls were enrolled in almost equal numbers.

General education in secondary schools encompassed six years of instruction divided into two three-year cycles. The first, or basic, cycle was compulsory; the second cycle was geared to university preparation. In addition to the academic track, public technical education schools provided secondary school education that was technical and vocational in nature. The two systems were parallel in structure, and there was little provision for transfer between the two. All sectors of society traditionally tended to prefer the academic course of study, which was regarded as more prestigious. As a result, academic secondary education had expanded more rapidly than technical education in the second half of the twentieth century. In 1987 there were 276 general secondary schools in Uruguay, including 118 private schools. However, the public high schools were much larger, so that in 1987 they actually contained 145,083 of the country's 175,710 secondary school students enrolled in both day classes and night classes. In addition, ninety-four technical education schools had a total enrollment of 52,766 students in 1987. Male and female enrollment at the secondary level was roughly equal, but females slightly outnumbered males overall (constituting, for example, 53 percent of the secondary school student body in 1982). It appeared that females were in the majority in the basic cycle but were very slightly outnumbered by males in the university preparatory cycle.

Uruguay had only one public university, the University of the Republic (also known as the University of Montevideo), founded in 1849, and only one private university, the Catholic University of Uruguay, established in 1984 and also in Montevideo. Education at the University of the Republic was free and, in general, open to all those possessing a *bachillerato,* or certificate awarded for completion of both cycles of general secondary education. Despite the free tuition, however, access to a university education tended to be limited to children of middle- and upper-income families because the need to supplement the family income by working, coupled with the expense of books and other fees, placed a university education out of the reach of many. Moreover, the fact that the only public university was in Montevideo severely limited the ability of those in the interior to attend university unless their families were relatively well off financially. In 1988 about 69 percent of university students were from Montevideo.

The number of university students continued to grow rapidly, from nearly 22,000 in 1970 to over 61,000 in 1988. Of that total, women accounted for about 58 percent. Most courses of study were intended to last from four to six years, but the average time spent at university by a successful student was usually considerably longer. As in the rest of Latin America, maintaining the status of student had various advantages, such as reduced fares on buses and subsidized canteens. This was one reason that the student population was so large yet the number of graduates relatively low. In 1986 only 3,654 students (2,188 women and 1,455 men) graduated from university, whereas 16,878 entered that year. Uruguayans exhibited a strong preference for the disciplines and professions they deemed prestigious, such as law, social science, engineering, medicine, economics, and administration.

Observers continued to note the discrepancy between university training and job opportunities, particularly in the prestigious fields. This gap contributed to the substantial level of emigration of the best-educated young Uruguayan professionals (see Emigration, this ch.).

Historical Origins and Evolution of Education

Uruguay pioneered universal, free, and compulsory primary education in the Americas under the influence of José Pedro Varela (president, 1875–76), whose writings convinced the government to pass the 1877 Law of Common Education. The model adopted for public schools was taken from the French system, and a centralized, nationwide system was established. A rigid separation into three branches of education grew up—primary, secondary, and university. Teacher training for grade school teachers was connected to the primary school system. The National Institute of Technical Education (Instituto Nacional de Educación Técnica—INET) grew up as an extension of the secondary school system. By the late 1950s, all three branches of the education system had established administrative autonomy, including complete control over their budgets. The Organic University Law of 1958 provided that the governing bodies of the University of the Republic would be elected by the members of the faculty, alumni, and students.

By the late 1960s, Uruguayan secondary schools and the various faculties of the University of the Republic had become extremely politicized. Student sit-ins, demonstrations, and even riots were commonplace. Classes and examinations were frequently disrupted. After 1973 the authorities vowed to put an end to this situation, and political purges in the education system became widespread. Some teachers were able to find work in private schools, but others either left the profession or emigrated. Entire branches of the university, such as the Institute of Social Sciences, were closed for a time. Academic standards suffered across the board as some of the best teachers and professors were fired and replaced by people with only mediocre qualifications.

Educational Reforms under Military Rule, 1973–85

In 1973, the year in which Uruguay descended into authoritarian rule, major changes were decreed in the education system. The National Council for Education (Consejo Nacional de Educación—Conae) was set up to oversee all three branches of education under the supervision of the executive branch of government. At the same time, the compulsory length of schooling was raised from six to nine years. The secondary curriculum was completely reorganized, as was the pattern of teacher training. Finally, the INET saw its status and budget upgraded. However, overall spending on education fell from 12.2 percent of the central government budget in 1974 to 7.3 percent in 1982.

Enrollments in primary education (both state and private) fell 6 percent from 1968 to 1981. From 1968 to 1982, secondary school enrollments grew 6 percent; however, about half the secondary school students in Montevideo (and 70 percent in the interior) dropped out before receiving any certification. Over the same period, there was a boom in technical schools; enrollments increased 66 percent in the interior and 27 percent in Montevideo. The major cause of this increase was the new *ciclo básico* (basic cycle), which added three years of compulsory secondary education to the six years of compulsory primary schooling. However, the drop-out rate remained about 50 percent. Enrollments in the University of the Republic doubled from 1968 to 1982, but the proportion of students graduating fell to just 8 percent.

In 1984, as something of a parting shot, Uruguay's military government formally granted university status to a Catholic college that had been expanding over the previous decade. This ended the University of the Republic's monopoly, which had lasted since its foundation in 1849. The new Catholic University of Uruguay remained extremely small, however, compared with its rival.

Education under the Colorados, 1985–88

Shortly after entering office in March 1985, Sanguinetti passed a decree aimed at restoring greater autonomy to the education system. Conae was replaced by the National Administration of Public Education, which oversaw three decentralized councils—one for primary, one for secondary, and one for technical education. Full autonomy was restored to the University of the Republic. Whereas total spending on education represented 7.4 percent of the national budget in 1984, by 1987 this had risen to 10.9 percent, equivalent to US$175 million.

From 1985 to 1988, the government agreed to rehire all teachers and professors who had lost their jobs during the political purges after 1973 (3,241 accepted the offer of returning to their old jobs, but 1,520 took retirement instead). In many cases, the rehiring of former teachers led to unnecessary numbers of staff, as the government undertook not to fire any of the replacement teachers that had been taken on under the military, although in some cases they lacked qualifications.

Clashes between the education authorities and the government were common after 1985, given the existence of a relatively conservative government and far more liberal teachers. Nevertheless, an element of balance between centralized control and decentralized initiative was successfully restored. Relations between the government and the University of the Republic were surprisingly smooth, and the latter's share of the national budget grew from 2.5 percent in 1984 to 4.3 percent (US$59 million) in 1988.

During the period of military rule, another phenomenon began to emerge—the establishment of private research institutes. These relied entirely on funds from foreign development foundations, such as the Inter-American Foundation (a United States agency), the International Development Agency (a Canadian agency), and various West European equivalents (see Political Forces and Interest Groups, ch. 4). The new institutes were comparatively small, usually only hiring a dozen or so full-time staff, but they constituted an important haven for academics who had lost their jobs for political reasons. Without these private centers, even more academics would have been forced into exile.

Among the new private research centers was the Latin American Center of Human Economy (Centro Latinoamericano de Economía Humana—CLAEH). By far the largest of the centers, the CLAEH was closely linked to the Christian Democrats. Apart from carrying out a broad range of sociological and economic research, it also conducted courses for university-level students and published what was for a time Uruguay's only social science journal. Somewhat more to the left was the Economic Research Center (Centro de Investigaciones Económicas—CINVE), which specialized in research on the economy, particularly that of the rural sector and the impact of the economic liberalization pursued under the military. Two other institutes with a more sociological agenda of research were the Center of Information and Studies of Uruguay

(Centro de Informaciones y Estudios del Uruguay—CIESU) and the Interdisciplinary Center of Development Studies, Uruguay (Centro Interdisciplinario de Estudios del Desarrollo, Uruguay— CIEDUR).

With the return to democracy in 1985, many of these centers found it hard to continue to win foreign grants to undertake their research, and most of their personnel attempted to return to their former jobs in higher education. Where possible, however, the teachers tried to retain both positions.

Religion

Roman Catholicism was the dominant religion in Uruguay, but Uruguay had long been a secular society. In 1981 the nation was divided into 221 parishes and had 204 diocesan priests. In addition, there were 374 monks and 1,580 nuns. About three-quarters of all babies were baptized in the church. In the 1963 census, 62 percent of Uruguayans had declared themselves Catholics. However, according to data compiled by the Uruguayan Bishops Conference in 1978, only 105,248 citizens regularly attended mass. This figure represented less than 4 percent of the population. Attendance at mass was, however, slightly higher in the interior of the country and substantially higher among women. There was also evidence that religious observance was higher among the upper classes than among the middle and lower strata of society. In the late 1980s, an estimated 66 percent of Uruguayans were professed Roman Catholics, but less than half of the adult population attended church regularly.

Uruguay's secularization began with the relatively minor role of the church in the colonial era, compared with other parts of the Spanish Empire. The small numbers of Uruguay's Indians, and their fierce resistance to proselytization, reduced the influence of the ecclesiastical authorities. After independence, anticlerical ideas spread to Uruguay, particularly from France, further eroding the influence of the church. In 1837 civil marriage was recognized, and in 1861 the state took over public cemeteries. In 1907 divorce was legalized, and in 1909 all religious instruction was banned from state schools. Under the influence of the radical Colorado reformer José Batlle y Ordóñez (1903-07, 1911-15), complete separation of church and state was introduced with the new constitution of 1917. Batlle y Ordóñez went as far as to have religious holidays legally renamed. Even as of 1990, Uruguayans referred to Holy Week as "Tourism Week."

Nevertheless, the separation of church and state ended religious conflict in Uruguay, and since that time Catholic schools have been allowed to flourish. A Catholic party, the Civic Union of Uruguay (Unión Cívica del Uruguay—UCU), was founded in 1912 but never won more than a low percentage of the national vote. By the 1960s, the progressive trend in the worldwide church was strongly felt in Uruguay under the influence of Pope John XXIII and Pope Paul VI. Particularly influential was the 1968 Latin American Bishops Conference in Medellín, Colombia, at which the concept of "structural sin" was put forward. By this doctrine, evil was seen as existing not only in the actions of individuals but also in the unequal organization of entire societies. The second Latin American Bishops Conference, held in Mexico in 1979, also had an important dynamizing and radicalizing impact in Uruguay. This time, the bishops called for a "preferential option for the poor." Sections of the Uruguayan church in fact became quite radical: when members of the National Liberation Movement-Tupamaros (Movimiento de Liberación Nacional-Tupamaros—MLN-T) were given amnesty in 1985, for a time they were housed in a Montevideo monastery while they readjusted to normal life.

One symptom of the growing progressive trend in the Uruguayan Catholic movement was the decision of the UCU to adopt the name Christian Democratic Party (Partido Demócrata Cristiano—PDC) in 1962. The new-found social conscience was strongly influenced by French Catholic philosophers—first Jacques Maritain and later Father Lebret. During the 1960s, the PDC moved further and further left, eventually espousing a form of "communitarian socialism" under its brilliant young leader, Juan Pablo Terra. In 1971 the PDC allied with the Communist Party of Uruguay and the Socialist Party of Uruguay to form the so-called Broad Front alliance. That caused conservative Catholics to form the Civic Union (Unión Cívica—UC) to offer religious voters a nonradical alternative, but the UC scarcely achieved any influence (see Political Parties, ch. 4).

During the twentieth century, Protestant sects began to grow in importance. Estimates put the Protestant proportion of the population at 2 percent or a little higher in the late 1980s. From 1960 to 1985, the number of Protestants is estimated to have increased by 60 percent. Over the same period, the number of Protestants grew 500 percent or more in many Latin American countries. Uruguay was thus considered a "disappointment" by evangelical crusaders.

Jews constituted a small proportion of the population (about 2 percent), with most living in Montevideo. The size of the Jewish community had dwindled since 1970, primarily because of emigration.

* * *

Very little has been published in English on Uruguayan society in recent years. Simon Gabriel Hanson's *Utopia in Uruguay*, published in 1938, provides a detailed history of social and economic reforms in the first three decades of the twentieth century. Russell H. Fitzgibbon's *Uruguay: Portrait of a Democracy* paints a rosy picture of Uruguay in the golden years of prosperity and social peace prior to the mid-1950s. George Pendle's *Uruguay: South America's First Welfare State* examines this period more concisely. English-language works discussing the crisis of Uruguay's welfare state in the 1960s include Marvin Alisky's *Uruguay: A Contemporary Survey* and M.H.J. Finch's more detailed and scholarly *A Political Economy of Uruguay since 1870*. Martin Weinstein's 1975 book on the rise of authoritarianism, *Uruguay: The Politics of Failure*, and his more recent volume on the return to democracy, *Uruguay: Democracy at the Crossroads*, provide ample information on the social situation.

Many of the most useful recent sources are journal articles or chapters in edited volumes. Arturo C. Porzecanski contributed a chapter on the problems of the Uruguayan welfare state to Carmelo Mesa-Lago's *Social Security in Latin America*. Lauren Benton discusses the evolution of housing and planning in Montevideo under military rule in "Reshaping the Urban Core." Alejandro Portes, Silvia Blitzer, and John Curtis examine the growth of the informal economy in Montevideo households in "The Urban Informal Sector in Uruguay." Graciela Taglioretti traces the increasing participation rate of women in the labor force in *Women and Work in Uruguay*. Among many important works, distinguished Uruguayan sociologist Aldo Solari and young colleague Rolando Franco have published an article on higher education, "Equality of Opportunities and Elitism in the Uruguayan University." The same authors contributed a chapter on "The Family in Uruguay" to Man Singh Das and Clinton J. Jesser's *The Family in Latin America*.

An extremely valuable source is Finch's *Uruguay*. Statistical data are available in various editions of the Uruguayan government publication *Anuario estadístico*. (For further information and complete citations, see Bibliography.)

Chapter 3. The Economy

Montevideo's harbor

URUGUAY IS A WEALTHY COUNTRY by Latin American standards, although its economic development has been sluggish since the 1950s. In 1990 the country had a gross domestic product (GDP—see Glossary) of approximately US$9.2 billion, or US$2,970 per capita, placing it among the highest-income countries in Latin America. Uruguay's small population (just over 3 million) and low population growth (0.7 percent per year) enabled its people to maintain a reasonable standard of living during the 1980s, despite the nation's unsteady economic performance. Like many other countries in the region, Uruguay faced a large external debt and an appreciable public-sector deficit, both of which impeded the growth of the economy. Other major limitations on growth were the continued dependence on a few agricultural products and one of South America's lowest levels of foreign and domestic investment.

Uruguay's economy developed rapidly during the first three decades of the twentieth century because of expanding beef and wool exportation. Rising trade income led to the creation of an advanced welfare state in which the government redistributed wealth and protected workers. After agricultural exports leveled off in the 1950s, the government's role in the economy expanded. With agriculture stalled and manufacturing potential limited by the small size of the domestic market, the public sector became the source of most new jobs in Uruguay. The economy operated behind high tariff barriers, barring competition from abroad. An alliance between the nation's two major political parties upheld this statist model through the 1960s, but lack of GDP growth and large public-sector deficits testified to its inefficiency.

Although the military government (1973–85) enacted major economic reforms during the 1970s, it operated with high fiscal deficits and borrowed extensively to pay for those deficits. In an effort to reorient the stagnated economy toward external markets, the government eliminated price controls and slashed tariffs while providing subsidies to exporters. These reforms of the goods market produced favorable results in the short run: exports, investment, and GDP all increased significantly. When the government went further, however, by deregulating the banking sector in hopes of removing inflationary pressures, the economy became unstable. In 1981 Uruguay's economy went into recession.

One source of instability was the growing "dollarization" of the banks. When foreign-exchange regulations were canceled, United States dollars (mostly from Argentine real estate investment) flowed into Uruguay. Uruguayan banks, in turn, loaned dollars to private companies and ranchers within the country. The danger in this system was the exchange rate: when the government allowed its currency, the Uruguayan new peso (for value of the Uruguayan new peso—see Glossary), to float against the dollar in 1982, the peso value of many Uruguayan loans suddenly tripled. Thus, Uruguay faced both a recession and a domestic debt crisis in the early 1980s.

In 1986–87 the economy recovered from the recession as real GDP increased by 6.6 percent in 1986 and 4.9 percent in 1987. The renewed emphasis on exports, including several new categories of goods, resulted in a positive trade balance. Real wages, which had fallen by 50 percent in the 1970s but risen by 15 percent in the early 1980s, increased again (but only marginally), as did employment (by 4 percent). These modest improvements could not mask fundamental problems, however. Inflation averaged over 60 percent per year in the 1980s, despite efforts to reduce it. In addition, the domestic debt was largely absorbed by the public sector, but in the process Uruguay's deficit and foreign debt became larger. Debt service alone absorbed about one-quarter of export earnings. During the last two years of the administration of Julio María Sanguinetti Cairolo (1985–90), fiscal pressures forced the government to abandon its growth-promotion strategy, and GDP did not increase. On the contrary, real GDP growth fell to 0.5 percent in 1988, 1.5 percent in 1989, and an estimated – 0.4 percent in 1990.

In 1989 Sanguinetti defended his administration's economic record in terms of what had *not* happened. In a speech to the General Assembly, he said that Uruguay's political and economic climate remained stable in contrast to its larger neighbors (Argentina and Brazil). The nation's economy "had not collapsed into regional hyperinflation, as was predicted; nor had the banking crisis that the government inherited destroyed the financial system; nor had the heavy external debt prevented the country from growing." The statement was an apt summary of both the government's cautious philosophy and of Uruguay's limited economic progress in the late 1980s.

The Sanguinetti government could claim credit for steering a sensible course during a difficult decade for Latin American nations. The government did not, however, make much progress addressing a fundamental limitation on the economy and the leading cause of the deficit: the size of the public sector. Powerful public-sector unions made it difficult for the government to reduce public employment. When, for example, the inefficient passenger rail service was discontinued in 1988 because of declining ridership, workers were not released but rather were transferred to other government jobs. The welfare-state model remained largely intact. By the last two years of the decade, however, economists and politicians were beginning to ask basic questions about the state's proper role in the economy.

An even more fundamental question, not addressed in the 1980s, was the economy's heavy dependence on a few livestock products, which were produced by primitive agricultural practices. Although exports could be diversified, for example, by producing not just wool but also woolen textiles and apparel, the supply of raw material depended on methods of raising sheep and cattle that had not changed significantly in two centuries. Livestock ranged over unimproved pastures whose carrying capacity was quite limited; production had actually decreased since the beginning of the twentieth century. The vulnerability of the sector was demonstrated in the late 1980s when a two-year drought (1988–89) decimated livestock herds.

Such fundamental issues were still in the background as Luis Alberto Lacalle de Herrera became president in March 1990. Lacalle indicated that his government would continue the cautious adjustment policies of its predecessor, seeking to reduce inflation and debt first and to resume growth second. Lacalle embraced privatization and drew up a bill to eliminate several state monopolies. Continued diversification of exports, including the possibility of exporting services, also appeared to hold good prospects for economic growth.

Growth and Structure of the Economy

Uruguay's recent economic history can be divided into two starkly contrasting periods. During the first, from the late 1800s until the 1950s, Uruguay achieved remarkable growth and a high standard of living. Expanding livestock exports—principally beef, mutton, and wool—accounted for this economic growth. Advanced social welfare programs, which redistributed wealth from the livestock sector to the rest of the economy, raised the standard of living for a majority of the population and contributed to social harmony. Booming livestock exports funded social programs and a state-led effort to build up new industries in Uruguay, such as domestic consumables (mainly food and beverages) and textiles. Thus, although Uruguay's economy was almost completely dependent on meat and wool exports, the strong earnings from those products helped to diversify the economy. As long as its exports continued to expand and world prices for those exports remained high, Uruguay's economic growth was ensured.

When export earnings faltered in the 1950s, however, the fabric of Uruguay's economy began to unravel. The country entered a decades-long period of economic stagnation. Export earnings first declined when world demand fell during the Great Depression of the 1930s. Prices later recovered somewhat, but a more important limitation on Uruguay's export earnings arose: livestock production reached its limits. Without room for continued expansion of traditional exports, and without a well-developed industrial sector, it became increasingly difficult for Uruguay to uphold the social welfare model that it had adopted in more prosperous times. The memory of those times, when livestock products earned enough to make Uruguay the "Switzerland of South America," made Uruguayans reluctant to completely reshape their economy. To understand that reluctance and its consequences, it is necessary to examine Uruguay's economic history in more detail.

Colonial Period

The foundation for Uruguay's livestock-based economy was laid well before the nation achieved independence. In 1603 Spanish colonists released cattle and horses on the empty plains of what is now Uruguay, then known as the Banda Oriental (eastern side, or bank, of the Río Uruguay). The livestock thrived in Uruguay's temperate climate, grazing on the natural pastures that still cover most of the countryside. By the early 1700s, there were millions of cattle in the area. During the "leather age," which lasted for the next century and a half, Uruguay's abundant livestock attracted traders and settlers from the nearby Argentine provinces. Hides became the area's chief export. Cattle raising, which seems to have begun almost by chance, quickly took hold of Uruguay's rural economy.

The success of simple livestock-ranching techniques in Uruguay during the colonial period was to have long-term consequences. Uruguay's temperate climate, natural pastures, and abundant land (because of its small population during the colonial period) combined to favor extensive methods of raising cattle. For ranchers, these methods held two economic advantages. Both investment and labor costs were kept to a minimum because cattle ranged free, subsisted on natural grass cover, and required little care. Well after independence in 1828, even when Uruguay had become an important exporter of livestock products, these advantages continued to exert a great deal of influence on the rural sector. Despite the limitations of extensive livestock raising, including low production levels per hectare and slow growth of stock, few ranchers ever became convinced that more intensive production techniques were worth the cost. As a result, the fundamental method of livestock production in Uruguay changed very little in over two centuries.

Postindependence Era

During the decades immediately following independence, however, political instability, not livestock production techniques, limited the development of Uruguay's rural economy. Until the mid-1800s, rival factions vied for control of the countryside, obstructing commerce and confiscating or destroying cattle and other property. Foreign investment, which was to play an important role in building up Uruguay's infrastructure, was delayed. And although the rural population was small to begin with, many settlers left the countryside in search of more peaceful surroundings. Those who remained operated cattle ranches (*estancias*) or practiced subsistence agriculture.

Rural struggles for political control thus slowed the growth of the livestock sector. By contrast, Montevideo, Uruguay's capital, where political struggles were less strident because of the city's booming trade and bustling social and cultural life, rapidly became a hub of economic activity. Montevideo was not founded until 1726, but its superb port allowed it to gain an increasing role in regional and international trade. In the 1800s, the Uruguayan capital became an important transshipment point because European importers and exporters preferred its port to that of nearby Buenos Aires (until the latter was improved in the 1870s). However, the volume of foreign traded goods passing through Montevideo had only a minimal impact on rural Uruguay. As a result, the city's development outpaced and diverged from that of the countryside. The different economic interests in the two areas helped drive a wedge between rural elites, who had amassed large landholdings and resented foreign involvement in the economy, and urban businessmen, who adopted outward-oriented attitudes and profited from trade. Later, profits from exports would become important to rural livestock producers as well, but the contrast between urban and rural economic (and political) orientations would persist.

The Export Model

After several decades of arrested development, Uruguay's economy underwent a series of important changes during the latter half of the 1800s. The consolidation of political control by the Colorado Party (Partido Colorado) and the division of the control of the departments in 1872 spelled the end of almost constant warfare and meant that the departments of Uruguay were finally united as one nation. Internal barriers to trade were removed, and the issuance of a national currency (the peso) in 1862 favored commercial activity. Political stability also allowed increased foreign involvement in the economy and encouraged technological advances. The framework for Uruguay's primary-product export economy, which supplied food and basic inputs to Europe's dynamic industrial sector, was erected during this period.

Livestock production changed in several ways as Uruguay adjusted to the export model. First, meat-packing technology was introduced in the mid-1860s, allowing canning of meat for export. Until then, beef was preserved only in a dry, salted form (*tasajo*), which appealed to a narrow export market (principally Brazil and Cuba, where it was fed to slave laborers). Second, livestock production was diversified when sheep ranching expanded rapidly, reflecting the British textile industry's demand for imported wool. After 1870 Uruguay had more sheep than cattle, largely because of an influx of sheep ranchers from France and Britain. A third change in the livestock sector came about in the 1870s with the introduction of barbed wire. For the first time, the boundaries of large *estancias* were marked off precisely, decreasing the number of ranch hands needed to watch over herds and driving many subsistence farmers off lands on the margins of large estates. Finally, the construction of railroad lines and telegraph networks provided the infrastructure that linked rural Uruguay to the thriving port of Montevideo.

These changes in the structure of the economy paved the way for a substantial increase in export earnings while reinforcing the importance of livestock production. In 1876 Uruguay had a positive balance of trade for the first time, and its export volume more than doubled over the next decade. Exports of wool increased dramatically, matching the value of leather exports by 1884. Residents of Montevideo were said to gauge the country's prosperity by counting the stacks of cowhides and bales of wool waiting to be loaded aboard ships. After 1900 the ability to ship frozen meat to Europe and the United States transformed the beef industry, added to Uruguayan export earnings as world demand for beef grew, and raised the importance of cattle production.

The nation's rising prosperity at the turn of the twentieth century rested firmly on rural livestock production. Paradoxically, however, it was in Montevideo that the most dramatic demographic and economic effects of growth were felt. The city's population increased, mainly because several waves of immigrants arrived from Europe. Most of these immigrants came from urban areas of Italy

Bags of wool ready for export in Montevideo
Courtesy Charles Guy Gillespie

and Spain, so it was natural that they tended to settle in Uruguay's urban center, where jobs were available. At the same time, the city's population was increasing because of the arrival of displaced laborers from the Uruguayan countryside. Both natives and immigrants made up a growing pool of labor for Montevideo's small but dynamic industries, many of which were owned by foreigners. Using mostly artisanal techniques, the city's workshops began to supply the home market with a variety of goods, such as footwear, clothing, wine, tobacco, paper, furniture, and construction materials.

Batllism

The government's protectionist policies—in the form of tariffs on imported manufactured goods, first imposed during the late 1800s—encouraged these light industries. However, it was Uruguay's most significant political figure, José Batlle y Ordóñez (1903–07, 1911–15), who devised an overarching government strategy that took into account the growing urban population and set the tone for the nation's economic development for much of the 1900s.

Two aspects of Batlle y Ordóñez's sophisticated political program were most relevant for the long-term development of the economy. First, the social components of Batllism raised the standing of the average laborer. The government enacted legislation that was unprecedented in Latin America: a minimum wage, a day of rest after six workdays, workmen's compensation, and old-age pensions. Second, and more significant over the long term, however, were Batlle y Ordóñez's efforts to give the state a multifaceted role in the economy. The state was to regulate the economy, perform key activities, protect laborers from unfair working conditions, and minimize the influence that foreign-owned companies would have in Uruguay (see Batlle y Ordóñez and the Modern State, ch. 1).

Under Batlle y Ordóñez's leadership, the state created or nationalized a wide range of service enterprises, officially known as autonomous entities (autonomous agencies or state enterprises; see Glossary), including an insurance company, public utilities, and mortgage banks. Later, the government became deeply involved in the production of goods, operating over twenty state enterprises, including the giant National Administration of Fuels, Alcohol, and Portland Cement (Administración Nacional de Combustibles, Alcohol, y Portland—ANCAP). By 1931 these state enterprises employed 9 percent of the nation's work force, including 16 percent of the workers in Montevideo.

Uruguay's novel economic policies bore fruit. Incomes rose on the strength of impressive export earnings. The value of exports doubled between 1900 and the onset of World War I, when beef exports, for example, reached 130,000 tons per year. Between 1926 and 1930, beef shipments continued to increase at a rapid rate, averaging 206,000 tons per year, a record that has not been equaled since then. During the same period, the Batlle y Ordóñez initiatives improved the lot of the worker, helped create a large middle class, and added to the productive capacity of the economy. The fact that all three developments—increased export earnings, improved conditions for labor, and successful state enterprises—occurred simultaneously helped Uruguayans to associate state intervention with prosperity.

The success of the export model, because of rising world demand and prices, was seen as the success of Batllism. However, as many observers have pointed out, the restructuring of the economy that occurred under Batlle y Ordóñez and his successors did not extend to the roots of that economy, the livestock sector. Because his political base did not reach beyond Montevideo into the countryside, and because he believed that market forces and property taxes would lead livestock producers to become more efficient, Batlle y Ordóñez essentially left the rural sector to its own devices. In doing so, he limited the extent to which his own bold reforms could transform the economy.

Stagnation

The precarious nature of Uruguay's primary-product export economy, so successful during the early decades of the 1900s, was gradually made clear for two distinct reasons. First, the sharp contraction of world demand for Uruguay's exports during the Great Depression showed the hazards of being at the mercy of external markets and foreign prices. Uruguay's export earnings fell by 40 percent between 1930 and 1932 as world demand contracted and importing nations adopted protectionist measures. Such a drastic decrease in earnings was only temporary, however. During World War II, prices recovered, making the export model appear viable again, if vulnerable. Still later, Uruguayan exporters were occasionally able to gain handsomely from world price increases. The most dramatic example of this phenomenon occurred during the Korean War (1950–53). Wool prices tripled temporarily as demand for cold-weather uniforms surged.

The volatility of export prices, which was itself troubling, also delayed recognition of the second, underlying limitation on Uruguay's export-based economy: the limited supply of livestock products. Production of beef stagnated by the mid-1930s, wool by the mid-1950s. With only minor modifications, ranchers continued to rely on the extensive production techniques used since the colonial period. Livestock production was therefore limited by the carrying capacity of the land. For many years, successful livestock producers had been able to expand their operations by simply purchasing or renting additional land, but after the tremendous expansion of both cattle ranching and sheep ranching during the early decades of the 1900s, this option was no longer available. Producers rejected the obvious alternative of increasing production levels by using more intensive techniques, such as fertilized pastures. According to a study published by the Economy Institute (Instituto de Economía) at the University of the Republic (also known as the University of Montevideo) in 1969, ranchers chose not to invest their profits in improved pastures because many more lucrative investments were available. Preferred investments included manufacturing (after World War II), urban real estate (during the 1950s), and overseas opportunities (leading to substantial capital flight during the 1960s).

The stagnation of livestock production undercut the export model that had brought Uruguay its prosperity. At first the nation was able to avoid complete economic paralysis by turning from livestock production to industrial development, from the dormant countryside to the dynamic city of Montevideo. Like most other Latin

American nations, Uruguay responded to the Great Depression by implementing a policy intended to encourage diversification away from primary products, reduce imports, and increase employment.

The so-called import-substitution industrialization (see Glossary) strategy raised tariff barriers to discourage imports and protect new manufacturing enterprises. In addition to increased protectionism, several other conditions in Uruguay favored the industrialization that accelerated beginning in the mid-1930s. Labor was plentiful in Montevideo; 100,000 immigrants had arrived from Europe during the 1920s. Equitable income distribution also meant that there was a sizable middle-class market for manufactured products. Finally, wealthy livestock producers were ready to invest in new enterprises.

Industry developed rapidly under these conditions. The number of firms, most of them employing ten or fewer workers, tripled from 7,000 in 1930 to 21,000 in 1955. Apart from the growth of traditional types of enterprises (food, beverages, textiles, and leather), there was also substantial progress in heavier industries (chemicals, oil refining, metallurgy, machinery, and electrical equipment). Workers earned good wages, and production increased more rapidly than employment, meaning that labor productivity was on the rise. During the 1940s, industrial output overtook livestock raising as a share of GDP.

But the industrial boom was short-lived. One sign of trouble was the fact that 90 percent of manufactured goods were consumed within Uruguay. Because domestic industries had grown up behind high tariff barriers, they were not competitive on world markets. This common shortcoming of the import-substitution industrialization strategy was particularly serious, given Uruguay's small internal market. Although income distribution was equitable, the potential for home-industry expansion was limited because consumption was limited. Most industries reached their full potential just two decades after the beginning of the industrialization process. During the mid-1950s, imports of machinery and industrial equipment that were essential for the further development of heavy industry leveled off and then declined. Industrial growth ceased. With the stagnation of both industrial production and livestock production in the mid-1950s, Uruguay's economy entered what would be a twenty-year crisis. Real per capita income, which had grown rapidly during the early 1900s, increased at an average of only 0.5 percent per year from the mid-1950s to the mid-1970s. The period was characterized by declining exports, a negative balance of payments, decreasing reserves, and growing inflation.

The prolonged nature of the crisis, i.e., the two-decade lack of fundamental economic restructuring, had much do to with the government policies that were set in motion during the Batllist period. As two of the three pillars of Uruguay's economy (livestock and industry) crumbled, the third (the public sector) bore an increasing burden. State enterprises expanded until, by the 1960s, they generated 30 percent of GDP and paid 40 percent of all salaries. Once-dynamic state enterprises became expensive public works projects. Elaborate formulas were devised to allow Uruguay's two principal political parties—the Colorado Party and the National Party (Partido Nacional, usually referred to as the Blancos)—to dispense public-sector jobs in proportion to votes received. Economically, a change of the ruling party meant very little. Both parties were allied in upholding the social welfare model, which amounted to keeping the state enterprises and the bureaucracy afloat. To do so, they incurred a large foreign debt and penalized the livestock sector through domestic price controls. The economy turned inward through continued protectionism and artificially high exchange rates. As a result, the once-vital export sector could not develop the momentum required to pull the economy out of the doldrums.

The protracted economic crisis became a political crisis in the late 1960s. Within Uruguay the welfare state government could provide no answers to the twin challenges of urban terrorism and growing inflation. Outside Uruguay military regimes in both of its larger neighbors (Argentina and Brazil) cast long shadows, and international economic conditions made the insulation of Uruguay's economy more difficult. As the military regime took power in 1973, two international economic factors were particularly relevant: the quadrupling of oil prices (Uruguay imported all of its petroleum) and the closure of European Community markets to imported beef. These factors helped convince the military government that a major restructuring of the economy was needed.

Restructuring under the Military Regime, 1973–85

The military government was at first able to redirect and revitalize the economy. During the first phase of stabilization and structural adjustment, from 1973 to 1978, government policies had two central goals: to reestablish an export-oriented growth policy and to eliminate inflation. In pursuit of the latter, the government tightened the money supply, sharply cut the public budget, and held real wages down. The effort was partially successful. Inflation declined from over 100 percent per year during the 1960s to about 50 percent per year in the 1973–78 period. To reorient the productive sectors of the economy, the government eliminated most price controls, lowered tariff barriers from a maximum of 346 percent in 1974 to 180 percent in 1977, and subsidized exports. Foreign-exchange and financial markets were also made more liberal, increasing Uruguay's integration with world markets. The immediate results were dramatic: from 1974 to 1978, GDP increased by an average of 3.9 percent per year, after two decades of stagnation. Real exports grew by 14 percent annually during the same period, and productive investment increased by 16 percent per year.

Dissatisfied with some aspects of the economy's performance, however, the government again adopted several measures between 1978 and 1982. These included passing a foreign investment act (designed to attract foreign investment), reducing government spending, and selling off a few state enterprises.

Inflation, which had dropped below 40 percent in 1976 but had since increased again, remained the primary target of the new stabilization policies. Authorities believed that two factors were fueling inflation: the influx of external funds (allowed under liberalized financial regulations) and the continuing price increases by local firms, still protected from foreign competition because tariffs had only been reduced partially. The government, then, saw continued inflation as a problem caused by incomplete economic liberalization and moved to accelerate reforms. Banks were largely deregulated as reserve requirements were eliminated and foreign currency deposits allowed. Import tariffs for most products were reduced, allowing increased foreign competition. Export subsidies were reduced or eliminated. In addition, the government began announcing moderate exchange-rate devaluations several months in advance in an attempt to slow inflation and discourage currency speculation.

These measures reduced inflation somewhat, but instead of stabilizing the economy, they disrupted the gradual process of economic recovery that had been under way for several years. Uruguayan firms, many of which had reoriented production toward exports after 1974, faced rising internal costs when subsidies were removed. At the same time, they became less competitive abroad because devaluations did not keep pace with inflation. Banks responded to deregulation by making risky loans, many of which became nonperforming as the expansion slowed. The public deficit increased, especially when the government stepped in to rescue several major banks. External debt increased when the government was forced to borrow abroad. A second oil shock in 1979 (the first was in 1973–74) and an Argentine devaluation in 1981 both hurt

Uruguay's trade balance. As the restructuring process broke down, capital flight became rampant.

The military government's attempt to regain economic stability during its last two years in office resulted in a severe recession. After increasing over several years to a high of 6.2 percent in 1979, GDP growth slowed to 1.9 percent in 1981 and plunged to −9.4 percent in 1982. Real GDP declined by one-sixth from 1982 to 1984. Unemployment increased to 13 percent, further increasing the burden on the nation's welfare system. During its last three years in office, the government's most significant accomplishment was far more modest than its earlier reforms: it reduced the public deficit from 18.4 percent of GDP in 1982 to 9.2 percent at the end of 1984.

As the military government prepared to leave power after a turbulent twelve years, five major issues confronted economic planners. First, the government had succeeded in reorienting production toward exports, but by the mid-1980s traditional export markets were growing less hospitable. For example, world beef prices had fallen, partly because of subsidized competition from the European Community. Second, the public sector, which played a large role in Uruguay's economy, faced a growing internal and external debt burden. This reduced savings available to finance private investment and made it difficult for the government to meet its social security obligations. Third, many firms and banks were financially weak, the former because of debts incurred before the recession and the latter because of nonperforming loans. Fourth, unemployment remained high. Finally, inflation, a primary target of the attempted reforms, had increased from 50 percent in 1983 to 72 percent in 1985. The first and second issues were concerned with enduring themes: the importance of livestock exports and the government's role in the economy. The third, fourth, and fifth issues were products of the reforms that had brought Uruguay out of stagnation without completely restructuring the economy.

The Sanguinetti Government

The civilian government that entered office in 1985 inherited an economy whose fundamental elements had not changed a great deal for many years. The economy was still based on agriculture. In 1988, midway through the Sanguinetti government's term of office, livestock, crop production, and fishing generated only 13 percent of GDP directly. But the largest industries in Uruguay—food processing and textiles—depended on agricultural inputs. Thus, the link between agriculture and industry, which generated 33 percent of GDP in 1988, was strong. Another inescapable feature

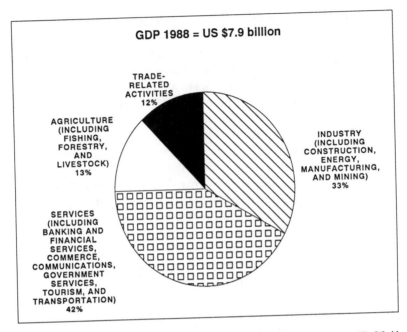

Source: Based on information from United States, Central Intelligence Agency, *The World Factbook, 1989,* Washington, 1989, 310; and Economist Intelligence Unit, *Country Report: Uruguay, Paraguay* [London], No. 1, 1990, 3.

Figure 6. Gross Domestic Product (GDP) by Sector, 1988

of the economy was the central role of government. Uruguayan national statistics included the government, which comprised not only agencies such as the Ministry of National Defense and the postal service but also, within the service sector, a large commercial bank and several insurance companies. The entire service sector—including activities such as private banking, transportation, and tourism—accounted for 42 percent of GDP. The external sector, i.e., activities involving foreign trade, generated the remaining 12 percent of GDP (see fig. 6).

The record of the Sanguinetti government was moderately successful. The administration entered office facing an economy just beginning to recover from a severe recession. That recovery continued, as real GDP growth averaged over 5 percent per year during the administration's first two full years in office (see table 9, Appendix). During 1988 and 1989, however, real GDP growth nearly ceased. In other areas, the record was similar. Unemployment fell from 13 percent in 1985 to 9 percent in 1987 but was reduced no further. Inflation fell at first, then increased again.

The lack of sustained economic progress during the late 1980s was not simply a result of the Sanguinetti government's policies, however. The government and the private sector inherited many serious difficulties in the mid-1980s: the growing external debt, a large government bureaucracy in deficit, a burdensome social security system, and a weakened currency. Because they could not immediately change these features, the government and the private sector chose to begin a cautious policy of readjustment. Fundamental restructuring was again delayed.

Economic Policy

Government policy has greatly influenced the development, or lack of development, of Uruguay's economy during the twentieth century. The government first became an important regulator of economic activity when it arranged for a portion of livestock export earnings to be transferred to the urban working class. As its interventionist role expanded during the early 1900s, the central government became the administrator of an elaborate social welfare system that was generous by Latin American standards. After the Great Depression, the government enacted tariff policies to promote domestic manufacturing and adopted the strategy known as import-substitution industrialization. The state also became an important participant in the economy. In a pattern repeated elsewhere in Latin America, the central government nationalized or established several of the largest service and manufacturing companies in the country (see Industry, this ch.). It became the single largest employer and producer in the nation.

The level of government involvement in the economy took on increasing significance after Uruguay entered a period of economic stagnation. When export earnings leveled off in the 1950s, the state's two roles in the economy became difficult to sustain yet vital to the population. Growing numbers of unemployed persons and retirees depended on the social welfare system, even as government revenues used to support that system declined. In addition, the overall economic slowdown made public-sector employment extremely attractive. Public employment, which was controlled by political parties rather than market forces, increased at 2.6 percent per year during 1955–61, while private-sector employment grew at only 0.9 percent. Government consumption expenditures for salaries and services remained high, but public investment was scaled back, penalizing future productivity. Despite this shift in the spending pattern, the state's income did not keep pace with its expenditures. By the 1960s, a public-sector deficit had developed, requiring borrowing from abroad and helping to fuel inflation.

The public-sector deficit was the hallmark of Uruguay's stagnated economy in the 1960s. Thereafter, efforts to reduce the deficit were a central feature of structural reforms. However, the web of government commitments within the economy—involving both administrative and productive activity—made this a difficult task. The military government (1973–85) partially succeeded at the larger task of reorienting the economy toward world markets but made only modest headway against the public-sector deficit. During the second half of the 1980s, the deficit was at first reduced but then increased again in the last two years of the Sanguinetti administration.

Fiscal Policy

The civilian government that entered office in 1985 faced a severe fiscal problem: the chronic public-sector deficit. It also faced a broader difficulty: an economy in deep recession. The deficit was believed to be perpetuating inflation. Inflation, in turn, prevented the economy from reaching a stable position conducive to renewed growth. Thus, the priorities of the Sanguinetti administration's economic plan—devised in cooperation with the International Monetary Fund (IMF—see Glossary)—were to reduce the deficit, bring down inflation, and improve the balance of payments.

These multiyear fiscal measures were considered essential for renewed growth, but the serious consequences of the recession called for immediate action to spur economic activity. Between 1981 and 1984, the recession had taken its toll on all sectors of the economy. GDP had declined by almost 17 percent; agricultural production by 12 percent; manufacturing by 21 percent; construction by 48 percent; and capital formation (investment) by 56 percent. Workers were especially hard-hit by the decline. Between November 1982 and March 1985, real salaries fell by 19 percent. In real terms, workers earned only half of what they had earned in 1968, and unemployment had increased to 13 percent. Unable to ignore these signs of distress, the Sanguinetti administration also adopted an economic growth policy.

Initially, the stabilization effort took precedence over efforts to boost economic activity. The idea was to break the inflationary momentum of the economy first and restore growth second. In fiscal terms, the goal was to reduce the public-sector deficit from 10 percent of GDP in mid-1985 to 5 percent of GDP by 1986. The scope of government involvement in the Uruguayan economy meant that the public-sector deficit had to be attacked on three fronts: the central government, by reducing expenditures and increasing revenues; the Central Bank of Uruguay, which accounted for about half of the deficit; and the state enterprises, many of which had run small deficits through most of the 1980s.

The results of the stabilization effort were ambiguous. On the one hand, the Sanguinetti government easily reached its fiscal targets. During its first two years in office, the government enacted tax increases that raised real government revenues by 58 percent. Meanwhile, real expenditures increased by only 43 percent (see table 10; table 11; table 12, Appendix). As a result, the public-sector deficit declined to about 3 percent of GDP, better than the government had planned. Simultaneously, however, inflation—the underlying target of the government's fiscal policy—hardly slowed at all. Inflation went from an annual rate of 72 percent in 1985 to 57 percent in 1987, but it increased to 85 percent in 1989. The persistence of inflation in the face of fiscal restraint did not reflect a failure of the Sanguinetti government's fiscal policy; rather, inflation persisted because of the government's monetary and exchange-rate policies, the instruments it used to promote economic growth (see Monetary and Exchange-Rate Policy, this ch.). Fiscal policy was also inadequate because the government expanded the money supply to pay for the fiscal deficit (8.5 percent by the end of 1989).

Monetary and Exchange-Rate Policy

The Sanguinetti administration turned to Uruguay's formerly strong export sector in devising its strategy for renewed economic growth. Through a combination of exchange-rate policy, liberal credit to exporters, and cultivation of new markets, the government hoped to revitalize the traditional export sector (primarily beef and wool) and promote the manufacture of nontraditional exports such as apparel.

The most important policy tool was the exchange rate. Initially, the government planned to allow the peso to float freely, in keeping with its philosophy of minimal market intervention. In practice, however, the monetary authorities carried out a "dirty float," repeatedly entering the currency market to lower the exchange rate of the peso. Devaluation translated into increased competitiveness. For a small country like Uruguay, facing world (United States dollar) prices for goods, a devaluation of the peso (more pesos per dollar) meant that an exporter would receive more pesos for a given quantity of goods. This effectively raised the profitability of exports (leaving aside other effects) and encouraged the growth of the sector.

Exports and GDP both increased after 1985, partly as a result of the more competitive exchange rate. But the policy also had

113

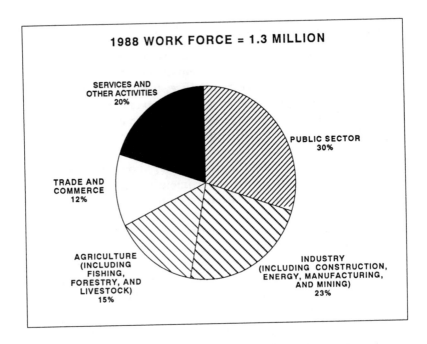

Figure 7. Employment by Sector, 1988

inflationary effects that counteracted the government's restrained fiscal policy. The government's intervention in the currency market consisted of buying foreign exchange and selling pesos. This raised the supply of pesos and lowered their price relative to other currencies (the exchange rate). But the intervention also increased the foreign-exchange component of the money supply, thus fueling inflation. The government attempted to compensate for this increase in the monetary base by decreasing other components of the money supply, a policy known as sterilization. However, an increasing share of Uruguayan bank deposits were denominated in United States dollars rather than pesos. Thus, the efforts to restrict the peso monetary base had little effect on the overall money supply, which continued to increase. As a result, the government could not fine-tune its export-promotion strategy to eliminate inflationary effects. Inflation persisted despite the decline of the public-sector deficit. In short, the government's notable accomplishments on the fiscal side were largely negated on the monetary side.

Labor

The labor force in Uruguay was small (1.4 million in 1990), about

80 percent urban, and educated at least to a high school level. In 1988 about 30 percent of workers were employed in the public sector, 23 percent in industry, 15 percent in agriculture, 12 percent in trade and commerce, and 20 percent in services and other activities (see fig. 7). During the 1970s, workers experienced a sharp decline in real wages, which they only partially regained in the 1980s. The problems of the labor force, reflecting the overall difficulties of the Uruguayan economy, led to widespread strikes and unrest that hindered economic growth during the 1980s. In view of Uruguay's fundamental structural difficulties, an accommodation with the labor movement remained an important issue for the government.

The Labor Movement

Several of the uncommon economic and political characteristics of Uruguay influenced the development of its labor movement during the early 1900s. First, because the only sizable concentration of workers was in Montevideo, the labor movement was largely restricted to that city and was thus not really a national phenomenon. Second, the small number of workers employed by most individual firms limited the tendency of workers to form mass organizations. Third, the government played a central role in labor policy. State enterprises and government organizations became the nation's largest employer. In addition, legislation established many private-sector labor policies that preempted organized labor.

Uruguay's laborers, like the economy as a whole, made great strides during the early decades of the 1900s. Ironically, this progress slowed the growth of a cohesive labor movement. President Batlle y Ordóñez, who firmly supported the working class and the right to strike, was an important figure for laborers during this period. His ideology of Batllism—in sharp contrast to the repression of labor in many other Latin American nations—aimed to reconcile labor and capital, or employees and owners. The Batllist government created the Office of Labor and ensured that a share of the increasing livestock export earnings was transferred to the urban working class. By the late 1920s, legislation limited the workweek and workday, established a minimum wage, and required that benefits be paid to injured or retired laborers. This congenial atmosphere gained the official labor movement only limited support. In 1926, for example, only 6,000 out of 65,000 industrial workers were dues-paying union members.

The cordial relationship between labor and government deteriorated as Uruguay's economic growth stalled in the 1930s. The government became less tolerant of unions. The unions, in turn, became more militant. Communism replaced anarchism as the dominant political ideology of labor leaders. During and after World War II, a sometimes-violent split between the communist and non-communist labor elements developed. This ideological division prevented the labor movement from speaking with one voice and limited its national impact. In contrast to Argentina, where the Peronist labor movement gained great political power during the 1950s, the labor movement in Uruguay remained fragmented.

An important question for the labor movement in Uruguay has been whether public-sector workers have the right to strike. Government employees—both in government agencies and in state enterprises—constituted the largest group of salaried workers in the country. Thus, the government's civil-service wage policy set the tone for wages in general. The government also participated directly in setting private-sector wage policy, along with unions and owners, through the tripartite advisory boards—the wage councils—established in the 1940s. When public employees tried to strike, the government responded harshly. After a 1952 strike in the petroleum refinery, for example, the government enacted a mild form of martial law.

The confrontation between government and labor became pronounced in the late 1960s. The Communist Party of Uruguay had come to dominate the unions after the Cuban Revolution, and the unions' objectives were as much political as they were economic. The government would not tolerate labor's leftist political program, especially given the charged atmosphere of the period. Nor was the government in a position to fulfill the unions' wage demands; a wage and price freeze was imposed, and the wage councils were abolished in June 1968. Strikes and repression became frequent. The confrontation reached its climax in 1973, when the major labor group, the National Convention of Workers (Convención Nacional de Trabajadores—CNT), organized a general strike to protest the military coup. The strike—the labor movement's last stand—dissolved within two weeks. The military regime that seized power in 1973 outlawed the CNT and arrested its leaders. Union activity ceased for almost ten years. During the 1970s, 12,000 public-sector workers and at least 5,000 private-sector workers were dismissed because of their trade union or political activities.

The military government allowed unions to resurface in 1981 through the Law of Professional Associations. Labor organizations were allowed to exist on three levels: by individual enterprise, by occupational category, and on a national scale. But the government took pains to depoliticize the labor movement. The secret ballot was to be used on the individual enterprise level, both for election of leadership and for strike votes. Leaders of previously outlawed organizations were admonished to limit their political activity. The law's timing was more important than these limitations, however. As economic activity slowed during the 1981–84 recession, union activity was minimal. Nevertheless, the unions did play a role in the "democratic counteroffensive" that led to the restoration of civilian rule in the mid-1980s. Successful general strikes before and after Sanguinetti's election helped dissuade the military from interfering in the political process.

Relations between labor and government were delicate during the Sanguinetti administration (see Political Forces and Interest Groups, ch. 4). The framework for relations was established before the civilian government took office, during the 1984–85 period of multiparty consultations, officially called the National Conciliatory Program (Concertación Nacional Programática—Conapro). A working group recommended that the incoming government adopt a three-part policy toward labor: repeal of the legislation that restricted union activity and collective bargaining; reinstatement of all public-sector employees who had been dismissed by the military regime for their union activity; and restoration of workers' purchasing power through periodic wage increases, but in a manner consistent with bringing down inflation. The new government quickly complied with the first two recommendations, but the third became a contentious issue.

Government Policy

The Sanguinetti administration attempted to balance the clear need to increase wages with the equally pressing requirement to control inflation. Thus, the government immediately declared a wage increase in March 1985 but took action designed to control future wage increases. The tripartite wage councils were reestablished to negotiate wages every four months for nonagricultural private-sector employees. The councils at first adopted wage increases that were slightly higher than inflation, so that real wages at the end of 1985 were an average of 15 percent higher than the year before. Nevertheless, there was a great deal of labor unrest: over 900 strikes occurred between March 1985 and September 1986. Workers were apparently frustrated by the slow increases in real wages and anxious to express their displeasure after a decade of repression.

After 1986 the number of labor disputes decreased, partly because of the government's bargaining strategy. The government tried to control wage increases by persuading all private-sector unions to sign twenty- to twenty-four-month contracts under which wages would be adjusted according to conditions within individual companies. This action helped lower the level of conflict between labor and government, but it may have made the task of restraining wage increases more difficult. In exchange for accepting longer wage contracts, unions demanded that workers be protected against inflation through "indexation," or automatic wage increases, to compensate for inflation. In 1986 about one-third of all workers were covered by indexed contracts; by the end of 1988, over half were. When Sanguinetti proposed in mid-1988 that wage increases be held to 90 percent of inflation, instead of the 100 percent or greater that unions had become accustomed to, most of the nation's work force joined a one-day work stoppage in protest. The position of workers was understandable: their average real wage (purchasing power) remained below its 1968 level (see Blue-Collar Workers, ch. 2). The wage issue, particularly the question of whether indexation was compatible with an anti-inflationary policy, was still unresolved when Lacalle took office in 1990.

Agriculture

Agriculture played a central role in Uruguay's economy. In 1988 agricultural activity (including fishing) directly generated 13 percent of GDP and provided over half the value of exports. Indirectly, agriculture was responsible for a much higher proportion of both GDP and exports. Many of Uruguay's most dynamic manufacturing enterprises—such as its tanneries and textile mills—depended on agricultural inputs. The close relationship between agriculture and manufacturing had a significant impact on Uruguay's economic development. For example, the sluggish performance of the large livestock sector in the 1980s contributed to slow overall economic growth (see table 13, Appendix).

Agricultural Stagnation

A troubling issue for the agricultural sector was the stagnation of production levels over several decades. Total agricultural production increased at an average rate of less than 1 percent per year from the 1950s to the 1980s. In 1989 the sector continued a 1 percent growth rate. This low growth was usually attributed to a lack of technologically advanced production methods, but that description applied mainly to the large livestock sector. Ranchers continued to rely on extensive production methods. By contrast, many crop and citrus farmers had adopted more advanced technology, using tractors, fertilizers, and pesticides. Similarly, poultry producers relied on advanced techniques, and some dairy farmers fertilized their pastures.

Alternative explanations of the agricultural sector's poor performance take note of the overall characteristics of Uruguay's economy. First, the small size of the internal market had forced most agricultural producers to be exporters. Agricultural products had become an important source of foreign exchange, but fluctuations in world prices and markets buffeted Uruguay's externally oriented agricultural sector. For example, wool prices fell when synthetic fabrics were developed. Additionally, the market for Uruguayan beef contracted when the European Community began subsidizing its beef producers in the 1980s.

A second reason for the lack of agricultural growth may have been the inconsistency of government policy. During the protectionist import-substitution industrialization phase in the 1950s, the government held agricultural prices down in order to lower industrial labor costs. This discouraged both agricultural production and investment. During the 1960s, the government reversed this pricing policy when it encouraged the export of certain agricultural products (poultry, dairy, and citrus products) through subsidies and other incentives. However, this export policy was itself reversed in the 1970s, in keeping with the military government's effort to open the economy to foreign competition. The abrupt withdrawal of subsidies made the production of several products unprofitable. With government policy toward it fluctuating in this manner, agriculture in Uruguay was on uncertain ground, and potential investors remained wary. Aided by a recovery in the livestock sector, however, agricultural output increased by an estimated 3.5 percent in 1990.

Land Use and Tenure

The general characteristics of Uruguay's land area helped determine the pattern of land use. The countryside is devoid of mountains—in contrast to most other Latin American nations—and is only 2 to 3 percent forested. Over 80 percent of the land can be used for some kind of agriculture. The natural grasslands for which Uruguay is famous lend themselves to the predominant agricultural activity: livestock production.

Although the land and temperate climate facilitated livestock production, the limited fertility of the soil hindered the production of crops. Livestock ranches covered three-quarters of the total land, especially in the departments of Artigas, Cerro Largo, Durazno, Flores, Lavalleja, Maldonado, Paysandú, Rivera, Rocha, Salto, and Tacuarembó (see fig. 1). The most productive wheat- and cereal-farming area was the southwest (Colonia, Río Negro, and Soriano departments); most of the rice was produced in the east (Treinta y Tres Department); and fruits, vegetables, and wine were produced in the departments of Canelones, Florida, and San José.

Uruguay was no exception to the Latin American pattern of concentrated landownership, but its small population had kept land distribution from becoming a major political issue. Agricultural enterprises could be roughly divided into two types, whose characteristics in the mid-1980s reflected the concentration of landownership and helped explain Uruguay's urban tendencies. The first type, family-operated (owned or rented) farms and ranches, made up 85 percent of agricultural enterprises in the country, employed 68 percent of rural workers, and produced 45 percent of all agricultural output. But this type of enterprise controlled only 25 percent of agricultural land (farming and livestock). The second type, larger commercial enterprises, controlled 75 percent of the land, employed 32 percent of rural labor, and produced 55 percent of output. These statistics indicate that smaller enterprises made more productive use of the land. However, the fact that such family-operated farms and ranches employed mostly family members rather than salaried workers tended to limit the development of the rural economy. The larger enterprises, by contrast, were mostly extensive livestock ranches that had little need of hired labor. As this second type of enterprise became more prevalent throughout the twentieth century, landownership became more concentrated, and the population of the countryside declined.

Agricultural production employed only about 15 percent of Uruguay's labor force in the late 1980s. The agricultural work force declined steadily as the number of small agricultural enterprises diminished. There were 87,000 farms and ranches in 1961, 77,000 in 1970, and only 57,000 in 1986. The importance of family-operated establishments is clearly seen in rural labor statistics. In 1980 two-thirds of the 160,000-person agricultural labor force was made up of landowners or their relatives; only 57,000 workers were wage earners. Not surprisingly, the labor movement had little impact on rural workers, although both the rice workers and the dairy workers were organized into unions.

Livestock Ranching

Uruguay's livestock herds did not expand appreciably after 1930. In 1908 there were 8 million cattle and 26 million sheep in the country. In 1981 the number of cattle peaked at 11 million, while the number of sheep had declined to 20 million. Because the land area dedicated to livestock raising has not changed significantly, these figures illustrated the lack of progress in the sector. The single

Herding cattle in Treinta y Tres
Department
Courtesy Inter-American
Development Bank

Inspecting a beef carcass
in Melo
Courtesy Inter-American
Development Bank

largest investment in cattle herds was complete by 1930, when Herefords were substituted for the original mixed breeds. Extensive ranching methods facilitated livestock raising because little investment was required. But these methods also limited the carrying capacity of the land and the size of the stock. By the 1970s, it took twenty-six Uruguayan cattle to yield one ton of beef, compared with about eighteen in Argentina and about thirteen in the United States or Western Europe. The production of wool and mutton per head of sheep was also low: 3.5 kilograms of wool per head, compared with over 5 kilograms per head in Australia or Argentina. In addition, both cattle and sheep herds were subject to losses because of limited efforts to prevent disease.

The vulnerability of the range-fed livestock herds was further demonstrated in the late 1980s when Uruguay experienced a severe drought. Millions of animals died or had to be slaughtered prematurely. The drought lasted longest in the center of the country, where most of the largest cattle ranches were located (the departments of Cerro Largo, Durazno, and Tacuarembó). The leading sheep-ranching departments in the northwest (Artigas and Salto) were not as severely affected.

Raising sheep for wool in Uruguay became less profitable during the 1960s. There was increasing worldwide competition from petroleum-based synthetic fibers. After the oil price increase in 1973, however, wool was once again in favor. Production surged from about 61,000 tons per year in the mid-1970s to 87,000 tons in 1986. Wool surpassed beef as Uruguay's most valuable export in the early 1980s. It also supplied the growing woolen textile and apparel industry, which earned additional foreign exchange.

Sheep, whose stock increased to almost 26 million by 1989, were also raised for lamb and mutton. The potential for Uruguay's export of sheep meat in 1989 was about 3 million head, as compared with annual exports of about 2 million head in the early 1980s. However, a severe drought in the first half of 1989 reduced the performance of this subsector by about 10 percent during that period.

Rising world beef prices stimulated the Uruguayan cattle industry in the late 1970s. At first, rising prices increased the profitability of cattle ranching but ultimately led to considerable instability in the sector. When many ranchers expanded their herds after the 1978-79 beef price increases, the price of pastureland grew almost tenfold. Because real interest rates were low or negative, ranchers were willing to borrow heavily to increase their landholdings. But beef prices soon leveled off, and many ranchers were left with large, unpayable debts. Land prices fell sharply; banks could not cover their loans even by foreclosing. As the bank crisis mounted, the Central Bank stepped in to provide refinancing in United States dollar-denominated loans. Most ranchers avoided bankruptcy but had to slaughter record numbers of cattle to service their debts. Many ranchers took the opportunity to switch to sheep ranching because wool appeared to face more stable world demand. Thus, Uruguay's cattle herds declined by 20 percent from 1981 to 1984.

Cattle ranchers rebuilt their herds during the latter half of the 1980s but were hindered by limited credit and severe drought. Damage from the prolonged drought had reached alarming proportions by the end of 1989, when the cattle stock was down to 9.4 million head. The number of cattle fell by 738,000 head between June 1988 and June 1989, the largest annual drop in fifteen years. About 2 percent of the total had died, and the rest had been killed and sold (50 percent more than usual). In the July-November 1989 period, the beef cattle herd was depleted by an additional 622,000 head. The increased slaughter rates allowed meat-packing plants to pay less for beef, decreasing ranchers' profits.

The continuing difficulty in the sector prompted the government to launch Operation Manufacture in March 1989. The program eased the ranchers' financial burden by extending them a special line of credit, lowering their tax rate by 20 percent, and providing for case-by-case assistance. The government also announced the opening of a line of credit with terms of up to eight years for herd replacement. Sheep ranchers, who suffered fewer losses from the drought, were not eligible for these government programs.

The dairy industry, based in the departments near Montevideo, expanded considerably in the 1980s. Milk production increased from 400,000 tons in 1979 to 635,000 tons in 1987. Even though many dairy farmers still relied on natural pastures, limiting the milk output per cow, Uruguay was more than self-sufficient in dairy products and exported to other Latin American countries. Most domestic milk processing and marketing was controlled by the National Dairy Products Cooperative, which distributed dairy products throughout the country.

Crop Production

Crop production in Uruguay has never been as important as livestock raising. Only about 8 percent of the land area was dedicated to growing crops in the mid-1980s, compared with 75 percent dedicated to livestock. The amount of land under cultivation has varied according to the world price of livestock products. When beef prices have declined, for example, ranchers have planted wheat or corn. Rising livestock prices in the 1980s resulted in a considerable decrease in the area dedicated to most crops. Because crop production had gradually become more efficient through mechanization, however, crop yields did not necessarily decline.

Although crop yields per hectare had generally increased, erosion of the thin topsoil layer became a significant problem in Uruguay during the 1980s. It was estimated that 30 percent of all arable areas had been adversely affected. The ill effects were most serious in areas that had been under continuous cultivation for long periods.

Rice surpassed wheat as Uruguay's most significant crop in the 1980s. In contrast to the general downward trend in farmed land area, the land dedicated to rice production increased from 55,000 hectares in 1980 to 81,000 hectares in 1988. Over this same period, production rose from 228,000 tons to 381,000 tons, a 67 percent increase. Only about 40,000 tons were consumed domestically; most of the rice was exported. The preferred farming system for rice production was closely connected to livestock raising. Rice was grown for two years; then the land was sown as pasture for four or five years to renew the fields and provide grazing for cattle. The most common variety produced was the American "Blue Belle" type. The drought that gripped Uruguay in 1988-89 caused rice producers to lose an estimated 6 percent of their crop, worth about US$2.4 million. The hardest hit areas were in the north, in the departments of Artigas, Rivera, and Tacuarembó.

Wheat production and hectarage both declined during most of the 1980s. This decline reflected the increasing land area dedicated to livestock production and the fact that Uruguayan wheat producers could not effectively compete with wheat producers in other countries. International competition became more important after the government discontinued its subsidies for wheat farmers during the economic liberalization of the 1970s. Uruguay was no longer self-sufficient in wheat production by the mid-1980s, when about 80,000 tons per year were imported. Wheat farming was largely mechanized by the 1980s, but advanced tractor equipment acted mainly to reduce the labor requirement on farms, rather than leading to huge production increases. Most farmers made only limited use of pesticides and fertilizers. Thus, wheat production per hectare was below that of most other countries. Nevertheless, the area dedicated to wheat farming rose in 1989, and production was expected to begin increasing again. Indeed, wheat production grew to 414,000 tons in 1988.

Corn production stagnated during the 1980–88 period. Like wheat farmers, corn farmers were adversely affected by the government's freeing of agricultural prices in the late 1970s. Unlike wheat, however, corn was not an important commercial crop; farmers used it primarily to feed their animals. No longer self-sufficient, Uruguay imported almost US$2 million worth of corn in 1988. Some farmers had substituted sorghum cultivation for corn because it provided roughly the same nutrition as corn but better withstood drought conditions.

Other crops produced in Uruguay in the 1980s included barley, soybeans, oats, sunflowers, peanuts, sugarcane, potatoes, flax, and cotton. Barley, soybeans, and sunflowers were produced mainly for export; the other crops were produced on only a small scale for the domestic market. Production of sugar was uneconomical, relying on a large government subsidy. Uruguay imported cotton (US$6.6 million in 1988) for its textile industry.

Citrus farming was a bright spot on the agricultural horizon in the 1980s. Citrus and produce farms were originally established around Montevideo to supply the city with fruits and vegetables. During the 1980s, these farms expanded, allowing Uruguay to become a net exporter of citrus fruit (oranges, lemons, and grapefruit). The exported value increased from US$5 million in 1980 to US$21 million in 1986. One large-scale citrus plantation added packing facilities and a juice-and-oil plant, with at least half of its production intended for export. The government encouraged such diversification of agriculture.

Fishing

Uruguay first began to develop a fishing industry in the 1970s. Previously, fishermen from other countries had taken advantage of the rich resources off Uruguay's coast, but there was no concerted national fishing effort. The military government enacted the five-year National Fishing Development Plan in 1974 as part of its attempt to develop new economic activities with export potential. Under the plan, administered by the government's National Fishing Institute, fishing expanded markedly. By the late 1980s, there were over 700 fishing vessels in the fishing fleet, compared with only 300 in 1974. Furthermore, the number of large oceangoing vessels increased from five to seventy during this period. Oceangoing vessels held more fish and allowed longer voyages to distant waters. The latter capability became important after most nations (including Uruguay and neighboring Argentina) extended their exclusive economic zone from 3 to 200 miles in the mid-1970s, restricting access to many coastal fisheries. As the fishing fleet expanded, port facilities were improved. The port facilities of Montevideo, Piriápolis, and Punta del Este were modernized, and an entirely new port was constructed at La Paloma.

The intensified fishing effort produced favorable results; the catch grew from 16,000 tons in 1974 to 144,000 tons in 1981, remaining at about 140,000 tons per year in the late 1980s. Not all aspects of the government's plan were successful, however. It called for sizable catches of species that could be processed (canned) for export, such as tuna and sardines. As of 1987, however, fishermen were only catching a few hundred tons of tuna per year, not enough to supply a cannery. The sardine catch was also very small. Although those two species proved difficult to catch, Uruguay's fishermen had success catching Argentine hake, Atlantic croaker, and striped weakfish. The fish-processing industry also developed as the catch increased. Processing capacity in the late 1980s was about 250,000 tons, considerably above the estimated annual catch of 200,000 tons for all kinds of fish, except the anchovy.

About half of Uruguay's catch was exported during the late 1980s, in line with the government's goal of increasing nontraditional exports. Argentine hake (a whitefish similar to cod) was the leading export. In 1988, however, Uruguayan processing companies reported that world prices for Argentine hake had fallen below production costs because of the competition from cod suppliers. Although prices later recovered, many companies began to process and export alternative species, such as anchovy, mullet, and bluefish. The industry's exports reached US$81 million in 1987, as compared with US$65 million in 1986 and US$1.2 million in 1974. The United States imported 30 percent of Uruguay's fish; Brazil imported 23 percent; and Japan, the Federal Republic of Germany (West Germany), Saudi Arabia, and Israel each imported between 4 and 6 percent.

In 1990 an important issue for the Lacalle administration was Uruguay's access to the fisheries of the South Atlantic near Antarctica, as well as to fishery resources in Argentina's coastal waters. Lacalle told *Visión* magazine in early 1990 that he strongly supported the idea of an international conference, under the auspices of the Food and Agriculture Organization of the United Nations, to regulate fishing in the South Atlantic.

Forestry

In the 1980s, estimates of Uruguay's natural forest ranged from 4,000 to 6,000 square kilometers of mostly small trees of limited or no industrial use; planted forest estimates ranged from 120,000 hectares to 137,000 hectares of pine and eucalyptus. There were an additional 70,000 hectares of palm, poplar, salix (a genus of shrubs and trees), and other species. Sawmills were inefficient and small, with a capacity of fewer than thirty cubic meters a day. Of

Harvesting oranges near Paysandú
Courtesy Inter-American Development Bank

the 220,000 cubic meters of sawn wood consumed per year, Uruguay imported about 66,000. Following the recovery of the construction industry from a recession in 1987, demand for sawn wood was increasing at a rate of about 2.5 percent per year in the late 1980s. Domestic use of firewood was important, increasing from about 1.4 million cubic meters in the mid-1970s to 2.8 million cubic meters in the mid-1980s. Firewood demand was growing at 5 percent a year in the late 1980s. A number of local industries converted to firewood from fuel oil for energy needs, resulting in significant savings.

Industry

Uruguay's industries, including construction, mining, and energy, generated 33 percent of GDP in 1988. These industries underwent most of their development behind high tariff barriers in the 1950s. As a consequence, the industrial sector was geared mostly to the domestic market. The small size of the internal market limited the growth of manufacturing and prevented many industries from achieving economies of scale. In addition, the substantial level of protection meant that Uruguayan consumers paid high prices for domestically produced goods, which faced no international competition. During the 1970s and 1980s, Uruguay's protectionist apparatus was partially dismantled, and industry began adjusting to the world market.

Background of Industrial Development

In the early twentieth century, Montevideo was home to many small artisanal workshops. These cottage industries were already protected by tariff rates of about 30 percent on most products. Rapid industrial growth did not occur until the 1930s, when the economic crisis caused by the Great Depression forced Uruguay, like other nations, to become more self-sufficient. Industry accounted for only 12 percent of GDP in 1930 but increased to 22 percent by 1955. The most dynamic growth occurred after World War II. During the presidency of "industrial populist" Luis Batlle Berres (1947–51), the government encouraged the development of industry through several policies: multiple exchange rates were introduced to allow manufacturers to import essential machinery at subsidized rates; import tariffs on competing goods were raised to prohibitive levels; and urban wage increases stimulated domestic demand (see Neo-Batllism, 1947–51, ch. 1). Industrial output doubled during the decade following World War II. The timing of the expansion was favorable. For part of the period, wool exporters earned record profits because cold-weather uniforms were needed for the Korean War. A share of those profits financed the industrial sector's imports of capital equipment.

The industrial boom was short-lived, however. Manufacturing output increased by only 14 percent between the mid-1950s and 1970. For the industries geared to the internal market, the main problem was the small size of that market. The food-processing and textile companies, however, produced goods for export as well as for internal consumption. For these enterprises, the stagnation of the agricultural sector was a serious blow. As M.H.J. Finch argues in his landmark study, *A Political Economy of Uruguay since 1870,* the lagging supply of agricultural inputs limited manufacturing output. The process of economic decline was circular: the decrease in exports meant lower domestic income and hence lower domestic demand for other manufactured products. Additional factors also contributed to the slowdown, such as the bias against exports, which was the result of an overvalued currency. In sum, import-substitution industrialization allowed manufacturing to increase, but only to a limited extent. More important, the policy insulated the economy and eroded much of Uruguay's capacity to export.

The military government that assumed power in 1973 attempted to revitalize the economy by reemphasizing exports. The government dismantled part of the protectionist structure surrounding industry, lowered trade taxes, and created incentives for nontraditional exports. The results were at first dramatic. Industry grew at a rate of about 6 percent per year from 1974 to 1980. The most dynamic manufacturing growth involved relatively sophisticated goods: electrical appliances, transport equipment, textiles, paper, and nonmetallic minerals. Manufacturers invested in new technology, and labor productivity increased rapidly. Argentina and Brazil became important export markets for manufacturers, proving that Uruguayan industry could compete outside of its own borders.

The expansion came to an abrupt halt in 1981, largely because of factors beyond industry's control. Macroeconomic instability—in part related to developments in the export markets of Argentina and Brazil—pitched the entire Uruguayan economy into recession. The reversal was particularly painful in the industrial sector because manufacturers had borrowed heavily for investments and were overindebted as the recession began. Financial costs actually exceeded labor costs for many manufacturing firms. Thus, lower real wages brought on by the recession were not enough to restore the firms' competitiveness. In 1983–84 the central government stepped in and took over part of the industrial sector's debt. This probably prevented widespread bankruptcies but also increased the public sector's financial burden. The lingering indebtedness of private firms was a major issue for the Sanguinetti government.

Autonomous Entities

The performance of the autonomous entities (autonomous agencies or state enterprises; see Glossary), which played a central role in Uruguay's economic development, was an even greater issue. Most of the autonomous entities were industrial or utility companies; others were service related (see table 14, Appendix). The two largest autonomous entities were also the two largest companies in Uruguay: the National Administration of Fuels, Alcohol, and Portland Cement (Administración Nacional de Combustibles, Alcohol, y Portland—ANCAP) and the National Administration for the Generation and Transmission of Electricity (Administración Nacional de Usinas y Transmisiones Eléctricas—UTE). In 1988 ANCAP, whose primary activity was refining and distributing imported crude oil, grossed US$470 million, had profits of US$12 million, and employed 6,700 workers; UTE grossed US$285 million, had profits of US$12 million, and employed almost 12,000 workers. (Based on their 1988 gross earnings, ANCAP and UTE were the 113th and 242d largest companies in Latin America, respectively.) Other important autonomous entities (and monopolies) included the National Administration of Ports (Administración

Nacional de Puertos—ANP; another name for the Montevideo Port Authority), the National Telecommunications Administration (Administración Nacional de Telecomunicaciones—ANTEL), and the State Railways Administration (Administración de los Ferrocarriles del Estado—AFE).

The Sanguinetti government's policy toward the state enterprises had two aspects. First, the government planned to invest US$1 billion in public-sector projects during the 1987–89 period, raising government investment from 2.9 percent of GDP in 1986 to 5 percent of GDP in 1987–89. This target was not met, however. Public investment in 1987 and 1988 increased only to 3.1 percent and 3.4 percent of GDP, respectively, because of the need to restrain spending. Second, the government planned to improve the fiscal health of the state enterprises, many of which were running deficits. A combination of utility rate increases and spending cuts (but no significant cuts in employment) made most state enterprises profitable by the late 1980s, easing the public-sector deficit slightly.

Private Firms

The two largest subsectors within manufacturing, both by output and by employment, depended on agricultural inputs. Food and beverage companies, which accounted for about 30 percent of the value of industrial output in 1987, included meat packers, soft drink companies, and wineries (see table 15, Appendix). These companies exported about one-third of their output. A new entry into the food-processing industry was the Azucitrus citrus plant in Paysandú, which opened in mid-1988. The textile and apparel industry, accounting for about 20 percent of manufacturing output, depended on supplies of both wool and leather for jackets and footwear. The capacity to export was an important asset, allowing firms to withstand fluctuations in domestic demand. For example, the textile industry's sales to the domestic market decreased 23 percent in 1988, compared with 1987, but its exports increased 36 percent during the same period. Other important manufactured goods included chemicals, most of which were exported; transportation goods, including a few thousand automobiles and trucks that were assembled each year; and metal products.

Construction

Activity in the construction industry fluctuated dramatically during the 1980s, appearing to be markedly affected by trends in GDP growth or contraction, but with a one- or two-year lag. One index of such activity, the quantity of private structures built, went from about 2.1 million square meters per year in 1980–81 (when the recession was beginning) to 500,000 square meters per year in 1985–86 (after the recession had ended). In the late 1980s, construction partially recovered. The industry achieved a 4 percent growth in 1988 because of a construction boom in Maldonado and Punta del Este, and it grew 11.7 percent in 1989. Continued moderate growth was expected because of infrastructure projects such as the modernization of ports and highways, to be financed by international organizations. An offsetting factor, however, was the government's need to reduce expenditures.

Mining

Mining has never played an important role in Uruguay's economy. However, Uruguay has exported granite and marble. In addition, semiprecious stones have been found in quantity. Investment in mining activities was expected to reach at least US$200 million during the first half of the 1990s. After Uruguay's General Assembly passed legislation allowing foreign investment in mining, two companies, Canada's Bond International Gold and Brazil's Mineração e Participação (Mining Copartnership), announced plans to search for gold, silver, and other metals. Bond International Gold was given exclusive rights to develop the Mahoma gold mine, expected to produce more than 900 kilograms per year. Part of the project was to be financed through a debt-for-equity conversion program. The National Mining and Geology Institute indicated that at least fourteen other areas in the country might contain deposits of precious or base metals.

Energy

Hydroelectricity and imported petroleum were the primary sources of energy in Uruguay. During the 1980s, the nation reduced its dependence on imported crude oil and increased its hydroelectric capacity. At the beginning of the decade, three-fourths of Uruguay's energy came from imported oil; by 1987 less than half did. This trend toward hydroelectric power was interrupted during 1988 and 1989 because of a severe drought. Oil-burning power stations had to be brought on-line temporarily, increasing energy costs. In addition, rotating power outages were instituted in Montevideo and other cities. Partly because of such conservation measures, total consumption of energy actually decreased during the late 1980s. Real growth in the utilities sector declined by 12.2 percent in 1989.

The single largest source of hydroelectricity was the Salto Grande Dam on the Río Uruguay, built and operated in cooperation with Argentina. The US$1 billion dam was completed in 1982 and supplied 1.8 million megawatt-hours of energy to Uruguay in 1987 (before the drought), or 40 percent of Uruguay's electricity. In 1989 the huge project was reported to be facing serious financial difficulties. The Uruguayan and Argentine state-owned power companies were US$45 million and US$250 million behind in payments, respectively, to banks and foreign creditors, and absorption of the debts by the two nations' central banks was expected.

Three other hydroelectric power sources were located on the Río Negro. Of these, the El Palmar Dam (located at Palmar), built and operated jointly with Brazil, was the largest and newest (in full operation since 1983); in 1988 it had a capacity of 330 megawatts. The Baygorria Dam and the Gabriel Terra Dam (the latter in operation since 1948) had a capacity of 108 megawatts and 128 megawatts, respectively, in 1988.

The Sanguinetti administration's policy was to improve the existing hydroelectric facilities rather than embark on new projects. Emphasis was placed on extending the electrical distribution network in rural areas. In 1988 the rural electrical network spanned 1,400 kilometers, more than double the 630 kilometers in 1984. The government approved a total of US$139 million in investments in 1988–89 by UTE, mostly in the distribution program.

Uruguay had no domestic oil resources, despite several exploration efforts. The nation imported mostly crude oil, which was then refined by ANCAP and a few small plants (see External Sector, this ch.). In 1985 ANCAP had a refining capacity of 40,000 barrels per day; its facilities were upgraded during the late 1980s.

Services

Uruguay's service sector, comprising the major subsectors of banking, transportation, communications, and tourism, as well as the activities of the large central government, accounted for 42 percent of GDP in 1988. Transportation, storage, and communications together accounted for about 6 percent of GDP, while banking and commerce accounted for about 15 percent. Thus, half of the so-called service sector consisted of government activity.

On the one hand, the service sector was a strong point in the economy because of the well-educated work force concentrated in Montevideo. On the other hand, the instability among banks, the lack of a modernized telecommunications system, and shortcomings in the nation's transportation infrastructure held back the sector's development. In the second half of the 1980s, these issues took on increasing importance as the government began promoting the idea of Uruguay as an international service center for the Southern Cone (Argentina, Bolivia, Chile, Paraguay, and Uruguay). The growing potential to export services and to integrate them across

*The spillway
at the Salto Grande Dam
The Fray Bentos
Bridge over the Río Uruguay
Courtesy Inter-American
Development Bank*

borders was considered a key element in the future development of Uruguay's outward-oriented economy.

Banking and Financial Services

Uruguay's banking sector was headed by the Central Bank of Uruguay (Banco Central del Uruguay; hereafter, Central Bank), founded in 1967 and charged with regulating the nation's banking and financial system and performing such standard central bank functions as controlling the money supply, regulating credit, issuing currency, controlling foreign exchange, and overseeing the operations of the nation's private commercial banks. The Bank of Uruguay (Banco de la República Oriental del Uruguay—BROU), founded in 1896, had performed some of the functions of a central bank prior to the creation of the Central Bank. An autonomous entity, it remained in 1990 the country's largest and most significant commercial bank. The banking sector also included the Social Welfare Bank (Banco de Previsión Social), the Commercial Bank (Banco Comercial), and several other state-owned banks, such as the Mortgage Bank of Uruguay (Banco Hipotecario del Uruguay) and the State Insurance Bank (Banco de Seguros del Estado), as well as a number of private commercial and savings banks.

In the late 1980s, Uruguay's financial sector was still feeling the effects of a profound banking crisis that had begun early in the decade. The crisis had its origins in the rapid expansion of credit to the private sector during the 1978–82 period. The unrestrained expansion of credit was made possible by the deregulation of the banks. As part of its effort to reorient the Uruguayan economy to the external market, the military government removed or reduced most restrictions on banks, including reserve requirements (which limit the amount of loans that can be made, relative to bank deposits), interest rate ceilings, and foreign currency regulations. The sudden removal of these and other restrictions encouraged banks to expand the supply of credit. The demand for credit also expanded because rising prices for exports convinced many ranchers and manufacturers to invest in land or equipment. The first signs of trouble came from the livestock sector. When world beef prices fell in 1980, rural land prices began to decline sharply, and ranchers began to have difficulty servicing their loans (see Livestock Ranching, this ch.).

The crisis became widespread after the economy went into recession in 1981. By 1982 one-quarter of all loans to the private sector were considered nonperforming. The increasing dollarization of credit complicated the situation. Banks that had received large United States dollar deposits also made loans in dollars in order to avoid exchange-rate risk. The trend toward dollarization increased in early 1982 because banks expected a major peso devaluation. By late 1982, about 60 percent of all loans were denominated in dollars. When the fixed peso exchange rate was finally abandoned toward the end of the year, leading to a large peso devaluation, many already-troubled private companies, which earned pesos on the domestic market, suddenly faced dollar-denominated loans whose peso value had tripled.

Government intervention was required to prevent widespread bankruptcies. BROU devised a two-part strategy for dealing with the crisis. First, it provided credit to the private banks so that loans could be refinanced. About one-fifth of all outstanding loans (worth US$400 million) were refinanced by late 1982, allowing debtors a two- or three-year grace period and a lengthened repayment schedule. The loans were still in dollars, however, so that further devaluations of the peso remained a difficulty for debtors. BROU's second action was to acquire many loan portfolios from the private banks. The government thus propped up several private banks, actually buying out four of the twenty-four banks in the country. This policy prevented a banking collapse but significantly increased BROU's obligations, making it responsible for a large share of the public-sector deficit.

The financial sector remained in a precarious condition as the Sanguinetti government took office. By the end of 1984, the banking system had a negative net worth. In 1985, however, the banking system raised US$400 million in new dollar deposits. Although overall economic conditions improved during the first three years of the Sanguinetti administration, credit remained restricted and interest rates high, making it difficult for even solvent borrowers to obtain new loans. The government continued its efforts to strengthen the banks. For example, it planned to spend US$160 million in 1989 to restructure the four banks bought during the height of the banking crisis so that they could be sold to the private sector. Critics charged that these banks were too highly indebted, inefficient, and overstaffed to be sold. As of mid-1989, all but one of the banks remained under the supervision of BROU, Uruguay's largest bank (a state enterprise). One bank, the Commercial Bank, was sold to a group of international investors in 1990.

Dollarization of the banking system continued to increase. The proportion of money held in United States dollar accounts reached 84 percent in 1989. The major source of these funds was Argentina, whose savers sought a safe haven and a dependable currency. Uruguayan savers placed deposits in dollars to avoid exchange-rate fluctuations. Thus, the openness of the banking system may have prevented some capital flight, but the dollarization of bank deposits made it difficult for the government to conduct a monetary policy because the money supply could not be tightly controlled. Nevertheless, the government did not restrict the banking system to deposits in pesos, encouraging instead the further internationalization of Uruguay's banks, most of which were foreign owned. In addition, liberal offshore banking rules (for transactions among nonresidents) were introduced in 1989.

Although Lacalle supported the idea of Uruguay as an international banking center, he indicated in early 1990 that his administration planned to introduce legislation under which bank secrecy i.e., anonymous accounts, would be lifted in cases where illegal drug-money laundering was suspected. The government was pressured to change that aspect of its banking regulations after an alleged Colombian "drug lord" told United States officials that he and others often used Uruguayan accounts.

Transportation and Communications

Uruguay's small size and relatively flat terrain have made development of an excellent transportation network easy. By most accounts, the country had one of the best domestic highway and rail systems in Latin America. The country's location in the Southern Hemisphere, far from many of its trading partners, however, and its lack of land links with neighboring countries have been a hindrance in the past to foreign trade and transportation. New technologies, including the introduction of refrigerated ships early in the twentieth century and later the airplane, have improved access to distant markets. Moreover, since the 1970s the country has made a concerted effort to upgrade links with neighbors, improving road connections to Brazil and constructing highway and later railroad bridges across the Río Uruguay to Argentina.

The highway network radiated out from Montevideo and in 1989 consisted of about 50,000 kilometers of roads, including 6,500 kilometers of the national network that received improvements during the 1985-89 period. Rural areas were served by a secondary network of 3,000 kilometers of gravel roads and 40,200 kilometers of dirt roads. Road transport carried an estimated 87 percent of all freight, and a modern bus system provided passenger links between most of the populated areas. Bridges at Fray Bentos and Paysandú spanned the Río Uruguay and provided for easy road transit to Argentina, and by the late 1980s newly paved roads to the northern border tied into the Brazilian road network (see fig. 8). In 1989 Uruguay was granted loans of US$84 million from the Inter-American Development Bank and US$81 million from the World

Bank (see Glossary) to modernize its international highways and to begin construction of Route 1, linking Montevideo with Buenos Aires.

Owing to the high cost of automobile ownership in Uruguay, traffic congestion in Montevideo remained low by the standards of other cities in the world. There was no subway system in 1990, but an extensive bus network operated on a twenty-four-hour basis. The city's electric trolleys had been allowed to decay, and the number of routes had been repeatedly reduced.

In 1989 the government-owned AFE maintained 3,000 kilometers of standard-gauge railroads. Montevideo was the center of the system with lines extending out to the north, northwest, and east. Three connections with the Brazilian rail system and a new link with Argentina that opened in 1982 allowed for easier shipment of goods to these countries. The rail authority, however, found it increasingly difficult to maintain passenger trains in the face of a decade of declining ridership. In 1988 all passenger service was discontinued under the government's five-year rationalization program designed to downsize the stagnant railroad subsector.

Carrasco International Airport, located twenty-one kilometers from Montevideo, was the country's principal airport. Capitán Curbelo Airport, near Punta del Este, also handled international flights to Brazil and Argentina. Fourteen other primarily commercial airports with paved runways were distributed throughout Uruguay. Uruguayan National Airlines (Primeras Líneas Uruguayas de Navegación Aérea—PLUNA) operated fourteen aircraft to domestic destinations and neighboring countries. Three Boeing 737s and one Boeing 707 were the workhorses of PLUNA's regional service. Uruguayan Military Air Transport (Transportes Aéreos Militares Uruguayos—TAMU), a small airline owned by the Uruguayan Air Force, maintained commercial flights on several domestic and foreign routes.

Despite improvements in land and air transportation since the 1960s, most foreign trade still went by water. Montevideo was the country's principal port, handling close to 60 percent of all cargo in the early 1980s. Other major ports included Colonia and Punta del Este on the Río de la Plata Estuary and Fray Bentos, Paysandú, and Salto on the Río Uruguay. Passenger ferries linked Montevideo and Buenos Aires with six-hour-long crossings via Colonia, and a modern high-speed hydrofoil traveled from Colonia to Buenos Aires in three and one-half hours.

River transport remained an important means of transportation, carrying about 5 percent of all freight, and the country counted over 1,600 kilometers of navigable inland waterways. The Río

Uruguay was by far the most important waterway, and ocean-going ships of up to 4.2 meters draught could travel north as far as Paysandú. Smaller vessels of up to 2.7 meters draught could travel upstream to Salto.

Broadcast facilities were numerous, and all parts of the country could receive at least one AM radio station or one television station. In 1990 there were ninety-nine AM stations, a quarter of which were in the Montevideo area. Ten of the AM stations broadcast on shortwave frequencies to reach a larger audience both domestically and abroad. All stations, except for one government-owned transmitter, were commercial, and broadcasts were in Spanish. Montevideo had four television stations; another twenty-two were scattered in towns across the country. Uruguayans had an estimated 1.8 million radio receivers and 650,000 television sets in 1990.

Improvement of the nation's telephone system was a priority for the Sanguinetti government. By 1990 there were over 345,000 telephones (at least 11 percent of the population, the highest per capita in South America), an increase of over 25 percent from five years earlier. The US$13 million expansion of service, about half of which took place in the country's interior, helped reduce the number of households and businesses on a waiting list for telephone service. The government's monopolistic communications agency, ANTEL, planned to invest US$100 million in the telephone system between 1989 and 1993, extending service to another 180,000 households in the country's interior. The basic elements of the nation's telecommunications network were expanded, and the system was modernized. In 1990 the government heeded the growing Latin American trend toward privatization of state enterprises when it began allowing private investment in the nation's telephone system. After years of depending on Argentine relay stations for its international telephone service, Uruguay installed its first satellite earth station in 1985. In 1990 it had two International Telecommunications Satellite Organization (Intelsat) earth stations. Telex and facsimile (fax) services were also expanded.

Tourism

Tourism in Uruguay generated an estimated US$300 million in 1989, equivalent to 22 percent of merchandise exports. The tourist industry depended mainly on visitors from Argentina. Thus, not only were tourist receipts seasonal (peaking in the warm summer months, January through March), they also fluctuated along with economic conditions in Argentina and relative exchange rates. In 1989 about 85 percent of the 1 million tourists were from Argentina; an additional 10 percent were from Brazil, and smaller

Artigas Boulevard,
a highway leading
to downtown Montevideo
Courtesy Inter-American
Development Bank

percentages came from Paraguay and Chile. Many of the visitors from Argentina owned property in Uruguay, especially in the resort area of Punta del Este, which drew half of all summer tourists.

In 1986 the Sanguinetti government created the Ministry of Tourism to regulate hotel and resort prices and to promote Uruguayan tourist attractions at international exhibitions. The ministry also developed programs aimed at attracting visitors and conventions to Uruguay during the low season, but with limited success. At the same time, the government supported the improvement of hotels, marinas, and camping facilities. To protect the beaches, a key tourist attraction, the Montevideo sewage system was being upgraded in 1990 so that it would discharge more than two kilometers offshore. Despite such efforts, tourism was expected to remain mostly regional because of the long distance from Europe and the United States, lack of services (Uruguay had no five-star hotels), lack of promotion, and restrictive transportation policies (for example, charter flights were difficult to get).

External Sector

Two concerns dominated Uruguay's foreign economic relations during the 1980s. The first, both a fiscal and an external problem, was the foreign debt. Uruguay's external debt of about US$6.7 billion (US$6.2 of this was foreign debt to the United States) in 1989 (US$4.2 billion belonging to the public sector) was not an

141

issue affecting international financial markets, like the much larger debt burdens of Brazil or Mexico (each over US$100 billion). Even so, Uruguay's indebtedness was onerous in comparison with the size of its economy and was one of the highest per capita debts in the region. For both the Sanguinetti and the Lacalle governments, debt reduction and debt rescheduling were priorities.

The second major concern was trade, primarily for its importance to overall economic growth. Trade-related activities were responsible for about 12 percent of GDP in 1988. Exports, which were the source of Uruguay's wealth in the early twentieth century, were seen as the key to the revival of the economy. Demand within Uruguay was simply too small to support large production increases. Trade was especially important in the 1980s because of the debt burden. In order to make payments on mostly dollar-denominated loans, Uruguay needed foreign exchange (dollars). Thus, the trade balance (the difference in value between exports and imports) took on added significance. To spur economic growth and to earn foreign exchange, Uruguay joined other Latin American nations in restraining imports and augmenting exports. Despite its positive trade balance, however, Uruguay's foreign debt continued to increase.

Foreign Debt

Uruguay began borrowing abroad on a large scale in the 1970s after the price of oil (its largest import) quadrupled. The oil price increase that prompted many developing nations to begin borrowing also made it easier for them to borrow; commercial banks were flush with petrodollars (foreign exchange obtained by petroleum-exporting countries through sales abroad) and were eager to make loans. Uruguay's debt increased from US$500 million in 1976 to as much as US$5.9 billion by the end of 1987. Although this debt was already large in proportion to Uruguay's GDP, international financial conditions made the loans appear beneficial for both the creditors (commercial banks and international organizations) and the Uruguayan government.

The most significant positive trend, from the point of view of both parties, was the decline in the late 1970s of the dollar's value, relative to major currencies. This decline meant that dollar prices of most internationally traded goods were rising, a fact that had double significance. First, Uruguayan exporters (like exporters in many other developing countries) were earning more dollars for a given basket of goods, making the country appear capable of repaying a large debt. Second, real interest rates (the nominal interest rate minus inflation) were negative. That is, the rate at which the dollar value of Uruguay's exports was rising (about 30 percent per year in 1979) was higher than the nominal United States interest rate (11 percent per year in 1979). Thus, it was becoming easier for Uruguay to service its external debt. Under these conditions, the government was inclined to continue borrowing abroad to finance its deficit and to fund development projects.

The situation changed dramatically in the 1980s for several reasons. First, the dollar appreciated significantly. This reversed the process that had occurred in the 1970s; the dollar price of Uruguay's exports fell. Second, the United States tightened its money supply. This prompted banks to raise interest rates on both old and new loans (the adjustable interest rate had become common in the 1970s). Both of these developments raised the real interest rate on Uruguay's debt. As the dollar appreciated, the peso declined, making the dollar value of Uruguay's GDP smaller and the ratio of debt to GDP larger (with both debt and GDP denominated in dollars). At the same time, lower export earnings made it more difficult for Uruguay to service its external debt. New loans were needed just so that the country could service old debt, even though foreign borrowing had become far less attractive than in the 1970s. In 1985 the total debt burden stood at US$4.9 billion; debt service (interest payments alone) consumed 34 percent of the nation's export income.

The debt crisis overshadowed all other economic difficulties in Uruguay during the late 1980s. The crisis was a vicious circle. Paying off the debt required higher growth and higher income. But the mere act of paying debt service on the huge amounts of principal reduced essential investment spending and precluded sustained economic growth. While the debt continued to grow, finding the means of servicing the debt became an economic priority; Uruguay was one of the few Latin American countries that did not default on its debt. While debt service became difficult, new external loans were no longer available (except to help service old debt) because Latin American debtors were no longer considered creditworthy. Thus, the government had to resort to inflationary means (''printing money'') to finance its public-sector deficit domestically. This directly contradicted the government's primary goal of eliminating inflation.

The Sanguinetti administration's debt policy focused on the most immediate difficulty for Uruguay: large debt-service payments. Through negotiations with its creditors, including the International Monetary Fund (IMF—see Glossary), the government was able to gain some breathing space. The debt-service burden declined to an estimated US$449 million in 1989 (28 percent of export earnings) from US$613 million in 1988 (44 percent of export earnings). However, the fact that debt was merely being rescheduled meant that the overall debt burden did not decrease. New financing actually added to the debt, which increased to US$6.7 billion by the end of 1989. Several projects to reduce the debt principal were carried out under the debt-for-equity program, but they were small compared with the total debt. During the 1988–89 period, the Central Bank approved fourteen investment projects that reduced the debt by an estimated US$78 million.

Substantive efforts to decrease a portion of the debt burden—the US$1.7 billion owed to commercial banks—began in March 1989 in the context of the United States government's Brady Plan. In an important departure from earlier United States policy, the Brady Plan (named after Secretary of the Treasury Nicolas Brady) officially recognized the need for debt reduction. Minister of Economy and Finance Ricardo Zerbino and Central Bank president Ricardo Pascale began debt negotiations with international creditors in September 1989.

The Brady Plan offered commercial banks holding Uruguayan debt three options. (The same three options applied in the case of other Latin American nations, with minor variations in the percentage terms of each option.) First, the banks could increase their current loans by 20 percent over four years, offering Uruguay new money in exchange for strengthened guarantees of repayment. Second, banks could exchange their debt for guaranteed bonds (backed by United States Treasury bonds) paying a fixed 6.34 percent interest. Finally, banks could opt to allow Uruguay to repurchase its debt for 56 percent of the debt's face value. In a tentative agreement reached in 1990, banks holding 28 percent of the debt chose the new money, banks with 33 percent of the debt chose to convert to fixed-interest bonds, and those holding the remaining 39 percent chose to allow Uruguay to repurchase its debt. The agreement was significant even though it affected only about one-fourth of Uruguay's debt. As the *Economist* reported, "Once a country has reached a Brady-plan deal, it is on the road to financial respectability."

Trade

Uruguay expanded its involvement in international trade considerably during the latter part of the 1980s. Exports doubled (in nominal dollar terms) from US$854 million in 1985 to US$1.6 billion in 1989. Imports increased at a slower rate, from US$675 million in 1985 to US$1.1 billion in 1989. The merchandise balance of trade reached a positive US$463 million in 1989, helping to offset the demands of debt service.

The largest export markets were Brazil (US$443 million in 1989), the European Community (US$363 million), the United States (US$177 million), and Argentina (US$78 million). Brazil (US$369 million), Argentina (US$177 million), and the United States (US$109 million) were the leading sources of imports in 1988. Uruguay's largest exports continued to be its so-called traditional products: wool (US$288 million in 1989), meat (US$225 million), and hides (US$129 million). While much attention continued to be focused on these three largest exports, a variety of nontraditional exports took on growing importance during the late 1980s. Goods such as processed foods, grains, fishery products, chemicals, and finished leather apparel together accounted for 60 percent of Uruguay's exports by the end of the decade.

Uruguay's largest import was crude oil. Imports of oil declined during much of the 1980s as Uruguay increased its reliance on hydroelectric power. Reduced oil prices in the late 1980s, combined with the reduction in the quantity of imports, helped improve the nation's overall trade balance. The value of oil imports declined from US$433 million in 1982 (40 percent of imports) to about US$120 million in 1988 (about 10 percent of imports). In 1989 the trend toward lower oil imports was reversed when the severe drought compromised Uruguay's capacity to generate hydroelectric power; oil imports increased to US$139 million. As a nation with no domestic sources of petroleum, Uruguay was particularly hard-hit by the oil price rise that accompanied the Persian Gulf crisis in late 1990. Domestic fuel prices were raised by over 50 percent during September and October 1990.

Several categories of industrial imports increased as Uruguay's manufacturing sector recovered from the recession. The largest increases were among semi-industrialized products, such as chemicals, rubber, and plastics, which increased from US$300 million in 1982 to US$500 million in 1987. Imports of capital goods (machinery and transportation equipment) dipped in the mid-1980s but recovered to US$150 million in 1987, indicating that manufacturing activity could increase. In 1989, however, imports of capital goods fell by 14 percent to US$137 million.

Balance of Payments

Uruguay's trade balance was positive and steadily improving during most of the 1980s. However, the current account balance remained negative until the mid-1980s because of the burden of debt service (see table 16, Appendix). In 1986, 1988, and 1989, the trade balance was large enough to make the current account balance positive. An exception to this pattern was 1987 because imports surged as the economy recovered from the recession. The capital account balance was positive for most of the 1980s because Uruguay continued to borrow from abroad to help cover its debt-service payments and because foreigners continued to deposit money in Uruguayan banks. Uruguay's reserves decreased during most years, but as of 1988 the nation still had substantial gold reserves—more than 80 tons. During the 1989 presidential campaign, at least one candidate proposed selling the gold reserves to pay off the foreign debt. Lacalle opposed such a plan, however.

Economic Integration

Economic integration with other Latin American nations was an important goal for Uruguay because of its small internal market. The idea of integration was enshrined in the nation's constitution, which states that "the Republic will seek to achieve social and economic integration of the Latin American nations, especially to provide for a common defense of products and raw materials."

Sanguinetti played an important mediating role in the early discussions of integration between Argentina and Brazil, a delicate process because of the traditional rivalry between the two larger nations (see Foreign Relations under Democratic Rule, 1985–90, ch. 4). Presidents Raúl Alfonsín of Argentina, José Sarney Costa of Brazil, and Sanguinetti held five trilateral meetings between 1986 and 1988, during which they signed several tariff-reduction agreements and discussed a long-term framework for regional economic integration.

The Uruguayan government predicted that the lower trade barriers would allow Uruguayan exports to Brazil and Argentina to increase by 80 to 90 percent by 1991. In practice, however, Uruguay's trade with its larger neighbors seemed to be affected more by exchange rates than by tariff and quota agreements. For example, Uruguay already had bilateral trade agreements with both Brazil and Argentina during the late 1980s, but in early 1990 exports to Argentina covered by the agreement actually declined. In contrast, exports to Brazil increased markedly during the first half of 1990 after the Brazilian government tightened liquidity and caused the Brazilian cruzeiro to appreciate.

Despite such early evidence that the trade agreements were having only a limited effect on regional commerce, Lacalle indicated in early 1990 that he expected Uruguay to continue to play a pivotal role in regional integration. He indicated further that he hoped the integration would be extended to include Paraguay and Bolivia. "We will try to open the Atlantic balcony to [those] inland countries," he said, "improving the operation of our ports, promoting the use of the Paraná-Paraguay waterway, and establishing free-trade zones near the ports for the manufacture of products from the South American 'hinterland'.'' Lacalle also said he proposed to President Andrés Rodríguez Pedotti of Paraguay the formation of a trinational fleet of merchant vessels to carry Uruguayan, Paraguayan, and Bolivian products to markets in North America, Europe, and Asia.

Thus, Lacalle envisioned Uruguay not only as a participant in trade agreements with its larger neighbors but also as a close partner with the smaller and apparently more stable economies of the region. A noteworthy aspect of Lacalle's plan was its stress on the development of the regional infrastructure. Lack of such an infrastructure—there was no railroad bridge between Uruguay and Argentina, for example, until the Salto Grande Dam opened in 1982—remained a serious impediment to regional integration.

Free-Trade Zones

The free-trade zones that Lacalle mentioned were already operating in Uruguay during the late 1980s as an important part of the Sanguinetti administration's strategy to encourage both foreign investment and regional trade. Under legislation passed in late 1987, free-trade zones such as the ones in Colonia and Nueva Palmira (in Colonia Department) became attractive sites for investors for several reasons: users were exempted from all Uruguayan taxes, except for social security taxes on Uruguayan workers; all imported goods and services entering the zones were exempt from customs duties or taxes; goods and services reexported from the zones were exempt from taxes; and commercial or government service monopolies were not applicable within the zones, so that no company was forced to deal with the State Insurance Bank, for example. Restrictions on free-trade zones prohibited companies from duplicating existing industries, such as textile manufacturing. Thus, the thrust of the program was to attract innovative companies to Uruguay. As of early 1990, the free-trade zones were attracting a good deal of attention, but it was too soon to tell what impact they would have on the Uruguayan economy.

* * *

A superb and very readable introduction to Latin American economic history, with references to Uruguay, is Celso Furtado's *Economic Development of Latin America,* which focuses on major themes such as import-substitution industrialization. For a more detailed picture of Uruguay's economic history until the 1970s, the best

English-language source is M.H.J. Finch's *A Political Economy of Uruguay since 1870.* Few English-language books have focused exclusively on Uruguay's more recent economic progress. A good source in Spanish is *La Crisis uruguaya y el problema nacional* by the Centro de Investigaciones Económicas.

Several references examine individual aspects of Uruguay's economy. Two good articles on the labor movement are Arturo S. Bronstein's "The Evolution of Labour Relations in Uruguay" and Juan Rial Roade's "Uruguay." Larry A. Sjaastad's "Debt, Depression, and Real Rates of Interest in Latin America" explains Uruguay's early involvement in the debt crisis.

Basic economic data on Uruguay are provided in the International Monetary Fund's *International Financial Statistics,* in the Inter-American Development Bank's *Economic and Social Progress in Latin America,* published annually, and in the *Latin American Regional Reports* series of periodicals. Two useful Uruguayan economic periodicals are *Guía financiera* and *Búsqueda.* (For further information and complete citations, see Bibliography.)

Chapter 4. Government and Politics

The Legislative Palace

ON MARCH 1, 1990, Uruguayans and representatives of many foreign governments witnessed the reaffirmation of Uruguay's revived democratic tradition: the transfer of power from one elected president to another. Having completed a full five-year term in office, Julio María Sanguinetti Cairolo (1985–90) of the liberal Colorado Party (Partido Colorado) transferred the presidential sash to Luis Alberto Lacalle de Herrera of the rival conservative National Party (Partido Nacional, usually referred to as the Blancos). Lacalle was elected to serve for the 1990–95 period as the country's fiftieth president.

An urbane lawyer, rancher, and senator, Lacalle was only the third National Party candidate ever to be elected president. After only five years as a National Party leader, he achieved what his legendary grandfather, Luis Alberto de Herrera, the National Party's dominant caudillo during the first half of the twentieth century, attained after a half-century of political battles: the defeat of the Colorados and the ascension of the Blancos to power. Technically, Lacalle became the first National Party president because Uruguay was formally ruled by a nine-member collegial executive (*colegiado*) when his party won its previous victories.

Uruguayan democracy had been reinstated five years earlier—after the 1973–85 period of military rule—as a result of Sanguinetti's victory in the November 25, 1984, election and referendum. Those national polls were held in accordance with the Naval Club Pact of 1984, a political agreement between the armed forces and four political parties: the Colorado Party, the National Party, the Broad Front (Frente Amplio, a leftist alliance), and the Civic Union (Unión Cívica—UC) (see The Military Government, 1973–85, ch. 1). The military regime, however, blocked the proposed presidential candidacies of the National Party's Wilson Ferreira Aldunate and the Broad Front's Líber Seregni Mosquera. Running, in effect, unopposed, Sanguinetti won approximately 41 percent of the votes, followed by the National Party's 34 percent, the Broad Front's 21 percent, and the UC's 2.5 percent.

Sanguinetti was the first Uruguayan president to be elected, albeit in a semidemocratic election, after the period of repressive military rule. He had been a lawyer, journalist, representative, minister of education and culture, and minister of labor and social welfare. During his term of office, Sanguinetti consolidated Uruguay's multiparty democracy, restored the country's prestige and respect abroad, increased its export markets, and avoided financial disorder. He symbolized Uruguay's political opening by visiting the Soviet Union and China in 1989.

In what proved to be its most active electoral year, Uruguay held two national elections in 1989. The first was a referendum on the government's amnesty law for abuses committed by the military regime. The second, the November 26 poll—the first totally free presidential elections to be held in Uruguay since 1971—demonstrated the country's return to its democratic tradition of free and honest elections.

Although voting was compulsory in Uruguay, the turnout in the November 26, 1989, elections was nonetheless impressive: 88 percent of the electorate of 2.3 million people participated. The high turnout did not necessarily mean that Uruguayan voters were among the most politically sophisticated in the world, although Uruguayans usually discussed and debated political issues exhaustively at all levels of society. The high voter turnout in 1989 demonstrated, however—as it had in 1984 when 88.5 percent participated—that Uruguay was a very politicized country and that it had one of Latin America's longest democratic traditions.

Despite Sanguinetti's accomplishments, his party's historic and decisive defeat reflected widespread dissatisfaction with two years of economic stagnation. The elections also challenged Uruguay's traditional two-party system of the Colorado and National parties. For the first time, a third party, the Broad Front, reached important levels by winning the country's second most powerful post (after president of the republic): the mayorship of Montevideo, which had over 40 percent of the country's population and more than two-thirds of its economic activity. The new Marxist mayor, Tabaré Vázquez, immediately began pressing Lacalle for greater municipal autonomy (see Democratic Consolidation, 1985–90, this ch.). The prospects for the success of a "co-habitation arrangement," i.e., harmonious cooperation, however, were doubtful because Uruguayans continued to support a strong presidential system and because Lacalle was assertive of his executive powers. Thus, in addition to the challenges posed by a resurgent political left, labor unrest, and economic crisis, the Lacalle government faced the possibility of political clashes with the municipal government.

Constitutional Background

Since achieving independence in 1828, Uruguay has promulgated five constitutions: in 1830, 1917, 1934, 1952, and 1967. When it became independent on August 27, 1828, the Oriental Republic

Welcome banner in Montevideo's Independence Plaza in honor of the 1983 state visit by King Juan Carlos I and Queen Sofía of Spain
Courtesy Charles Guy Gillespie

of Uruguay (República Oriental del Uruguay) drew up its first constitution, which was promulgated on July 18, 1830.

The 1830 constitution has been regarded as Uruguay's most technically perfect charter. Heavily influenced by the thinking of the French and American revolutions, it divided the government among the executive, legislative, and judicial powers and established Uruguay as a unitary republic with a centralized form of government. The bicameral General Assembly (Asamblea General) was empowered to elect a president with considerable powers to head the executive branch for a four-year term. The president was given control over all of his ministers of government and was empowered to make decisions with the agreement of at least one of the three ministers recognized by the 1830 constitution.

Like all of Uruguay's charters since then, the 1830 constitution provided for a General Assembly composed of a Chamber of Senators (Cámara de Senadores), or Senate (Senado), elected nationally, and a Chamber of Representatives (Cámara de Representantes), elected from the departments. Members of the General Assembly were empowered to pass laws but lacked the authority to dismiss the president or his ministers or to issue votes of no confidence. An 1834 amendment, however, provided for *juicio político* (impeachment) of the ministers for "unacceptable conduct."

As established by the 1830 constitution, the Supreme Court of Justice (Corte Suprema de Justicia), and lesser courts, exercised the judicial power. The General Assembly appointed the members of the high court. The latter—with the consent of the Senate in the case of the appellate courts—appointed the members of the lesser courts. The constitution also divided the country into departments, each headed by a governor appointed by the president and each having an advisory body called a Neighbors' Council (Consejo de Vecinos).

Although the 1830 constitution remained in effect for eighty-seven years, de facto governments violated it repeatedly. In the 1878–90 period, the Blancos and Colorados initiated the framework for a more stable system through understandings called "pacts between the parties." This governing principle, called coparticipation (*coparticipación*), meaning the sharing of formal political and informal bureaucratic power, has been formally practiced since 1872.

In 1913 President José Batlle y Ordóñez (1903–07, 1911–15), the father of modern Uruguay, proposed a constitutional reform involving the creation of a Swiss-style collegial executive system to be called the *colegiado*. A strong opponent of the one-person, powerful presidency, Batlle y Ordóñez believed that a collective executive power would neutralize the dictatorial intentions of political leaders. It met intense opposition, however, not only from the Blancos but also from members of his own Colorado Party. The proposal was defeated in 1916, but Batlle y Ordóñez worked out a deal with a faction of the Blancos whereby a compromise system was provided for in the second constitution, which was approved by plebiscite on November 25, 1917.

In addition to separating church and state, the new charter, which did not become effective until 1919, introduced substantial changes in the powers of the presidency. The executive power consisted of the president, who controlled foreign relations, national security, and agriculture, and the National Council of Administration (Consejo Nacional de Administración), or *colegiado,* which administered all other executive governmental functions (industrial relations, health, public works, industry and labor, livestock and agriculture, education, and the preparation of the budget). The *colegiado,* embodying the political mechanism of coparticipation, consisted of nine members: six from the majority party and three from the minority party. The first *colegiado* (1919–33) was thereby established without eliminating the office of president.

The history of successive constitutions is one of a lengthy struggle between advocates of the collegial system and those of the presidential system. Although the 1917 constitution worked well during the prosperous time after World War I, recurring conflicts between the president and the *colegiado* members made the executive power ineffective in coping with the economic and social crises wracking the country. These conflicts eventually led to the presidential coup of 1933. The ad hoc government suspended the constitution and appointed a constituent assembly to draw up a new one.

The 1934 constitution abolished the *colegiado* and transferred its power to the president. Nevertheless, presidential powers remained somewhat limited. The executive power once again was exercised by a president who had to make decisions together with the ministers. The 1934 charter established the Council of Ministers (Consejo de Ministros) as the body in which these decisions were to be made. This council consisted of the president and the cabinet ministers. The constitution required the chief executive to appoint three of the nine cabinet ministers from among the members of the political party that received the second largest number of votes in the presidential election. The General Assembly, for its part, could issue votes of no confidence in cabinet ministers, with the approval of two-thirds of its members.

The constitution divided the Senate between the Blancos and the Colorados or, as political scientist Martin Weinstein has pointed out, between the Herrerist faction of the Blancos (named after Luis Alberto de Herrera) and the Terrist wing of the Colorados (named after Gabriel Terra; president, 1931–38). The party that garnered the second largest number of votes automatically received 50 percent of the Senate seats. In addition, the 1934 charter empowered the Supreme Court of Justice to rule on the constitutionality of the laws. This system, which lasted eighteen years, further limited the power of the president and his government.

Although Uruguay returned to a more democratic system in 1942, the failure of political sectors to reach an agreement on the proposed constitution drafted that year resulted in the postponement of constitutional reform. On July 31, 1951, a formal pact between the rightist Batllist faction of the Colorados—the Colorado and Batllist Union (Unión Colorada y Batllista—UCB)—and the Herrerist Movement (Movimiento Herrerista) of the Blancos called for a plebiscite on constitutional reform. The plebiscite the following December 16 drew less than half of the 1.1 million voters to the polls, but the collegial system was approved by a small margin.

As the culmination of an effort to reestablish the *colegiado* and the plural executive power, a fourth constitution was promulgated on January 25, 1952. It readopted Batlle y Ordóñez's original proposal for coparticipation by creating a nine-member *colegiado*, this time called the National Council of Government (Consejo Nacional de Gobierno), with six majority-party seats and three minority-party seats. The presidency of the council rotated among the six members of the majority party. The chief executive could nominate only four of the nine ministers from his own party faction; the General Assembly selected the other five through separate votes in both chambers. An absolute majority (more than two-thirds), however, of the full membership of the two legislative chambers had to support the appointments. It thereby ensured that either the Colorados or the Blancos would get the minority seats on the *colegiado*. The 1952 constitution also provided for impeachment of the president by the General Assembly.

This nine-member *colegiado,* which headed the executive branch from 1954 to 1967, was ineffective because the president lacked control over the ministers and because the majority was seldom united. During most of this period, the National Party held power, having been elected in 1958 for the first time in over ninety years and again in 1962 when a different faction of the party was elected. The ineffectiveness of these governments caused the public to turn against the *colegiado* arrangement.

In the elections of November 27, 1966, nearly 59 percent of Uruguayans voted to amend the 1952 constitution and to reestablish a presidential system of government, thus ending a fifteen-year experiment with the *colegiado.* The new constitution, which became operative on February 15, 1967, and has remained in effect since then, created a strong one-person presidency, subject to legislative and judicial checks. In free and fair elections held in 1968, Uruguayans approved the new charter and elected the Colorado Party to power again.

The 1967 constitution contains many of the provisions of the 1952 charter. However, it removed some of the General Assembly's power to initiate legislation and provided for automatic approval of bills under certain conditions if the legislature failed to act. If, on receiving a bill, the president has objections or comments to make, the bill must be returned to the General Assembly within ten days. If sixty days elapse without a decision by the General Assembly, the president's objections must be considered as accepted. The 1967 document also established the Permanent Commission, composed of four senators and seven representatives, which exercises certain legislative functions while the General Assembly is in recess.

The 1967 charter can be amended by any of four different methods. First, 10 percent of the citizens who are registered to vote can initiate an amendment if they present a detailed proposal to the president of the General Assembly. Second, two-fifths of the full membership of the General Assembly can approve a proposal presented to the president of the General Assembly and submitted to a plebiscite at the next election (a yes vote of an absolute majority of the full membership of the General Assembly is required, and this majority must represent at least 35 percent of all registered voters). Third, senators, representatives, and the president of the republic can present proposed amendments, which must be approved by an absolute majority of the full membership of the General Assembly. And finally, amendments can be made by constitutional laws requiring the approval of two-thirds of the full membership of each chamber of the General Assembly in the same legislative period.

In 1976, however, the military government issued a series of constitutional decrees that amended the 1967 constitution by creating the Council of the Nation (Consejo de la Nación) to serve as the supreme governmental body, with executive and legislative functions. It consisted of the thirty members of the Council of State (Consejo de Estado, the body created by the regime in June 1973 to act in lieu of the General Assembly, which dissolved by the regime) and the twenty-eight senior officers of the armed forces (sixteen from the army, six from the navy, and six from the air force). The Council of the Nation appointed the president of the republic and the members of the Council of State, the Supreme Court of Justice, and the Tribunal of Administrative Claims, which had been dissolved in 1985. Eight institutional acts substituted for many of the functional provisions and guarantees of the 1967 constitution. For example, in addition to giving the Council of the Nation the power to appoint the president of the republic and to set general policy for the country, institutional acts deprived previous officeholders and candidates of their political rights and permitted the arbitrary dismissal of public employees.

Under the 1976 constitutional amendments, the president exercised executive power, acting with the concurrence of one or more ministers as appropriate or with the National Security Council (Consejo de Seguridad Nacional—Cosena). The Cosena had been formed in 1973 and consisted of the commanders of the army, navy, and air force, plus an additional senior military officer, and the ministers of national defense, interior, and foreign affairs. It participated in any decision related to the "national security" or in any formulation of overall plans or objectives.

157

The constitutional decrees declared generally that the maintenance of the national security was of "exclusive competence," i.e., the sole prerogative, of the armed forces. These decrees deprived local governments of all budgetary powers. The Council of State continued to pass laws that the executive normally would have submitted for approval. Only the executive could initiate the procedure for approval of legislation on budgetary or other matters that could be related in any way to national security. The decrees also created the Ministry of Justice, responsible for relations between the executive and judicial powers.

In 1980 the military regime drew up a charter that would have provided for a strong, continuing role for the military along the lines of the 1976 constitutional decrees, including legitimizing the Cosena's new role. The document also would have greatly reduced the roles of the General Assembly and political parties. In a plebiscite held November 30, 1980, however, Uruguayans, by a margin of 57 percent to 43 percent of the popular vote, rejected the new military-drafted constitution. Nevertheless, a new thirty-five-member Council of State was installed on August 20, 1981, before President Gregorio Alvarez Armelino (1981–85) took office. Its powers were expanded to include responsibility for calling a constitutional assembly, a plebiscite, and general elections.

In discussions held during 1983, the military commanders and the leaders of the Colorado and National parties prepared a new text of the 1967 constitution. Accords negotiated by the military, the Colorados (but not the Blancos), and most of the Broad Front in July and August 1984 provided for a return to democracy without the Cosena.

Following the return to civilian rule in 1985, Uruguay's human rights record quickly improved. One of the Sanguinetti government's first acts in this area was—with the approval of the newly restored General Assembly—to grant amnesty to all political prisoners, who consisted chiefly of members of the National Liberation Movement-Tupamaros (Movimiento de Liberación Nacional-Tupamaros—MLN-T). In the late 1980s, there were no credible reports of human rights violations, according to the United States Department of State.

Since 1985 Uruguay's democratic governments have respected the sixty-five articles in the 1967 constitution concerned primarily with the rights of citizens. The document provides for freedom of religion, thought, speech and press, peaceful assembly and association, collective bargaining, movement within the country, foreign travel, emigration and repatriation, respect for political rights, and the inviolability of property and privacy. The constitution does not provide for a state religion, although Roman Catholicism predominates, or for capital punishment (that was abolished during Batlle y Ordóñez's second term). There are two forms of citizenship: natural (persons born in Uruguay or those who were of Uruguayan parents and were registered residents) and legal (individuals established in Uruguay with at least three years' residence in the case of those with family in Uruguay or five years' residence for those without family there). Primary and secondary education is both free and compulsory. Every citizen eighteen years of age or older has the right and obligation to vote, which is compulsory (see The Electoral Process, this ch.).

Uruguay has long been one of the most egalitarian countries in the world. Women's suffrage was enacted in 1932. In 1946 a statute was passed repealing all laws that established legal differences in the rights of women. Uruguayan women, who constituted one-third of the work force in the 1980s, enjoyed complete equality under the law. Nevertheless, some barriers still existed in practice because of traditional social patterns and restricted employment opportunities. Women often received less pay than men, especially in less skilled jobs. By early 1990, very few women held high political positions, but women had served in the cabinet, the Supreme Court of Justice, and the diplomatic corps, including at the ambassadorial level, and a few had served as alternates in the General Assembly.

Governmental Structure

Uruguay is a republic with three separate branches of government (see fig. 9). The 1967 constitution institutionalizes a strong presidency, subject to legislative and judicial checks. The electorate exercises sovereignty directly through elections, initiatives, or referendums and indirectly through representative powers established by the constitution.

The Executive

Executive power is exercised by the president of the republic, acting with the advice of the Council of Ministers. The vice president of the republic serves as the president of the General Assembly and the Senate. The president and vice president are elected for five-year terms by a simple majority of the people through a unique voting system. Candidates must be at least thirty-five years of age, native born, and in full possession of their civil rights. After a period following their election, the president and vice president are sworn in before both chambers of the General Assembly and take office on March 1. Neither may be reelected until five years after the completion of their terms.

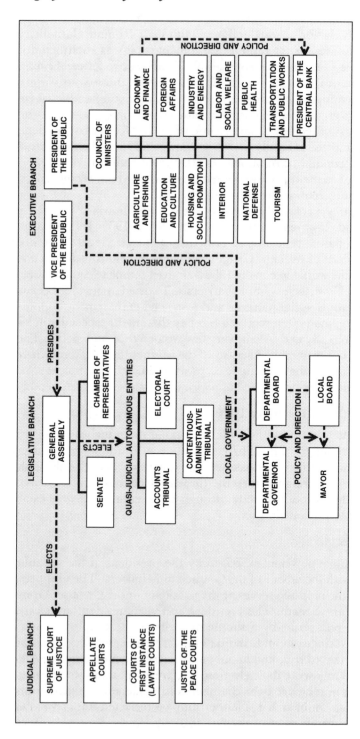

Figure 9. Governmental Structure, 1990

The president's duties include publishing all laws and enforcing them, informing the General Assembly of the state of the republic and of proposed improvements and reforms, making objections to or observations on bills sent by the General Assembly, proposing bills to the chambers or amendments to laws previously enacted, conferring civilian and military offices, and removing civil servants (with the consent of the Senate) for "inefficiency, dereliction of duty, or malfeasance." The key civilian appointments made by the president are cabinet members.

A 1986 constitutional amendment returned to the presidency the power to command the armed forces and appoint the armed forces commander. The chief executive grants promotions to members of the armed forces, with the consent of the Senate for promotions to colonel or higher ranks. The president also is responsible for maintaining internal order and external security. Although the constitution does not give the president sweeping powers in cases of emergency, Article 168 empowers the chief executive "to take prompt measures of security in grave and unforeseen cases of foreign attack or internal disorder." In such an event, the president is required to explain his action to a joint session of the General Assembly or, if it is in recess, to the Permanent Commission within twenty-four hours.

Other presidential powers include decreeing the severance of diplomatic relations with another country and declaring war if arbitration or other pacific means to avoid it are unsuccessful. The president appoints ambassadors and other foreign service diplomatic personnel. The chief executive may not leave the country for more than forty-eight hours without authorization from the Senate. The president may not be impeached unless found guilty of violations of articles of the constitution or other serious offenses.

The Council of Ministers includes the cabinet ministers (appointed by the president) and the president of the Central Bank of Uruguay. Each appointee must be approved by a simple majority in each chamber of the General Assembly. Cabinet members must be native-born citizens in full possession of their civil rights and at least thirty years of age. They may be removed from office by impeachment proceedings initiated by the Chamber of Representatives and approved by the Senate.

When all the cabinet ministers or their deputies meet and act jointly, the body is known as the Council of Ministers. Presided over by the president of the republic, who has a vote, the Council of Ministers is responsible for all acts of government and administration. In addition, a number of autonomous entities (autonomous agencies or state enterprises; see Glossary) and decentralized services are important in government administration (see Public Administration, this ch.).

The principal duties of the cabinet members are to enforce the constitution, laws, decrees, and resolutions; to formulate and submit for the consideration of superior authority any laws, decrees, and resolutions they deem appropriate; to effect—within the limits of their functions—the payment of the national debt; to propose the appointment or discharge of employees of their ministries; and to perform any other functions entrusted to them by laws or by measures adopted by the executive power. They may attend the sessions of either chamber of the General Assembly and their respective standing committees, and they may take part in debate, but they may not vote.

The Legislature

The bicameral General Assembly enacts laws and regulates the administration of justice. The General Assembly consists of the thirty-member Senate—thirty senators and the vice president of the republic, who presides over it as well as the General Assembly and has both a voice and a vote in Senate deliberations—and the ninety-nine-member Chamber of Representatives. If the vice president ever assumes the presidency, the senator heading the list of the party that received the most votes in the last election will succeed to the presidency of the Senate.

Members of both legislative bodies are directly elected every five years by a system of proportional representation. The Chamber of Representatives represents the nineteen administrative subdivisions of the country, with each department (*departamento*) having at least two representatives. The members of the Senate are also elected by the people, but with the entire nation representing a single electoral district. Members of the General Assembly must be natural citizens or legal citizens with seven years' exercise of their rights. Senators must be at least thirty years of age, and representatives at least twenty-five years of age. Uruguay does not have a residency requirement for election to the Senate or the Chamber of Representatives. Consequently, almost all of the country's politicians have lived and worked in Montevideo. Military and civil service personnel or public officials may not be candidates for either chamber of the General Assembly unless they resign their positions at least three months before the election. In 1988 there were no female members of the General Assembly, but several served as alternates.

The Chamber of Representatives can impeach any member of either chamber, the president, the vice president, cabinet ministers,

President Lacalle
Courtesy Embassy of Uruguay, Washington

judges of the Supreme Court of Justice, and other judges. The Senate is responsible for trying these impeachment cases and can deprive a person of a post by a two-thirds vote of its membership. In addition, the Senate, in session from mid-March to mid-December, spends much time considering nominations for, appointments to, and removals from office submitted by the executive. In other respects, the Senate and the Chamber of Representatives have equal powers and duties. Members of either of the two chambers can initiate a bill. Both chambers must approve a proposed bill before it can be sent to the executive power to be published. The latter branch, however, has ten days to make objections to or observations on the bill. If the president objects to only part of a bill, the General Assembly can enact the other part.

Among the most important duties of the Chamber of Representatives—in joint session with the Senate—are the election of the members of the Supreme Court of Justice and three quasi-judicial autonomous entities: the Accounts Tribunal, the Contentious-Administrative Tribunal, and the Electoral Court. These ordinary administrative courts hear cases involving the functioning of state administration. In addition, the Chamber of Representatives is empowered to grant pardons and settle disputes concerning legislation on which the two chambers disagree. The Chamber of Representatives also has the exclusive right to impeach members of both chambers, the president and vice president of the republic, the cabinet ministers, and members of the courts for violations of the constitution or other serious offenses. Impeachment proceedings must be tried before the Senate.

The Accounts Tribunal, which is a functionally autonomous appendage of the General Assembly, is responsible for determining taxes and reporting on the accounts and budgets of all the state organs. It is authorized to intervene in all matters relating to the financial activities of the state organs, departmental governments, and autonomous agencies, and it is authorized to report to the appropriate authority all irregularities in the management of public funds or infractions of budgetary and accounting laws. It is authorized to certify the legality of expenditures and payments and append pertinent objections whenever necessary. In the departmental governments and autonomous agencies, officials acting under the supervision of the tribunal perform the same duties. The tribunal's opinions cover all the organs of the state, including departmental governments. An annual report must be submitted to the General Assembly. The Accounts Tribunal consists of seven members appointed by a two-thirds vote of the full membership of the General Assembly. Their elective qualifications are the same as those of a senator. Their term of office ends when the succeeding General Assembly makes new appointments, but they may be reelected.

The Contentious-Administrative Tribunal hears pleas for the nullification of final administrative acts that are considered contrary to law or an abuse of authority made by the administration, state organs, departmental governments, autonomous entities, and decentralized services. It also has jurisdiction over the final administrative acts of the governments of the departments and of the autonomous entities. Its functions are only to appraise the act itself and to confirm or annul it, without alteration. Its decisions have effect only in the cases before it. The Contentious-Administrative Tribunal can act in cases of conflict of jurisdiction based on legislation and on differences that arise among the executive, the departmental governments, and the autonomous entities.

The qualifications necessary for election to the Contentious-Administrative Tribunal, the manner of appointment, the remuneration, and the term of office are the same as those established for the members of the Supreme Court of Justice. The tribunal is composed of five judges appointed by the General Assembly for ten-year terms. It also has an "attorney general for administrative claims" (appointed by the president), whose qualifications, remuneration, and term of office are decided by the tribunal. The attorney general is heard at the final hearing of all matters within the jurisdiction of the tribunal.

The Electoral Court, a quasi-judicial autonomous entity, supervises national, departmental, and municipal elections and has competence over all electoral acts and procedures. It rules in the last instance on appeals and complaints; it also judges the election of all the elective posts and the holding of a plebiscite (on constitutional issues) or referendum (on political issues). Of the Electoral Court's nine members, the General Assembly appoints five and their alternates by a two-thirds vote in joint session and elects the other four members and their alternates equally from the two political parties having the highest number of votes. The court has eighteen alternates in addition to the nine full members. Members serve four years until the succeeding legislature selects their replacements (see The Electoral Process, this ch.).

The Judiciary

Like all previous charters, the 1967 constitution establishes the judicial branch as an independent power of the state. The Supreme Court of Justice heads the judiciary, both civilian and military. Lower civilian courts include six appellate courts (for civil matters, criminal matters, and labor matters), courts of first instance (sometimes referred to as lawyer courts [*juzgados letrados*]), and justice of the peace courts.

During the military regime (1973–85), the Ministry of Justice administered the courts, and military officers were appointed to the highest courts. As a result of the 1984 Naval Club Pact, which clipped the powers of the military courts, the judicial branch regained its autonomy when Sanguinetti assumed office on March 1, 1985. That May the General Assembly, despite the opposition of the Colorado Party, declared all posts of the Supreme Court of Justice vacant on the grounds that none of the justices had been legally appointed. Accordingly, all of the military officers appointed by the military regime to the high court or the appellate courts retired from their positions. Sanguinetti then formally abolished the Ministry of Justice, retaining only the minister of justice post. Nevertheless, there was a continuing public debate during his administration over the need to reform the legal and judicial systems.

Located in Montevideo, the Supreme Court of Justice manages the entire judicial system. It prepares budgets for the judiciary and submits them to the General Assembly for approval, proposes all legislation regarding the functioning of the courts, appoints judges to the appellate courts, and nominates all other judges and judicial officials. It has the power to modify any decisions made by the appellate courts and is the only court allowed to declare the unconstitutionality of laws passed by the General Assembly. It alone decides on conflicts affecting diplomats and international treaties, the execution of the rulings of foreign courts, and relations among agencies of the government. The president of the Supreme Court of Justice is empowered to attend meetings of the committees of both chambers of the General Assembly and has a voice in discussion but has no vote.

A conference of the two chambers of the General Assembly appoints the five members of the Supreme Court of Justice. The justices must be between forty and seventy years of age, native-born citizens in full possession of their civil rights, or legal citizens with ten years' exercise of their rights and twenty-five years of residence in the country. They also must have been a lawyer for ten years or must have been a judge or member of the Public Ministry for eight years. (The Public Ministry consists of the public attorneys, headed by the "attorney general of the court and attorney of the country," who acts independently before the Supreme Court of Justice.) Members serve for ten years and may be reelected after a break of five years. At the appointment of the president, two military justices serve on the Supreme Court of Justice on

18th of July Avenue in downtown Montevideo
Courtesy Inter-American Development Bank

an ad hoc basis and participate only in cases involving the military (see Military Justice, ch. 5).

Each of the appellate courts, also located in Montevideo, has three judges appointed by the Supreme Court of Justice with the consent of the Senate. To be a member, one must be at least thirty-five years of age, a native-born citizen or legal citizen for seven years, and a lawyer with at least eight years of experience or otherwise engaged in a law-related profession for at least six years. An appellate court judge is obliged to retire by age seventy. These courts do not have original jurisdiction but hear appeals from lower courts. The appellate courts divide responsibilities for civil matters (including matters concerning commerce, customs, and minors), as well as for criminal and labor affairs.

In Montevideo Department, the judges of first instance, sometimes referred to as lawyer judges (*jueces letrados*), decide on the appeals to lower-court rulings. In 1990 Montevideo Department had forty judges of first instance, including eighteen who decided on civil matters, four on minors, three on customs, ten on criminal cases, and five on labor cases.

Outside Montevideo Department, the first decision on all cases of civil, family, customs, criminal, or labor law is submitted to the municipal judges of first instance. Each department has up to

167

five municipal judges of first instance, located in the major cities. They rule on most minor cases, with the exception of those that are within the competence of the justices of the peace. Both municipal judges of first instance and the Montevideo Department judges of first instance must have previously served as justices of the peace.

At the lowest level, each of the country's 224 judicial divisions has a justice of the peace court. The Supreme Court of Justice appoints the 224 justices of the peace for four-year terms. They must be at least twenty-five years of age, native-born citizens or legal citizens for two years, and in full possession of their civil rights. Those who serve in Montevideo Department and the capitals and major cities of other departments must be lawyers; those in rural areas must be either lawyers or notaries. Their jurisdiction is limited to cases involving eviction, breach of contract, collection of rent, and all small-claims commercial and business cases.

The law recognizes only one category of lawyer. In order to practice law, an individual must first obtain the degree of law and social sciences from the Faculty of Law and Social Sciences of the University of the Republic (also known as the University of Montevideo). The degree is granted by the university after the successful completion of six years of studies. Candidates must be at least twenty-one years of age, listed in the Register of Lawyers maintained by the Supreme Court of Justice, not be under indictment for a crime penalized by corporal punishment, and not have been convicted of a crime. A public defender system was established in 1980 with the placing of lawyers in all courts to assist those unable to pay for their services. Public defenders—appointed jointly by the president and the minister of justice—protect the society's interests.

Public Administration

Uruguay traditionally has had a sizable civil service organization. Civil service regulations determine conditions for admission to the service as a career. In accordance with these regulations for service in the national government, departmental governments adopted regulations for their own civil service personnel. Permanent career status is achieved after a fairly short probationary period.

The Sanguinetti government reestablished the National Office of the Civil Service (Oficina Nacional del Servicio Civil—ONSC), which the military regime had abolished, as the technical advisory organ specializing in administrative reform matters. The ONSC publicizes its ideas on change and reform by sponsoring academic, public, and international seminars and roundtables.

The ONSC's duties include controlling the entrance of personnel into the public administration and streamlining public institutions. Under Sanguinetti, the ONSC also implemented course requirements for civil service managers and, with the assistance of France's National School of Public Administration (Ecole Nationale d'Administration Publique), created a ''training course for high executives of the central administration.'' During the first twenty years since its creation in 1969, the ONSC trained or provided technical assistance to some 4,000 public employees, more than one-third of them between 1986 and 1988.

Following ONSC guidelines, the Sanguinetti government restructured the civil service and reassigned 1,787 workers. At the end of 1988, the state employed a total of 271,124 workers (approximately 20 percent of the labor force), who included 1,281 members of the legislative branch, 106,455 members of the executive branch, 5,132 members of the judicial branch, 117,423 members of the autonomous entities, and 40,833 members of the departmental governments.

Over twenty autonomous entities administer certain national industrial and commercial services (see table 14, Appendix). These agencies are divided into two general classifications: the first is concerned with education, welfare, and culture; the second, with industry and commerce.

Local Government

Uruguay's administrative subdivisions consist of nineteen departments (*departamentos*), which are subordinate to the central government and responsible for local administration. They enforce national laws and administer the nation's social and educational policies and institutions within their departments. These departments have limited taxing powers, but they can borrow funds and acquire property. They also have the power to establish unpaid five-member local boards or town councils in municipalities other than the departmental capital if the population is large enough to warrant such a body.

Executive authority is vested in a governor (*intendente*), who administers the department, and in a thirty-one-member departmental board (*junta departmental*), which carries out legislative functions. These functions include approval of the departmental budget and judicial actions, such as impeachment proceedings against departmental officials, including the governor. At the municipal level, a mayor (*intendente municipal*) assumes executive and administrative duties, carrying out resolutions made by the local board (whose members are appointed on the basis of proportional representation of the political parties). The governor is required to comply with and enforce the constitution and the laws and to promulgate the decrees enacted by the departmental board. The governor is authorized to prepare the budget, submit it for approval to the departmental board, appoint the board's employees, and, if necessary, discipline or suspend them. The governor represents the department in its relations with the national government and other departmental governments and in the negotiation of contracts with public or private agencies.

Like the governor, the members of the departmental board and the mayor are elected for five-year terms in direct, popular elections. A governor can be reelected only once, and candidates for the post must meet the same requirements as those for a senator, in addition to being a native of the department or a resident therein for at least three years before assuming office. Departmental board members must be at least twenty-three years of age, native born (or a legal citizen for at least three years), and a native of the department (or a resident for at least three years).

The board sits in the capital city of each department and exercises jurisdiction throughout the entire territory of the department. It can issue decrees and resolutions that it deems necessary either on the suggestion of the governor or on its own initiative. It can approve budgets, fix the amount of taxes, request the intervention of the Accounts Tribunal for advice concerning departmental finances or administration, and remove from office—at the request of the governor—members of nonelective local departmental boards. The board also supervises local public services; public health; and primary, secondary, preparatory, industrial, and artistic education. Although Montevideo is the smallest department in terms of area (divided into twenty-three geographic zones that generally coincide with the electoral zones), its departmental board had sixty-five members in 1990; all other departments had thirty-one-member boards and a five-member executive council appointed by the departmental board, with proportional representation from the principal political parties.

The Electoral Process

Uruguayans take voting very seriously. Voting, which is obligatory, is not restricted by race, sex, religion, or economic status. Other rules governing suffrage include mandatory inscription in the Civil Register and a system of proportional representation. These rules also include prohibition of political activity (with the exception of voting) by judicial magistrates, directors of the autonomous entities, and members of the armed forces and police.

In addition, the president of the republic and members of the Electoral Court are not permitted to serve as political party officials or engage in political election propaganda; all electoral boards must be elected; a two-thirds vote of the full membership of each chamber is needed to adopt any new law concerning the Civil Register or elections; and all national and local elections are to be held every five years on the last Sunday in November.

Uruguay's electoral processes are among the most complicated known. The unusual Uruguayan electoral system combines primaries and a general election in one event. Primary and general elections combine proportional representation with a "double simultaneous vote" (*doble voto simultáneo*). This system, as established by the Elections Law of 1925, allows each party's *sub-lemas*, or factions, to run rival lists of candidates.

Traditionally, under Uruguayan law the results of political elections are tabulated in an unusual fashion. Under the 1982 Political Parties Law, each party is allowed to present three tickets, or single candidates, each representing a different *sub-lema*, for executive and legislative posts, and these factions do not need the party's approval of their candidates. A voter selects a faction and a list of candidates within that *sub-lema*. The votes of all the factions are given to the party (*lema*) to which they belong, and the presidency goes to the candidate of the *sub-lema* that receives the most votes within the winning party. Thus, even if a given ticket garners more votes than any other slate running for election, it cannot win unless its party also wins. The governing party is actually the majority group within the party that won the last elections. The disadvantages of this system are that it discourages intraparty selectivity in choosing presidential candidates, often allows politicians who receive only a minority of the vote to rise to power, blocks the rise of new parties and new leadership while encouraging fractionalization, and often results in a multiplicity of alliances or combinations of national and local candidates for office.

Election of members of the General Assembly is even more complicated. Election of the ninety-nine members of the Chamber of Representatives is based on the population in the country's nineteen departments, whereas the thirty members of the Senate are elected at large from the nation. Seats are allocated on the basis of each party's share of the total vote, but each party usually has various lists of candidates, among whom prior agreements have been made to unify or transfer votes. As a result, there have been frequent complaints that voters never know for whom they are ultimately voting in the congressional races. Electoral fraud, however, is precluded by the traditional method of decentralized vote-counting at thousands of vote-counting tables.

In addition, the Electoral Court supervises the entire registration and voting process, registers parties and candidates, has final jurisdiction in all election disputes, and supervises the functioning of the various departmental electoral boards. It also supervises the National Electoral Office in Montevideo, which has the responsibility for organizing and maintaining the Civil Register of all eligible voters in the country. One Electoral Court exists at the national level and one in each department capital.

Before an election, the General Assembly allocates a sum of money for the Electoral Court to distribute among the political parties in proportion to the number of votes a party received in the last election. These funds help to defray campaign costs. Party-proposed ballots must be presented to the Electoral Court at least twenty days prior to an election. After making the final verification of ballots, the Electoral Court can annul an election, but only if gross irregularities are found.

Political Dynamics

Political Parties

The Colorado and National parties and, to a lesser extent, the Broad Front coalition, were the three major political entities in 1990. Until the 1971 elections, the Colorado and National parties together accounted for 90 percent of the votes cast; the remaining 10 percent of the votes were divided among various small parties. Some of the minor parties have followed the lead of the major parties and sought to enhance their electoral chances through coalitions, such as the Broad Front. The traditional two-party system was threatened for the first time by the Broad Front's victory in the Montevideo municipal elections in 1989, its first win on the national level.

As previously noted, a system of coparticipation (*coparticipación*) in the government between the ruling party and the principal opposition has characterized Uruguayan politics since 1872. According to Weinstein, this term best described Uruguay's unique political process and was still widely used among Uruguayans in the 1980s. Coparticipation meant that the two traditional parties and their members were entitled to divide and share the governing of the country. Indeed, in order to govern, the majority party had to make alliances with other parties because being the majority party in a proportional representation system did not necessarily mean that it had a simple majority in the General Assembly. For example, the Colorado Party almost always governed in alliance with a section of the National Party. During the first years of the Sanguinetti administration, the National Party refrained from systematic opposition, thereby helping to ease the legislative passage of government policies. The Colorado Party was expected to do the same for the Lacalle government. Sharing political power also has been determined by the principle of parity (*paridad*), meaning that the losing party's participation in the government was based on the relative electoral strength of the two parties.

Each party permitted internal ideological divisions because each party could run multiple presidential candidates and its own slate of legislative nominees. Factions, or *sub-lemas*, fielded different lists of candidates for general elections. Voters expressed a preference for a list rather than an individual candidate, and they voted for a party. The winning list of the party that received the most votes won the presidency and a percentage of the seats in the Senate and the Chamber of Representatives corresponding to the percentage of votes that the party as a whole received. National and departmental elections were held simultaneously every five years. Campaigns were funded in part by government subsidies given to the parties and factions in accordance with their voting strength in the previous election.

Traditional Parties

Uruguay is one of the few Latin American countries with two political groupings—the Colorado and National parties—as old as the country itself. Most Uruguayans consider themselves either Colorados or Blancos from birth, and affiliation with one of the two major parties or their major *sub-lemas* is a part of one's family heritage. The two parties traditionally maintained a rough equilibrium, and their factions had their own leaders, candidates, followers, policies, and organizational structures. These *sub-lemas* embraced persons of various political orientations and social backgrounds. In general, however, the Colorado Party traditionally was associated with the city, labor unions, and secularist and "progressive" movements, whereas the National Party identified with the interior farming groups and the more religious and conservative groups.

The cleavage between Montevideo and the rural interior influenced party affiliation and political attitudes to a greater extent than did differences in social status and income. (The coastal region often held the balance of power between Montevideo and the interior.) Although three-fourths of all voters remained loyal to the traditional parties in the 1984 elections, the support of these parties in Montevideo weakened gradually during the 1980s. The decline of the National Party in Montevideo was the most pronounced; it won none of the capital's twenty-three electoral zones in 1984 and made no headway against the Broad Front in 1989. Despite internal fractionalization, both traditional parties maintained the structures typical of more cohesive modern parties, including conventions, general assemblies, party steering committees, and caucuses. The fundamental units of the factions of both parties were the neighborhood clubs, guided and controlled by professional politicians.

Vague ideological differences between the major parties still existed in the 1980s, but the differences involved not so much politics as allegiance to certain leaders and traditions. Although the Colorados traditionally were more liberal than the Blancos, both parties had liberal and conservative factions. In the General Assembly, the left wings of both parties often lined up in opposition to both right wings on important votes. The Colorados also were more anticlerical in the early twentieth century, but this distinction lost most of its significance as both parties broadened their bases of support. The urban-based Colorados were considered more cosmopolitan in outlook than the rural-based, tradition-oriented, and economically conservative Blancos. In general, the followers of Batlle y Ordóñez in the Colorado Party were more willing than the Blanco leadership to undertake political, social, and economic innovations.

The Colorado and National parties each had various *sub-lemas* in late 1990. The Colorado Party's factions included the right-of-center United Batllism (Batllismo Unido—BU), which was in the majority for thirty years until August 1990; the left-of-center BU sector, called the Social Action Movement (Movimiento de Acción Social—MAS), led by Hugo Fernández Faingold; Unity and Reform (Unidad y Reforma), or List 15, led by Jorge Batlle Ibáñez; the antimilitary Freedom and Change (Libertad y Cambio), or List 85, led by Enrique E. Tarigo, Sanguinetti's vice president; the Independent Batllist Faction (Corriente Batllista Independiente—CBI), led by Senator Manuel Flores Silva; Víctor Vaillant's "progressive" Batllist Reaffirmation Movement (Movimiento de Reafirmación Batllista—MRB), a CBI splinter group; the rightist Colorado and Batllist Union (Unión Colorada y Batllista—UCB), or List 123; and Democratic Traditionalism (Tradicionalismo Democrático—Trademo), a sector of the National Republican Association (Asociación Nacional Republicana—ANR).

The UCB was subdivided into three main groups: the minority right-wing and promilitary Pachequist faction led by Jorge Pacheco Areco (president, 1967–72); the sector led by Pablo Millor Coccaro, Pacheco's principal rival; and the National Integrationist Movement (Movimiento Integracionista Nacional—MIN), which was formed in early 1986 and led by Senator Pedro W. Cersósimo. Following the 1989 elections, Millor's sector caused a political storm within the UCB when it announced that it would henceforth operate autonomously, although still recognizing Pacheco's leadership. Pacheco's faction, for its part, founded the National Colorado Movement (Movimiento Nacional Colorado—MNC) on May 11, 1990.

As a result of the primaries of the Colorado Party in early August 1990, Batlle Ibáñez's Unity and Reform *sub-lema* ousted the faction led by former President Sanguinetti from the leadership of the Colorado Party. Batlle Ibáñez's faction obtained five seats on the party's fifteen-member National Executive Committee, followed by Pacheco's four seats, Sanguinetti's three, and Millor's three.

The National Party was divided into at least five factions. The Herrerist Movement (Movimiento Herrerista), or faction, of the National Party emerged in the 1930s. Lacalle founded the Herrerist National Council (Consejo Nacional Herrerista—CNH) in 1961. The CNH joined with Senator Dando Ortiz's sector in 1987 to form the right-of-center Herrerist Movement. After Wilson Ferreira Aldunate's death in March 1988, Lacalle assumed the presidency of the Herrerist Movement.

Other National Party factions included Carlos Julio Pereyra's left-of-center La Rocha National Movement (Movimiento Nacional de La Rocha—MNR), the second largest National Party *sub-lema;* the centrist For the Fatherland (Por la Patria—PLP), founded in 1969 by Ferreira as a personalist movement, reorganized into a more democratic party in 1985, and led by Senator Alberto Sáenz de Zumarán after Ferreira's death in 1988; Renovation and Victory (Renovación y Victoria—RV), led by Gonzalo Aguirre Ramírez, a constitutional lawyer; and the People's Blanco Union (Unión Blanca Popular—UBP), founded in the late 1980s by Oscar López Balestra, a member of the Chamber of Representatives. The CNH, MNR, and PLP were all antimilitary factions.

Additional minor parties included the White Emblem (Divisa Blanca), a conservative party led by Eduardo Pons Etcheverry; Juan Pivel Devoto's Nationalist Popular Faction (Corriente Popular Nacionalista—CPN), which broke away from the National Party in late 1986; the Barrán National Party (Partido Nacional-Barrán); the ultrarightist Society for the Defense of Family Tradition and

Property (Sociedad de Defensa de la Tradición Familia y Proprie-dad—TFP); the Humanist Party (Partido Humanista), which ap-peared in 1985; and the Animal Welfare Ecological Green Party (Eto-Ecologista—Partido Verde—EE–PV), which emerged in 1989.

Broad Front

In February 1971, Colorado Party dissident senators Zelmar Michelini (who was assassinated in 1976) and Hugo Batalla formed the left-of-center Broad Front (Frente Amplio) coalition in a bid to break the historical two-party system of Colorados and Blan-cos. The Socialist Party of Uruguay (Partido Socialista del Uru-guay—PSU), one of Uruguay's oldest left-wing parties (founded in 1910 by Emilio Frugoni), was one of its principal members.

Another core Broad Front member, founded in 1921, was the Communist Party of Uruguay (Partido Comunista del Uruguay—PCU). Rodney Arismendi, PCU general secretary since 1955, returned to Uruguay in November 1984 after many years as a resi-dent of Moscow; he died in 1988 and was replaced by Jaime Pé-rez, a former union leader. One of Sanguinetti's first acts after taking office was to lift the restrictions on the PCU (which had been banned) and its Moscow-line newspaper *El Popular*. The PCU had only an estimated 7,500 members in early 1990, but its apparatus controlled the majority of the country's labor unions.

The Broad Front had a strong following in Montevideo, with a presence in all social classes and all generations. Under military rule (1973–85), the alliance's leader, General (Retired) Líber Seregni Mosquera, was arrested, the Broad Front was outlawed, and its activists were persecuted. When national elections were held in 1984, the military banned Seregni from running. Nevertheless, with Juan José Crottogini as its candidate, the Broad Front received slightly more than 21 percent of the total vote, compared with 18.5 percent in the 1971 national elections.

The Broad Front coalition generally agreed with the Sanguinetti government's foreign policy and political leadership stances, but it was fundamentally opposed to its economic policies. For exam-ple, the Broad Front favored increasing real incomes and opposed the government's export-oriented policy.

Internal power struggles between moderate and radical sectors weakened the Broad Front in the late 1980s. By late 1987, the Chris-tian Democratic Party (Partido Demócrata Cristiano—PDC) and the People's Government Party (Partido por el Gobierno del Pueblo—PGP) were feuding with other coalition members over their demand that the alliance be redefined to give their own positions greater weight. The PDC and PGP wanted to reduce the hegemony of the Marxist groups and their undue influence on Seregni's public stances. In 1988 a PDC faction broke away and sought an understanding with one of the factions of the National Party. The PDC and PGP then proposed that the alliance should field two presidential candidates in the November 1989 elections: Seregni and PGP leader Batalla. The Broad Front's radical Marxist and communist sector, however, opposed the idea of running two candidates because they regarded the front as a party and not a coalition. In December 1988, therefore, the leftist parties of the alliance decided that Seregni would be the Broad Front's sole candidate; but the PGP backed Batalla. The PDC and PGP withdrew from the alliance in February and March 1989, respectively, over the issue of presidential candidacies and the leftist control of the organization. Batalla's PGP, which accounted for about 40 percent of the alliance's electoral votes in 1984, had been responsible for eleven of the Broad Front's twenty-one representatives and three of its six senators.

By May 1989, the Broad Front consisted of fourteen parties. Smaller ones included the People's Victory Party (Partido por la Victoria del Pueblo—PVP) and the Uruguayan Revolutionary Movement of Independents (Movimiento de Independientes Revolucionario Oriental—MRO), a pro-Cuban group founded in 1961. Five parties were accepted as members in May 1989: the National Liberation Movement-Tupamaros (Movimiento de Liberación Nacional-Tupamaros—MLN–T), the 26th of March Movement of Independents (Movimiento de Independientes 26 de Marzo—26 M), the Trotskyite Socialist Workers' Party (Partido Socialista de los Trabajadores—PST), the Grito de Asencio Integration Movement (Movimiento de Integración Grito de Asencio), and a faction of the PDC.

The MLN–T—a former urban guerrilla organization established in 1962 and disbanded by the armed forces in 1972—was given amnesty by the General Assembly in March 1985. The MLN–T reorganized and appeared in the political arena in July 1986 but was not legally recognized until May 1989. With several hundred members, it was politically insignificant. In order to run candidates in the November 1989 elections, the MLN–T, together with other ultra-leftist forces—the PVP, PST, and MRO—created the People's Participation Movement (Movimiento de Participación Popular—MPP).

In 1989 the Broad Front also included a subcoalition called the Advanced Democracy Party (Partido de Democracia Avanzada), which served as a front for the PCU; the People's Broad Front Movement (Movimiento Popular Frenteamplista—MPF); the

Broad Front Unity Faction (Corriente de Unidad Frenteamplista—CUFO); the Pregón Movement (Movimiento Pregón); Alba Roballo's left-wing Liberal Party (Partido Liberal), a *sub-lema* that joined in April 1989; the Nationalist Action Movement (Movimiento de Acción Nacionalista—MAN), a nationalist organization; the Popular and Progressive Blanco Movement (Movimiento Popular Blanco y Progresista—MBPP), a moderate left-wing party; and the Movement for the People's Government (Movimiento por el Gobierno del Pueblo—MGP), which became, in August 1986, the tenth political party of Uruguay to be created. The MGP subsequently merged with the PGP and adopted a social democratic program.

The Broad Front was organized like a communist party. It had a party congress with decision-making powers, under which was a central committee-like body called the national plenum. A president, Seregni, headed the 108-member national plenum, which met at least once every two months. A political bureau, which included the president, exercised day-to-day authority.

New Sector

After breaking away from the Broad Front in early 1989, the PDC and PGP joined with the Civic Union (Unión Cívica—UC) to form a coalition called the Integration Movement (Movimiento de Integración—MI). The MI nominated the PGP leader, Batalla—a senator, journalist, and lawyer—as its 1989 presidential candidate. On July 24, these three social democratic parties comprising the MI—the PGP, PDC, and UC—formally created a left-of-center electoral alliance within the MI called the New Sector (Nuevo Espacio), which reaffirmed Batalla as its presidential candidate.

Juan Guillermo Young and Carlos Vassallo, dissidents from the conservative Civic Union of Uruguay (Unión Cívica del Uruguay—UCU), a Catholic party founded in 1912, founded the PDC in 1962, when the UCU officially became the PDC. A left-of-center party, the PDC advocated social transformation through democratic means. The PDC soon fractionalized. In 1971, when the PDC joined with the PCU and PSU in the Broad Front, PDC dissidents, including former UCU members, broke away and formed the UC, an anti-Marxist social Christian party. The UC recognized a Christian democratic faction that also split from the PDC in 1980. From November 1982 to August 1984, the military regime banned the PDC for its policy of casting blank ballots.

In the second half of the 1980s, the UC was divided between its traditional sector, the Progressive Faction (Corriente Progresista), led by Humberto Ciganda and made up of other longtime leaders, and the Renewal Faction (Corriente Renovadora), led by members of the Chamber of Representatives Julio Daverede and Heber Rossi Passina, UC secretary general Héctor Pérez Piera, and youth leaders. One leader of the UC's Progressive Faction, the late Juan Vicente Chiarino, served as Sanguinetti's defense minister. The withdrawal of the UC's presidential candidate, Ciganda, from the November 1989 elections widened the split within the party.

Democratic Consolidation, 1985–90

The Sanguinetti Administration

The Sanguinetti government pursued a moderate and pragmatic approach to the nation's problems. Having inherited a US$4.9 billion foreign debt accrued almost entirely during the military regime, the Sanguinetti government focused on foreign trade. On April 1, 1986, after several months of negotiations among the principal parties—the ruling Colorados, the Blancos, the Broad Front, and the UC—the leaders signed an agreement to promote the country's economic and social development.

In August 1986, Sanguinetti, with the backing of his Colorado Party, submitted an unrestricted amnesty bill for the military and police to the General Assembly as an extension of the pardon granted to the Tupamaros. The government was able to obtain only fifty-five of the necessary sixty-six votes, however, so the proposal was rejected. The ruling Colorado Party then voted in favor of the bill sponsored by the National Party, which recommended trials only for those responsible for serious human rights violations. The Senate rejected the National Party bill as well, setting the stage for the worst political crisis in twenty months of democratic government. Lacking a majority in either of the two chambers, Sanguinetti met with opposition National Party leader Ferreira to attempt to reach a political solution on a number of points: the human rights issue; the extreme lack of expediency in General Assembly deliberations; interparty differences over the proposed national budget; and frequent clashes between the government and the opposition. In the first step leading to a resolution, the government and the National Party reached an agreement on the budget report, which the General Assembly subsequently approved.

In December 1986, after acrimonious debate (including fistfights in the Chamber of Representatives), the General Assembly approved the government's alternative to an amnesty, consisting of a "full stop" to the examination of human rights violations committed by 360 members of the armed forces and police during the military regime. According to Amnesty International, thirty-two

Uruguayan citizens "disappeared," and thousands were victims of persecution and torture during that period. Groups opposed to what they called the "impunity" law—including the MNR, the Broad Front, the Tupamaros, the UC, and the most important labor confederation—launched a campaign, spearheaded by the MNR, to force a referendum on the issue. Led by human rights activists, university professors, and artists, these groups laboriously collected the required 555,701 "recall" signatures, all of which had to be certified by the Electoral Court. The measure carried by only 230 signatures. According to the constitution, the signatures of at least 25 percent of the electorate are needed for the holding of a referendum to revoke a law passed by the General Assembly.

Those who favored keeping the full-stop law—including the ruling Colorado Party and the Ferreira-led For the Fatherland (the principal National Party faction)—argued that the amnesty had given the country four years of stability and military obedience to democratic rule. They warned that a repeal could spark an army revolt. Nevertheless, the MRB supported the call for a referendum on the full-stop law. In the obligatory April 16, 1989, referendum—in which 85 percent of the population participated—Uruguayans voted by a decisive 57 percent to 43 percent to keep the full-stop law in effect and thereby maintain a peaceful democratic transition. Although the referendum's aftermath was characterized by tranquillity and a spirit of reconciliation, it highlighted Uruguay's growing generation gap. Approximately 75 percent of Montevideo residents between eighteen and twenty-nine voted against the full-stop law.

The November 1989 Elections

Of the dozen candidates running for the presidency in the elections of November 26, 1989, the two front-runners were the National Party's Lacalle and the ruling Colorado Party's Batlle Ibáñez (see table 17, Appendix). Both were from political families and were grandsons of the founders of their respective parties. The tradition of public service went back even further for Lacalle; his great-grandfather, Juan José de Herrera, was minister of foreign affairs in Blanco governments in the nineteenth century. Batlle Ibáñez—a lawyer, senator, and leader of the Colorado Party's majority sector, United Batllism (Batllismo Unido—BU)—descended from three presidents: his great-grandfather Lorenzo Batlle y Grau (1868–72), his great–uncle José Batlle y Ordóñez (1903–07, 1911–15), and his father, Luis Batlle Berres (1947–51).

The personalities of Lacalle and Batlle Ibáñez, rather than policy differences, dominated the campaign, although the issues debated

Flag-wavers outside the Legislative Palace on March 1, 1985,
President Sanguinetti's inauguration day
Courtesy Charles Guy Gillespie

were the ones that traditionally distinguished the two parties.
Whereas the Colorado Party emphasized the role of the government in promoting the national welfare, the National Party focused
on Uruguay's people and society as being primarily responsible
for their own destiny. The more controversial issues included
"privatization" of state enterprises—such as the telephone company and ports—and the extension of university education to the
interior. Both Batlle Ibáñez and Lacalle advocated reducing the
state's economic role, seeking foreign investment, and taking on
the leftist-led unions. One difference was that Batlle Ibáñez favored
paying the country's foreign debt, whereas Lacalle favored renegoti-
ating it (see Foreign Policy in 1990, this ch.). In a televised debate
in October 1989, Batlle Ibáñez repeatedly noted their agreement
on issues, while Lacalle distanced himself from his opponent, thereby apparently outscoring him. In general, the campaign was very
respectful and lacking in "dirty tricks."

Other 1989 presidential candidates included, on the Blanco side:
Carlos Julio Pereyra, leftist leader of the MNR; Alberto Sáenz de
Zumarán, a strongly antimilitary centrist endorsed by the Social
Christian Movement (Movimiento Social Cristiano—MSC); and
the CNH's Francisco Ubilles. On the Colorado side, candidates

181

included Sanguinetti's former minister of labor and social welfare, Hugo Fernández Faingold, the MAS leader; and Jorge Pacheco Areco, the former president (1967–72) and later ambassador to Paraguay, as well as leader of the Colorado and Batllist Union (Unión Colorada y Batllista—UCB), who ran on a ticket with Pablo Millor Coccaro, whom he selected late in the campaign. Pacheco's authoritarian and austere administration had been widely disliked, and Pacheco had spent his previous seventeen years out of the country—even serving as an ambassador for the military regime—but many Uruguayans still nostalgically identified him with a long-gone period of economic stability and security.

Of the National Party's three candidates—Pereyra, Zumarán, and Lacalle—Lacalle initially had the least support among party members (20 percent), as compared with Pereyra (28 percent) and Zumarán (46 percent), according to a poll commissioned by a weekly news magazine, *Búsqueda,* in July 1988. This standing was reversed, however, by September 1989 when, according to a poll in Montevideo published by *Búsqueda,* 52 percent of those questioned voted for Lacalle, 34 percent for Pereyra, and 10 percent for Zumarán.

The total number of people duly registered to vote in the November 26, 1989, presidential elections was 2.4 million, of which 47.3 percent were Montevideo city residents and 52.7 percent were from the country's nineteen departments. In an upset for the Colorado Party, Lacalle and his running mate, Gonzalo Aguirre Ramírez, won after their party garnered 37.7 percent of the 2 million votes cast, compared with the Colorado Party's 29.2 percent, the Broad Front's 20.6 percent, and the New Sector's meager 8.6 percent. Other parties, including the EE–PV, received a total of 3.9 percent.

The other big winner was the Broad Front, whose mayoral candidate, Tabaré Vázquez, captured Montevideo's municipal government. Vázquez, a cancer specialist and professor of oncology, as well as a member of the PSU's central committee, became the city's first Marxist mayor by obtaining 35 percent of the total vote.

The Colorado Party lost not only the elections but also ten departments and fifteen seats in the Chamber of Representatives. The National Party took seventeen departments, obtaining thirty-nine of the ninety-nine seats in the Chamber of Representatives; the Colorado Party, thirty; the Broad Front, twenty-one; and the New Sector, nine. Of the thirty Senate seats, the Blancos won twelve, the Colorados nine, the Broad Front seven, and the New Sector two. Aguirre's own fledgling RV party overtook the veteran PLP and equaled the MNR by winning 112,000 votes, thereby winning two seats in the Senate and three in the Chamber of Representatives.

The Lacalle Administration

A climate of labor unrest, imminent economic crisis, and growing activism on the political left confronted Lacalle when he assumed office on March 1, 1990. Lacking a parliamentary majority, he formed a "European-style" coalition, called National Coincidence (Coincidencia Nacional), with the Colorado Party, the first such interparty sharing of power in a quarter-century. Nevertheless, the two parties were able to agree only on sharing four cabinet appointments and supporting the new government's fiscal-reform measures.

Lacalle gave the posts of ministers of housing and social promotion, industry and energy, public health, and tourism to the Colorado Party in exchange for the necessary support in the General Assembly for approving various controversial projects regarding education, the fiscal deficit, and the right to strike—measures that labor unions and the left opposed. Lacalle chose Mariano Brito, a law professor with no previous government service, as his defense minister; Enrique Braga, one of his principal economic advisers, as his economy and finance minister; Héctor Gros Espiell, a lawyer-diplomat, as his foreign affairs minister; and Juan Andrés Ramírez, a lawyer-professor who had not previously occupied any key position, as his interior minister.

At the top of Lacalle's policy priorities were regional economic integration and moving Uruguay toward a market economy, largely through privatization of inefficient state enterprises and through free trade (see Foreign Policy in 1990, this ch.). Unlike his predecessor, however, Lacalle found himself confronted with a Marxist mayor of Montevideo, whose Broad Front coalition was opposed to economic restructuring. By mid-1990 the prospects for a "cohabitation arrangement" between the neoliberal, right-of-center president and Vázquez appeared poor. Shortly after taking their respective offices, the two leaders publicly clashed on departmental government prerogatives. Vázquez sought to pursue autonomous policies in areas such as transportation, public works, and health and to decentralize power in Montevideo Department. Lacalle opposed Vázquez's attempts to expand his departmental powers, arguing that a more powerful mayor of Montevideo would undermine the position of the executive branch. The confrontation that effectively ended the co-habitation arrangement took place over Montevideo's new budget, which Lacalle threatened to block.

Political Forces and Interest Groups

The Military

Prior to the 1973 coup, the military exercised influence but had

Punta del Este, host city to international conferences
Courtesy Inter-American Development Bank

rarely intervened directly in the political system. The fact that all of the defense ministers who served between 1959 and 1971 were military men indicated a degree of military influence. By 1984, when the military negotiated with the political parties on a transition to democratic government, the armed forces were considered a de facto political force (see The Growth of Military Involvement in Politics, ch. 5). As Uruguay returned formally to democratic rule in 1985, the armed forces continued to exercise a degree of tutelage over national affairs, despite their depoliticized role. Sanguinetti's defense minister was a retired lieutenant general, Hugo M. Medina (the only military defense minister to serve in the 1980s), who as army commander in chief had refused to serve subpoenas on military officers. A poll commissioned by *Búsqueda* in September 1986 found that an overwhelming majority of Montevideo's population believed, to varying degrees, that the military was still a factor in political power; only 10 percent believed that the military had no power.

Some observers and political party leaders commented on alleged military pressure to defeat a call for prosecution of military officers for human rights abuses. The issue arose in December 1986 after the General Assembly approved the full-stop amnesty law, which exonerated 360 members of the armed forces and the police accused of committing human rights abuses during the military regime. In one demonstration of possible continued military influence, Defense Minister Medina reflected military opinion in condemning the April 1989 referendum to decide the validity of the amnesty law. Medina emphasized that ''the dignity of the national army'' should not be violated. General Washington Varela, head of the Military Academy, warned that the army would ''close ranks'' if the amnesty were rescinded.

Amnesty appeared to be firm, but the question of whether or not the military would retain its traditionally apolitical role in the future was less certain. Stating that ''the Pandora's box of military intervention has been opened in Uruguay,'' Martin Weinstein opined in 1989 that the military would continue to exercise a veto power over government action in human rights and military affairs and possibly assume a tutelary role in areas such as economic policy and labor relations. Military influence in the latter two areas, however, had not yet manifested itself in 1990. In order to demonstrate his authority over the military, Lacalle appointed a civilian as his defense minister and exercised his presidential prerogative to appoint armed forces commanders of his own choosing, regardless of seniority. His appointments of the air force and naval commanders were third and fourth in seniority, respectively, among serving officers.

Labor Unions

In March 1985, Sanguinetti abrogated laws and decrees issued by the military regime that had banned the labor unions, the immunity of labor union leaders, and the right of public and private workers to strike. He also restored the legal status of the primarily communist-led National Convention of Workers (Convención Nacional de Trabajadores—CNT), dissolved by the military regime in 1973; in 1983 the Interunion Workers' Assembly (or Plenum) (Plenario Intersindical de Trabajadores—PIT) adopted the name PIT-CNT to show its link with the banned CNT. The long-repressed labor movement took advantage of its newly granted freedom by staging strikes and marches during the first six months of democracy.

The communist-led Uruguayan labor movement, which claimed to represent about 300,000 of the 1.3 million Uruguayan workers, also called general strikes in the late 1980s, as well as strikes in specific job areas, mostly involving civil service workers or those in state enterprises. In 1986 Sanguinetti's government and the Colorado Party signed a "nonaggression" pact with the PCU. Under the Colorado-Communist Pact (the "Co-Co Pact"), militant labor members of the Colorado Party and the PCU formed alliances whenever the National Party promoted a movement within a labor organization. Nevertheless, the powerful main labor organization, the PIT-CNT, staged three general strikes in 1986.

The attitudes of the leadership of the Moscow-oriented World Federation of Trade Unions (WFTU), which was affiliated with the PIT-CNT, were among the main issues discussed by candidates in the 1989 presidential campaign. The leading candidates endorsed proposals for legislation to require secret strike votes and other union regulation. Labor activity in Uruguay was virtually unregulated. The WFTU supported the PCU and other leftist political groups united in the Broad Front. In November 1989, the movement was preparing for a showdown with the mainstream political leaders over whether or not to espouse a more market-oriented economy with foreign investment. Although the PIT-CNT's leadership opposed increasing foreign investment, the organization was becoming fractionalized among those influenced by *perestroika* (restructuring) in the Soviet Union, those who rejected it, and non-Marxists seeking to challenge leftist domination of the movement.

Lacalle advocated regulating labor union activities, including the right to strike. In his view, the decision on whether or not to strike should be made by the workers in a secret vote, after the failure of obligatory reconciliation efforts. Shortly after Lacalle took office, Minister of Labor and Social Welfare Carlos Cat, who ran for mayor of Montevideo in the 1989 elections, met with representatives of business organizations and the PIT–CNT but failed to reach an agreement. The PIT–CNT demonstrated its right to strike with a six-hour general work stoppage on July 25, 1990, to protest the government's austerity and privatization programs.

Despite Lacalle's efforts to regulate the sector, Uruguay's labor movement in 1990 had significant clout as an interest group, mainly with regard to its highly disruptive strike tactics. Like leftist political organizations in general, however, the labor unions' continued use of the same rhetoric and methods that got results during the military regime were seen by some Uruguayan journalists and sociologists as major contributors to both emigration and apathy among young Uruguayans.

The Roman Catholic Church

The Roman Catholic Church has had only a minimal role in Uruguay because of a strong anticlerical bias bequeathed by Batlle y Ordóñez. Unlike many other Latin American countries, religion has not interfered in politics to any significant extent. Although 66 percent of the population was nominally Roman Catholic in 1990, less than half were practicing Catholics. The church's main political wing was the PDC, which advocated social transformation through democratic means. In addition, there were numerous lay organizations engaged in enhancing the church's social relevance. These included the Catholic Workers' Circle, Catholic Action, the Christian Democratic Youth Movement, and the Catholic Family Movement. The conservatives had few representatives among the clergy.

The election of Lacalle, a devout Catholic, may have reflected ascending Catholic influence in the nation. Another indicator of rising Catholic influence was the establishment in 1984 of the Catholic University of Uruguay in Montevideo, the country's only private university. However, the limits of Catholic influence in Uruguay were highlighted in early 1986 by the failure of a proposal by Catholic conservatives in the Colorado and National parties to ban the film *Hail Mary,* which the church hierarchy regarded as ''pornographic and blasphemous.''

Students

Student organizations have had little influence on their own, but they often supported the demands of labor unions and other groups.

Government and Politics

The University of the Republic, Uruguay's only public university, played a key role as an opposition force during the administrations of Pacheco (1967–72) and Juan María Bordaberry Arocena (1972–76). Shortly after taking office, Sanguinetti ordered the restoration of the legal status of the Federation of Uruguayan University Students (Federación de Estudiantes Universitarios del Uruguay—FEUU). The military regime, whose generals regarded the university as a center of leftist subversion, had banned the FEUU. University of the Republic student elections were held twice during the Sanguinetti administration, and student groups resumed campus political activities. As a result of the June 1989 university elections, leftists retained their dominance in 1990.

The Media

Uruguay's long tradition of freedom of the press was severely curtailed during the twelve years of military dictatorship, especially its final years under Lieutenant General Gregorio Alvarez Armelino (1981–85). During his administration, more than thirty news organizations, including radio stations, publications, and television stations, were closed. On his first day in office in March 1985, Sanguinetti reestablished complete freedom of the press. His government also abrogated a regulation that compelled all international news agencies to supply a copy of all disseminated political news to the Ministry of Interior.

Although newspapers have played an important role in the evolution of Uruguayan party politics, they were generally affiliated with and dependent on one or the other of the traditional parties. This combination of party dependence before the military regime and censorship during it prevented the press and the media in general from developing into a Fourth Estate. After freedom of the press was restored in 1985, however, Montevideo's newspapers (which accounted for all of Uruguay's principal daily newspapers) greatly expanded their circulations and presumably increased their influence (see table 18, Appendix). Most of the twenty-five to thirty interior newspapers were biweekly, except for a couple of regional dailies.

Well over 100 periodicals were published in Uruguay. *Búsqueda* (Search) was Uruguay's most important weekly news magazine. Founded in 1971, *Búsqueda* had close links to civilian economic officials in the Sanguinetti and Lacalle governments and served as an important forum for political and economic analysis. A right-of-center, independent publication, *Búsqueda* had a liberal editorial policy that espoused free markets, free trade, and private enterprise and competition. Although it sold only about 16,000 copies

189

a week, its estimated readership exceeded 50,000. The educational economic status of its readers placed them among the top 3 or 4 percent of the population.

Other periodicals included the PDC's *Aquí,* a weekly founded in late 1984; the monthly *Cuadernos de Marcha,* founded in 1985 by Carlos Quijano—who founded the former weekly procommunist newspaper *Marcha* in 1939—and associated with the Broad Front; *Zeta,* a weekly founded in 1986 and affiliated with the PGP; and *Mate Amargo,* a fortnightly published by the Tupamaros with an estimated readership of 53,000. An additional 100 periodicals were imported from foreign countries.

Fifteen foreign wire services had offices in Montevideo. Persons affiliated with the National Party established Uruguay's first private international news agency, PRESSUR, in 1984. The Sanguinetti government had its own official news service, the Presidential Information Service (Servicio Presidencial de Información—SEPREDI), presumably retained by Lacalle with a new staff. The leading press associations were the Association of Newspapers of Uruguay, the Uruguayan Press Association, and the National Association of Uruguayan Broadcasters (Asociación Nacional de Broadcasters Uruguayos—ANDEBU).

Other Interest Groups

Latinamerica Press reported that West German foundations had a heavy presence in Uruguay, where more than 100 research institutes, all funded from abroad, were engaged in nearly 500 projects. The report noted that the Colorado Party had developed close ties to the Hanns-Seidel Foundation over the years; the PDC and several Christian democratic business associations were connected to the Konrad Adenauer Foundation; the National Party received support from the Friedrich Naumann Foundation; and the PIT–CNT and PGP received financial support from the Friedrich Ebert Foundation.

What influence, if any, these foundations had on government policies was unclear, although their presence presumably enhanced West German-Uruguayan relations. However, when Sanguinetti visited the Federal Republic of Germany (West Germany) in 1987 and signed a technical assistance agreement with the right-wing Hanns-Seidel Foundation, a scandal erupted in Montevideo over whether West German development foundations were using their funds to influence Uruguayan politics. The agreement provided for assistance by the Hanns-Seidel Foundation to the Ministry of Interior in the development of an antiterrorism computer system.

Foreign Relations

Uruguay's foreign policy has been shaped by its democratic tradition, its history of being a victim of foreign intervention, its status as the second smallest republic in South America (after Suriname), and its location between the two rival giants of the region: Argentina to the west and Brazil to the north. In the nineteenth century, Argentina and Brazil did not accept Uruguay's status as an independent republic, and they often invaded Uruguayan territory (see Beginnings of Independent Life, 1830–52, ch. 1). The British and French consuls, for their part, often exercised as much power as the local authorities. Thus, Uruguay's international relations historically have been guided by the principles of nonintervention, respect for national sovereignty, and reliance on the rule of law to settle disputes. The use of military force anywhere except internally was never a feasible option for Uruguay.

According to Bernardo Quagliotti de Bellis, a Uruguayan professor of law, his country had historically defined its foreign policy as based on five principles: affirmation of the right of self-determination of peoples; active participation in the process of political cooperation that attempts to look within and outside the region; coordination of positions on everything possible; recognition of the complexity and the diversity of the problems at hand; and flexibility combined with a sense of precaution.

Beginning with Batlle y Ordóñez's government in the early twentieth century, Uruguay has been active in international and regional organizations. It joined the United Nations (UN) in 1945 and has been a member of most of its specialized agencies. In 1986 Uruguay was elected to membership in the UN's Economic and Social Council. In December 1989, Uruguay signed the United Nations Convention against Illicit Traffic in Narcotic Drugs and Psychotropic Substances. Uruguay belonged to thirty-one other international organizations as well, including the Organization of American States (OAS), the General Agreement on Tariffs and Trade (GATT—see Glossary), the International Telecommunications Satellite Organization (Intelsat), the Latin American Economic System (Sistema Económico Latinamericano—SELA), and the Latin American Integration Association (Asociación Latinoamericana de Integración—ALADI; see Glossary). Uruguay was a signatory of the Inter-American Treaty of Reciprocal Assistance (Rio Treaty), the Treaty for the Prohibition of Nuclear Weapons in Latin America (Tlatelolco Treaty), and the Río de la Plata Basin Treaty.

Uruguay has had strong political and cultural ties with the countries of Europe and the Americas. It has shared basic values with them, such as support for constitutional democracy, political pluralism, and individual liberties. Historically, Uruguay has enjoyed a special relationship with Britain because of political and economic ties beginning in 1828 (see The Struggle for Independence, 1811–30, ch. 1). Bilateral relations with Argentina and Brazil have always been of particular importance. In 1974 and 1975, Uruguay signed economic and commercial cooperation agreements with both countries.

Traditionally, relations between Uruguay and the United States have been based on a common dedication to democratic ideals. Although it initially attempted neutrality in both world wars, Uruguay ultimately sided with the Allies. In World War I, Uruguay did not break relations with Germany and lift its neutrality policy until October 1917. By that time, the government of Feliciano Viera (1915–19) had recognized "the justice and nobility" of the United States severance of diplomatic relations with Germany in early 1917. In 1941 President Alfredo Baldomir (1938–43) allowed the United States to build naval and air bases in Uruguay. The United States also trained and supplied Uruguay's armed forces. In January 1942, one month after Japan attacked Pearl Harbor, Uruguay broke relations with the Axis. The United States reciprocated with generous loans. As a condition for admission to the San Francisco conference, where the United Nations Charter was drawn up, Uruguay declared war against the Axis on February 15, 1945. That year it also signed the Act of Chapultepec (a collective defense treaty of the American republics) and joined the Inter-American Defense Board (IADB). In 1947 it signed the Rio Treaty, a regional alliance that established a mutual defense system.

During the 1973–85 period of military rule, Uruguay's traditionally democratic diplomacy was replaced by "military diplomacy" as determined by the "Doctrine of National Security." This military diplomacy gave priority to the serious problem of national and regional subversion and to historical conflicts affecting regional diplomatic stability, such as the issues of dams between Argentina and Brazil, sovereignty over the Beagle Channel, Bolivia's attempts to regain access to the Pacific from Chile, the Ecuador-Peru border dispute, and South Atlantic security.

Foreign Relations under Democratic Rule, 1985–90

With the return of democratic government in 1985, Uruguay's foreign policy underwent an abrupt change. After taking office, Sanguinetti vowed to maintain and increase diplomatic relations with every nation "that respects the international rules of noninterference in the internal affairs of other countries." He carried out this policy by renewing relations with Cuba, Nicaragua, and China and by strengthening relations with the Soviet Union. Sanguinetti's first foreign affairs minister, Enrique Iglesias, conducted an intensive and successful diplomatic offensive to restore his country's prestige. Once again, Uruguay began to host important international meetings, such as the September 1986 GATT conference and the second meeting of the presidents of the Group of Eight (the successor organization of the Contadora Support Group) in October 1988, at the seaside resort of Punta del Este. More world leaders visited Uruguay during the Sanguinetti administration than ever before in Uruguay's history.

An important element of the Sanguinetti government's foreign policy was the promotion of a more just world economy and of a more free and open trade system. Guided by Iglesias, Sanguinetti reintegrated Uruguay into the region, renewed and strengthened diplomatic and commercial relations with countries that were ignored for ideological reasons during the "military diplomacy" period, negotiated new markets for Uruguayan products, instigated a new round of negotiations in GATT, and designed a new Latin American strategy for dealing with the foreign debt. In April 1988, after Iglesias's election as president of the Inter-American Development Bank (IDB), Luis A. Barrios Tassano became Sanguinetti's second foreign affairs minister. Barrios described Uruguayan foreign policy as "pluralist, multifaceted, nationalist, and flexible."

The United States

Although Uruguay was critical of unilateral United States military intervention in Latin America and elsewhere, bilateral relations during the 1985–90 period were excellent. The United States, which had expressed deep concern about the human rights situation beginning with the administration of Jimmy Carter, strongly supported Uruguay's transition to democracy. In March 1985, Secretary of State George P. Shultz attended Sanguinetti's presidential inauguration. As a member of the Contadora Support Group, Uruguay participated in meetings on Central American issues in 1985–86, particularly United States support for the anti-Sandinista resistance guerrillas in Nicaragua. The Sanguinetti government regarded United States aid to the anti-Sandinista Contra rebels in Nicaragua as an obstacle to peace in Central America. It also opposed the presence of United States troops in Honduras.

Despite his government's criticism of United States military actions in Honduras, in Nicaragua, and against Libya in April 1986, Sanguinetti received a warm welcome at the White House during an official five-day state visit to the United States in June 1986, the first by a Uruguayan president in more than thirty years. During the visit, which was dominated by trade discussions, Sanguinetti criticized United States protectionist policies, such as the decision to subsidize grain exports to the Soviet Union. Nevertheless, he departed Washington satisfied that the administration of President Ronald W. Reagan had adopted a more flexible policy toward Uruguayan exports. Shultz again paid an official visit to Uruguay on August 5, 1988, for talks with Sanguinetti, Barrios, and several opposition leaders. The official talks centered on trade issues.

Although Uruguay's relations with Panama at the time of the United States military intervention there in December 1989 were at their lowest possible level—without an ambassador—Sanguinetti was again critical of the United States. He characterized the United States military operation as a "step backward."

Latin America

Sanguinetti favored the formation of a bloc of debtor countries in Latin America to renegotiate the foreign debt. To that end, in the late 1980s Uruguay joined the Cartagena Consensus (of which Iglesias was secretary) on the foreign debt. Uruguay hosted the temporary secretariat of the Cartagena Consensus follow-up committee, a group of Latin America's eleven most indebted countries.

Uruguay also participated in the Group of Eight, a permanent mechanism for consultation and political coordination that succeeded the Contadora Support Group in December 1986. Like the Contadora Support Group, the Group of Eight advocated democracy and a negotiated solution to the Central American insurgency. It consisted of Argentina, Brazil, Colombia, Mexico, Panama, Peru, Uruguay, and Venezuela. The Sanguinetti government advocated a diplomatic solution to the insurgency in Central America based on the Caraballeda Declaration, a document drawn up on January 12, 1986, by the Contadora Support Group.

The Sanguinetti administration, after direct negotiations with Cuba, resumed Uruguay's commercial and cultural ties with the island nation in April 1985 and diplomatic and consular relations on October 17, 1985. It also reestablished diplomatic relations with Nicaragua. Uruguay had discontinued its diplomatic and consular relations with Cuba on September 8, 1964, in compliance with the decision of the OAS General Assembly, which sought to isolate the regime of Fidel Castro Ruz.

The Sanguinetti government's differences with Cuba's political, social, and economic system, as well as with some foreign policy issues, remained. For example, Sanguinetti disagreed with Castro's

Embassy of the United States, Montevideo
Courtesy Edmundo Flores

proposal to discontinue payment on the Latin American foreign debt. Sanguinetti believed that the resulting financial and commercial isolation would provoke much worse problems. In his view, the Cartagena Consensus, rather than a meeting in Havana, was the appropriate forum in which to discuss the debt issue. Both countries strengthened bilateral relations, however, by signing commercial agreements in May 1986 and March 1987 and by signing a five-year economic, industrial, scientific, and technical cooperation agreement on the latter occasion.

Sanguinetti considered regional integration in the Río de la Plata Basin the key to Uruguay's foreign policy. Uruguay's efforts at promoting integration were aided in the late 1980s by the emergence of democratic governments in Argentina, Bolivia, Brazil, Chile, Peru, and Paraguay. Sanguinetti sought a closer relationship with Argentina, Brazil, and Paraguay in the belief that Uruguay's future was closely linked to the possibility of the integration of the Río de la Plata Basin. Although the Sanguinetti government supported Argentina's claim to sovereignty over the Falkland Islands (Islas Malvinas), it adopted a neutral stance in the conflict between Argentina and Britain (which waged the South Atlantic War over the islands from April to June 1982) and made known its desire that military bases and other facilities not be installed in the South

Atlantic. In May 1985, Argentina and Uruguay signed the Declaration of Colonia, which established the framework for promoting economic and social integration between the two countries. Sanguinetti initiated a similar program of integration with Brazil. In August 1985, the Brazilian and Uruguayan presidents strengthened bilateral relations by holding the first meeting of the General Coordinating Commission and signing thirteen bilateral accords. The presidents of Argentina, Brazil, and Uruguay met in Brasília in 1986 to advance their integration process. In January 1990, Sanguinetti hosted an official visit by the Paraguayan president, Army General Andrés Rodríguez Pedotti, during which integration matters such as the River Transport System (consisting of the Río Paraguay-Río Paraná-Río Uruguay waterway) were discussed.

Other Regions

Since 1926 and renewed in 1943, Uruguay has had diplomatic and trade relations with the Soviet Union, longer than any other South American nation. Relations were at a relatively low level during the military regime. In May 1985, the Sanguinetti government authorized the reopening of the Soviet-Uruguayan Cultural Center and, in September 1986, the opening of an office of the Soviet airline Aeroflot (Air Fleet) in Montevideo, with flights to Moscow beginning in 1987. During a meeting with Soviet foreign affairs minister Eduard A. Shevardnadze at the UN on September 24, 1985, Sanguinetti asked for the Soviet Union's support for Uruguay's desire to join the group of nations operating in Antarctica (which Uruguay subsequently joined). Shevardnadze later visited Uruguay in October 1987.

In the first visit of a Uruguayan president to the Soviet Union, Sanguinetti visited Moscow in March 1988 and held a "cordial and frank" two-hour meeting with General Secretary Mikhail S. Gorbachev. Sanguinetti's visit strengthened trade, economic, and cultural relations, to include the establishment of a joint Soviet-Uruguayan company. Sanguinetti also visited certain East European countries, including the German Democratic Republic (East Germany), and established trade relations.

Optimistic about trade prospects, Uruguay established diplomatic and formal commercial relations with China on February 3, 1988. By 1990 China was Uruguay's fourth largest trading partner. Although both countries had conducted bilateral trade, diplomatic relations had been nonexistent since 1949. With the opening of diplomatic ties with China, Uruguay simultaneously severed relations with Taiwan. In November 1988, Sanguinetti paid a six-day official visit to China at the head of an eighty-member delegation and signed four agreements designed to further strengthen bilateral relations. China's President Yang Shangkun reciprocated with a visit to Uruguay in May 1990. The Sanguinetti government also established trade ties with Malaysia and Singapore and was planning to reopen Uruguay's mission in India.

When Sanguinetti assumed office, Uruguay had only four resident ambassadors in all of the Middle East and Africa. By 1988 Uruguay had opened resident missions in Algeria and Côte d'Ivoire, had reestablished relations with Tanzania, and had established ties with Oman, Qatar, and Bahrain. In May 1986, the Sanguinetti government criticized what it termed the sovereignty and territorial integrity violations committed by the South African government against neighboring countries. It also denounced apartheid and stated its support for the peoples and governments of Botswana, Zambia, and Zimbabwe against South African aggression. Although the Sanguinetti government announced in May 1986 that it was unwilling to recognize the Palestine Liberation Organization (PLO), which it characterized as a terrorist organization, it accorded an official reception at the Ministry of Foreign Affairs to a PLO delegation participating in the first parliamentary congress of socialist parties in Latin America and the Caribbean in June 1989.

Foreign Policy in 1990

The general direction of Uruguayan foreign policy was not expected to change significantly under President Lacalle. His newly designated foreign affairs minister, Héctor Gros Espiell, told reporters in January 1990 that although there would be specific changes, adjustments, and differing viewpoints, the Lacalle government intended to maintain the general guidelines of Uruguay's existing foreign policy. Gros Espiell, the former head of Uruguay's School of Diplomacy, also noted, however, that under the new Foreign Service Law to be submitted to the General Assembly by the Lacalle government, the foreign service would be entirely revamped to make its operations more responsive to the national interests.

Gros Espiell also explained that the Lacalle government's foreign policy would emphasize the trend toward regional integration and that Uruguay would continue pursuing its integration policy with Argentina and Brazil. According to Gros Espiell, the Río de la Plata Basin would be Uruguay's first priority in foreign policy, with the Buenos Aires-Montevideo-Brasília axis functioning in coordination with the Montevideo-Asunción-La Paz axis. In talks with the presidents of Argentina, Brazil, and Paraguay in early 1990, Lacalle discussed ways to increase regional integration in the Río de la Plata Basin. One of Lacalle's foreign policy goals was to integrate Bolivia and Paraguay into the Brazilian-Uruguayan-Argentine integration agreements and grant them free port facilities.

Lacalle favored using the Group of Eight and ALADI as instruments for promoting, with Argentina, a new Latin American integration process. In January 1990, he worked toward this through what he called the Group of Seven (because Panama's membership was suspended in February 1988) with the intention of organizing, within five to ten years, a true Latin American common market. The Lacalle government wanted the Group of Eight (whose name was changed in 1990 to the Group of Rio) to expand to include Bolivia, Chile, Ecuador, and Paraguay.

Lacalle told United States president George H.W. Bush during their unofficial meeting at the White House on February 5, 1990, that Uruguay could play an important role in the Río de la Plata Basin, but this role did not materialize in 1990. The Lacalle government reportedly had become uneasy over what it perceived to be a lack of interest toward integration with Uruguay shown by Argentina and Brazil (see Economic Integration, ch. 3).

Both pro-United States and pro-free market, Lacalle was expected to enjoy excellent relations with the Bush administration. Lacalle's support of the United States varied, however, depending on the issue. When the United States military intervened in Panama in December 1989, Lacalle refused to recognize the new Panamanian government of Guillermo Endara. After the United States troops retreated to the former Canal Zone and their number was reduced to preintervention levels, Lacalle announced in March 1990 that his government would normalize relations with Panama by recognizing the Endara government. In keeping with its traditional position condemning the use of force, the Lacalle government denounced the invasion of Kuwait by Iraq in early August 1990, urged action by the UN Security Council, and endorsed the UN sanctions against Iraq.

On other issues, Lacalle favored the United States policy position on the foreign debt problem and negotiated Uruguay's external debt based on a proposal presented by Secretary of the Treasury Nicolas Brady in March 1989. The Brady Plan called for creditor banks to write off a portion of a developing country's indebtedness in return for guaranteeing repayment of the remaining debt (see Foreign Debt, ch. 3). Lacalle enthusiastically endorsed President Bush's Enterprise for the Americas Initiative (see Glossary), made on June 27, 1990, for promoting the development of Latin America by opening a free-trade partnership with the region, either on a bilateral or on a multilateral basis. Lacalle was somewhat

President Lacalle addressing the Organization of American States, Washington, September 1990
Courtesy Organization of American States (Roberto Ribeiro)

ambivalent, however, toward the United States policy on drug trafficking. He viewed the issue as two sided, involving not only the Latin American producing countries but also the principal consuming country, the United States.

* * *

Although few books on Uruguay's government and politics in the 1980s were available in 1990, Uruguay has been the subject of considerable scholarly research. M.H.J. Finch and Alicia Casas de Barrán's *Uruguay* lists comprehensively and evaluates succinctly major sources, including recent doctoral dissertations, on all aspects of Uruguay. A dated but still historically useful book is Russell H. Fitzgibbon's *Uruguay: Portrait of a Democracy.* A more up-to-date introduction to the country is Martin Weinstein's *Uruguay: Democracy at the Crossroads;* his earlier book, *Uruguay: The Politics of Failure,* analyzes the causes of Uruguay's descent from a model democracy to a military dictatorship. The human rights abuses committed by the military are detailed in Lawrence Weschler's *A Miracle, a Universe: Settling Accounts with Torturers.* An incisive fact-filled chapter on Uruguay's party system may be found

199

in *Party Politics and Elections in Latin America* by Ronald H. McDonald and J. Mark Ruhl. In-depth analyses of the political party system in the 1970s and early 1980s can be found in two Yale University doctoral dissertations: Charles Guy Gillespie's "Party Strategies and Redemocratization," and Luis E. González's "Political Structures and the Prospects for Democracy in Uruguay." Gillespie's *Negotiating Democracy: Politicians and Generals in Uruguay* focuses on Uruguay's transition to democracy. An informative monograph on the November 1989 elections is Weinstein's "Consolidating Democracy in Uruguay: The Sea Change of the 1989 Elections." (For further information and complete citations, see Bibliography.)

Chapter 5. National Security

The colonial fortress museum of Santa Teresa National Park near Laguna Negra in Rocha Department

As OF 1990, URUGUAY FACED no external threat. Its defense posture was based on the country's geostrategic position as a buffer state. Defense planners recognized that the nation could never independently deter invasion, however unlikely, by either of its two giant neighbors—Argentina and Brazil—and instead counted on obtaining aid from one should the other attack. As a result, the armed forces were chiefly organized to cope with internal threats, although Uruguay had no terrorist or insurgency problem in the 1980s and 1990.

During the 1960s and early 1970s, an urban guerrilla movement—the National Liberation Movement-Tupamaros (Movimiento de Liberación Nacional-Tupamaros—MLN-T)—posed a significant threat to national security. The military ruthlessly suppressed the Tupamaros in 1972 after the police proved unable to do so. Although the Tupamaros had been brought under control by then, the military seized control of the government of Juan María Bordaberry Arocena (1972–76) in 1973 in order to suppress all activity it interpreted as threatening the public order. The military's effort to rationalize and legitimize its role as political arbiter was rejected in a 1980 referendum. The defeat was attributable to the country's strong national democratic tradition and to public bitterness over human rights abuses under military rule. The military, itself divided over the armed forces' proper role in national political life, accepted the public's decision, and civilian rule was restored completely in 1985.

After the resumption of civilian rule, the armed forces occupied a position much like that during the period before military rule; they were under the control of the civilian government and were largely excluded from national political and economic decision making. The armed forces continued to embrace a conservative and anticommunist political orientation. The military leadership, however, expressed its commitment to a pluralist democratic system on several occasions during the late 1980s and in 1990.

Acknowledging reluctantly that the nation faced no serious threat to internal order and sensitive to the dictates of a constrained national economy, during the late 1980s the military accepted an approximately 20 percent reduction in personnel, as well as a sigficant reduction in spending. As of 1990, armed forces strength was about 25,200, somewhat higher than the level maintained during premilitary rule.

The army was deployed geographically under regional headquarters; it was organized and equipped principally as a counterinsurgency force. The navy operated a coastal and riverine patrol fleet; it was supported by a small naval air arm. The air force provided counterinsurgency air support and transport and logistics services. Equipment in all three services was aging or obsolete, and, because of shortages of spare parts, some equipment could not operate. The straitened national economy, however, made replacement or modernization of the armed forces inventory unlikely in the near term.

Public order in the late 1980s was chiefly disturbed by occasional—and usually not very lengthy—public demonstrations or labor actions. Little violence was associated with such activities, and for the most part the National Police were able to maintain public order and contain ordinary crime without resorting to unusual force. The National Police were divided into local commands under a departmental chief in each of the country's nineteen departments.

Criminal justice was the responsibility of the national government. The Supreme Court of Justice administered the national judiciary and the country's criminal courts. Constitutional guarantees regarding civil rights and the right to a fair trial were routinely honored. Political prisoners were granted amnesty in 1985 and released from prison; there have been no credible reports of political arrests or human rights abuses since that time.

The Origin and Development of the Armed Forces

The military history of Uruguay is rooted in seventeenth- and eighteenth-century clashes between settlers from Spain's Viceroyalty of the Río de la Plata, ruled from Buenos Aires to the west, and settlers from Portugal's Viceroyalty of Brazil to the northeast (see The Struggle for Independence, 1811–30, ch. 1). At stake was the territory on the east bank of the Río Uruguay known as the Banda Oriental (eastern side, or bank), which formed a buffer between the two viceroyalties. In 1720 Spanish colonists built a fortress at Montevideo as an overt manifestation of their interest in the Banda Oriental and to put a stop to Portuguese expansion.

Evolution of the Army

The first armed forces associated with the Banda Oriental, or what was to become Uruguay, developed after the Spanish hold on Buenos Aires ended in 1810. Montevideo, the only Spanish stronghold in the area, soon became embroiled in the conflict, and residents of the interior of the Banda Oriental rebelled against Spanish rule. Led by José Gervasio Artigas, the independence movement

The colonial Watchman's Tower at Maldonado
Courtesy Prints and Photographs Division, Library of Congress

was started by a band of guerrillas that first joined with the independent government in Argentina to help free Montevideo from Spanish rule. General Artigas prematurely declared Uruguay independent in 1815 and formally took control of the new national army, which consisted of one battalion of ethnic European settlers and one battalion of freed slaves (see Artigas's Revolution, 1811–20, ch. 1).

After Uruguay became an independent state in 1828, the new nation's army consisted of a poorly organized irregular militia, of which a substantial portion of personnel were inducted slaves or minor criminals condemned to service. The army was employed in a short campaign in 1832 against a remnant Indian force. The low quality of the army's personnel and its poor public image, however, made it neither an influential force in politics nor an effective military establishment.

Independence did not bring peace or an end to foreign military intervention. Uruguay was plagued by chronic disorder and repeated insurrections supported by various foreign powers (see Beginnings of Independent Life, 1830–52, ch. 1). Most of the disorder derived from political factionalism, as evidenced in the 1836 struggle between forces led by the nation's first president, General José Fructoso Rivera (1830–35, 1838–43), and his successor, General Manuel Oribe (1835–38), who was backed by Argentina. In 1838 Rivera's army prevailed, and Oribe fled to Buenos Aires. Oribe returned in 1842, however, and, using Blanco and Argentine forces, commenced a nine-year siege of Montevideo that attracted French, British, and Italian intervention. The siege and the war between Colorado forces in Montevideo and Blanco forces outside the capital, known as the Great War (Guerra Grande, 1843–52), helped forge the identities of what were to become the nation's two dominant political parties (see Political Parties, ch. 4).

The end of the nine-year siege of Montevideo was followed by renewed conflict and foreign intervention. The Uruguayan Army in 1852 consisted of infantry, cavalry, and artillery elements and had a total strength of some 1,800 personnel; it was nonetheless unable to control the private political armies kept by local caudillos. In 1858 the country established the National Guard, in which males between seventeen and forty-seven years of age were required to serve. The main effect of the National Guard, however, was to provide local caudillos with better-trained personnel for their armies, which operated under the auspices of various factions of the Colorado Party (Partido Colorado) or the National Party (Partido Nacional, usually referred to as the Blancos).

Foreign intervention on behalf of the Blancos by Francisco Solano López, the Paraguayan dictator, embroiled Uruguay in a bloody war between the Triple Alliance of Argentina, Brazil, and Uruguay on the one side and Paraguay on the other side. During the War of the Triple Alliance (1865–70), some 3,000 Uruguayan troops joined the more professional armies of Brazil and Argentina. The Uruguayan Army emerged from the experience with somewhat more professional standards.

After the challenge of facing a foreign threat ended, the pattern of armed Colorado-Blanco clashes resumed. The war had strengthened the sense of national identity, but party loyalty remained intense, and for many Uruguayans it surpassed loyalty to the state. The army, itself highly politicized, worked to control banditry, engaged in public-works projects, and was active in controlling clashes between the private political armies. The number of combatants in the interparty struggles was never large, and the clashes were punctuated by a number of peace pacts that ended specific uprisings and formally redistributed power held by the dominant Colorados in Montevideo to accommodate Blanco aspirations outside the capital.

The party clashes peaked around the turn of the twentieth century. A serious Blanco rebellion in 1897 ended in a "pact between the parties," but, as in the past, the Blancos used the opportunity to consolidate their power and improve their armed strength. After Colorado president José Batlle y Ordóñez (1903–07, 1911–15) moved to check Blanco growth, Blanco rural leaders rose up in 1904 in the last of the armed conflicts between the two parties (see The New Country, 1903–33, ch. 1).

After the defeat of the Blanco uprising, the army replaced the private armed forces of the caudillos as the nation's dominant armed force. Batlle y Ordóñez appointed and promoted only loyal officers; by 1915 almost all army officers were Colorados. In recognition of the politicization of the army and its growing influence, Batlle y Ordóñez and other civilian leaders followed a careful policy of balancing frequent transfers of loyal and suspected units in and out of Montevideo with increased investment in weaponry and increased personnel. As a result, the army nearly doubled in size between 1904 and 1914; it grew from about 6,000 to 12,000 personnel. Its position as the nation's preeminent military force was strengthened after Uruguay made it illegal to address nonmilitary persons with a military title, which had formerly been a common practice among Blanco forces.

As the prospect of further revolution subsided, the active-duty forces were reduced through attrition in an effort to circumscribe the army's political role. The army was spared serious budget cutting but was reorganized into smaller units intended to be expanded in wartime. The increase in the number of units meant more officers and more promotions; at the same time, the increase in the number of units also made it harder for officers to forge a unified political force. The government and the armed forces leadership placed new emphasis on developing an apolitical and professional military institution, and as a result the army essentially withdrew from the political arena.

After World War I, the army came under the influence of a French military mission, and officers began to train at the Military Academy at St. Cyr, France, and at various specialty schools of the French army. Under a French plan, the country was divided into four military regions, and the military air arm was strengthened. Modern equipment, including aircraft, was imported from various European sources. The army was used to support a coup by President Gabriel Terra (1931–38) in 1933 but did little except to prevent legislators from entering the General Assembly (the nation's bicameral legislature).

During World War II, the United States replaced France as the nation's foremost foreign military influence. United States assistance under the Lend-Lease Agreement focused primarily on aviation. The armed forces spent the 1950s and 1960s pursuing a program of gradual equipment modernization.

Development of the Navy

The Uruguayan Navy was formally established in 1860, and its forces saw action during the War of the Triple Alliance, principally in a transport capacity. The modern Uruguayan Navy, however, owes its professional development to the establishment in 1885 of the Military Academy, which offered training to naval and other officers. By 1910 navy strength was some 1,300 in all ranks, and vessels included gunboats (some armed with torpedoes), steamers, and various other small craft. The separate Naval Academy was established in 1916.

After World War I, many of the navy's aging vessels were withdrawn from service, and replacement was slow. The Naval Air Service was formed in 1925, but the first aircraft were not acquired until 1930. The only significant purchase of vessels between the wars was three patrol vessels and a training ship. Personnel declined to fewer than 1,000.

After the outbreak of World War II and the December 1939 Battle of the Río de la Plata, the government decided to strengthen the navy and the Naval Air Service (see Baldomir and the End of Dictatorship, ch. 1). During the 1940s and 1950s, the navy, and naval aviation in particular, benefited from United States military assistance. In 1959 Uruguay—along with the United States, Argentina, Brazil, and Venezuela—participated in the first large multinational exercise involving Latin American navies. Although the air arm (renamed the Naval Aviation Service in 1951) accounted for 50 percent of naval personnel in 1952, by the late 1960s naval air assets had begun to be withdrawn from service, and few modern replacements were acquired. At the same time, the fleet underwent a modest expansion, and a battalion of marines was added. During the 1970s, the government acquired a small number of vessels to replace aging equipment. In 1981 three large patrol craft were purchased new from France. The sole addition in the late 1980s was a frigate purchased used from the French navy and commissioned in late 1988. In early 1990, the Uruguayan Navy received two decommissioned United States Coast Guard cutters for coastal patrol and antinarcotics work under a United States Department of State antinarcotics program. Acquisitions were insufficient to offset the number of retired vessels, however, and a further reduction of the navy's assets seemed likely as more vessels had to be withdrawn from service.

Creation of an Independent Air Force

Military aviation began in 1913 as the Military Aeronautics Branch of the army, and as early as 1916 a flight training school was established near Montevideo. By the 1930s, the service comprised one bomber and three reconnaissance flights. It operated out of bases at Paso de Mendoza near Montevideo, at Durazno, and at the Military Air School at Pando in Canelones Department. Beginning in the late 1940s, United States military assistance focused on military aviation, and the inventory of military aircraft increased in number and quality. The Air Force Academy was established at Pando in 1950, and aviation instruction formerly conducted at the Military Academy was discontinued. In late 1953, the Uruguayan Air Force, which had continued to function as an integral part of the army, was established as an autonomous organization, equal in status with the army and the navy.

During the 1950s, the air force inventory was relatively well developed. As equipment aged, however, economic constraints prevented replacement, and the inventory grew smaller. By 1990 the air force had shrunk to a very modest size (about 100 aircraft) and operated largely obsolete equipment. Given the nation's continued economic problems and the low-threat environment, the air force appeared likely to remain a well-trained, professional force but one that was poorly equipped.

The Growth of Military Involvement in Politics

Until the 1960s, the military was mostly ignored by politicians and played a marginal role in Uruguayan political life. A military career lacked prestige and respect. Officers came mainly from the lower middle class in the small towns and cities of the interior; troops were recruited from the lowest strata of the rural sector, mainly from the *estancias* (ranches) or from the ranks of the unemployed in the urban shantytowns (*cantegriles*).

In the second half of the 1960s, the military began to function in a limited law enforcement capacity after the national economy suffered a serious downturn and public discontent increasingly came to disrupt internal order. Initially backing up the National Police in confrontations with union members, students, and other protesters, the military was drawn further into the struggle as the decade progressed, manning road blocks, conducting searches, and eventually becoming targets themselves. The most significant threat to public order was the growth of the urban guerrilla movement known as the MLN–T, whose adherents were more commonly known as Tupamaros.

The armed forces leadership was divided internally over the military's new role, but antipathy toward the Tupamaros' Marxist political philosophy was strong among the politically conservative, staunchly anticommunist military leadership. Initially, the police had been charged with handling the problem, but as the disorder worsened, many in the armed forces grew impatient with the police's lack of success. When President Jorge Pacheco Areco (1967–72) called on the army to take over responsibility for the problem on September 9, 1971, the Army Intelligence Service began to draw up a military offensive. After the Tupamaros escalated the guerrilla campaign in April 1972, President Bordaberry, Pacheco's successor, and the General Assembly declared a state of ''internal war'' against them. The army was prepared, and the insurgency was crushed within a few months (see Pachequism, 1967–72, ch. 1).

By this time, however, the armed forces leadership had agreed that the military's duty to the nation required it to pursue a level of internal order that was untroubled by leftist, student, labor, or other opposition or protest. The suspension of constitutional protections during the state of internal war was therefore prolonged by new legislation that put harsh controls on the press and on dissent. The new laws also stated that persons charged with crimes against the national security were denied normal legal protections and were subject to preventive detention and trial in military courts. In June 1973, the military compelled President Bordaberry to accept suspension of the democratic process and institute military rule through the creation of the National Security Council (Consejo de Seguridad Nacional—Cosena), made up of the commanders in chief of the army, navy, and air force, plus an additional senior military officer, and the ministers of national defense, interior, and foreign affairs. The General Assembly was abolished on June 27 and replaced with the thirty-member Council of State (Consejo de Estado). A new armed forces organic law, adopted in February 1974, assigned the military the role of protector of the nation's traditional way of life against a communist threat. Beyond that general mission, however, the military had no coherent ideological agenda or any organized plan for national development. No charismatic military leader emerged to centralize power. Instead, decision making was characterized by consensus among senior officers, who were determined to use the military's new powers to impose internal order (see The Military Government, 1973–85, ch. 1).

Until the 1972–73 period, the Uruguayan armed forces were among the least politicized in Latin America. The military had little experience in political affairs and no corporate political philosophy beyond a belief in democracy and an antipathy toward communism and extreme leftist political thought. Many within the armed forces viewed the military's assumption of power in 1973 as a necessary but unfortunate interruption of the nation's democratic tradition. A significant element within the military was never comfortable with the institution's expanded role, however. Nonetheless, during the period of military rule, senior and sometimes mid-level officers served in positions of responsibility in various government agencies, the National Police, some businesses, and autonomous entities (autonomous agencies or state enterprises; see Glossary). In general, military personnel assigned to such posts found themselves poorly prepared in terms of either training or education to take on new responsibilities.

During the 1973–80 period, the military moved ruthlessly against all it deemed a security threat. An estimated 6,000 citizens were tried in the military courts, and critics charged that tens of thousands were detained, denied legal rights, or abused or tortured. During the same period, the military grew from some 22,000 to an estimated 30,000, and military officers began to serve as heads of state enterprises and as governors of departments.

In 1980 the military government attempted to legitimize the armed forces' political role by submitting to public referendum a new constitution that effectively gave the armed forces veto power within a restricted democracy. The regime publicly campaigned that the constitution moved the nation toward democracy. The government also identified opposition to the referendum with support for communism or, conversely, with support for continued military rule. Nonetheless, opposition positions were permitted expression, and the proposed constitution was rejected by 57 percent of the populace.

The armed forces leadership then instituted a process of slow disengagement from economic, political, and administrative positions of power. Surprising many local and foreign observers, the president of the Council of the Nation (Consejo de la Nación, consisting of the Council of State and twenty-eight military officers), which became the supreme governing body in 1976, appointed a retired military general as president of an interim administration designed to initiate a process to return the country to civilian leadership in 1985. In March 1984, the military negotiated the Naval Club Pact with most of the nation's political parties to design the transition, which included reestablishment of the General Assembly. In March 1985, a new civilian president, Julio María Sanguinetti Cairolo (1985–90), was inaugurated. After 1985 the military leadership devoted itself to the management of a depoliticized and professional armed forces establishment.

The process of the military's withdrawal from national political life was difficult. There were charges in the 1985–86 period, for instance, that the armed forces intelligence services continued to monitor opposition groups as potential sources of subversion. Such charges had died down by the late 1980s, after passage of a new armed forces law that reaffirmed the supremacy of civilian command and after senior military leaders made public statements of allegiance to civilian democratic rule.

The most difficult issue facing the nation in the wake of the return to civilian rule was how to treat military officers who had committed offenses during the period of military rule. In an effort to calm military and police fears and to put the nation's troubled past behind it, the Chamber of Representatives passed, by a vote of sixty to thirty-seven, an amnesty bill on December 22, 1986, to prevent prosecution of nearly all such offenses. Almost immediately, opponents of the law launched a movement to bring the bill to a public referendum. After protracted legal deliberations, the bill was placed before the voters in 1989, and the public voted to retain the amnesty provisions. As of the end of 1990, the military continued to play a very minor role in the national economic and political life, and officers were no longer seconded to serve in the civilian administration.

The Armed Forces in the National Life

The armed forces continued to contribute to national development through civic-action programs in 1990. The army's engineers were heavily involved in road building, repair, and maintenance; bridge construction; maintenance of the internal telecommunications network; and construction of public-works projects, such as schools and government buildings. The army's Military Geographic Service was responsible for all mapping. The navy trained and supervised the nation's merchant marine and operated navigational aids along inland waterways. The navy also conducted oceanographic studies, and its port facilities provided support and repair to Uruguay's fishing and merchant fleets. The air force controlled and maintained the country's airports and regulated civil aviation. It also transported passengers and cargo to isolated areas.

All services provided disaster-relief assistance. The army, for instance, constructed emergency dams and provided transportation in times of special need. The air force was active in search-and-rescue operations, air evacuation, and airlifts of emergency supplies. The navy provided surface and air rescue operations at sea, and in times of flooding it provided emergency transportation.

Manpower

Unlike most Latin American countries, entrance into the armed forces was entirely through voluntary recruitment; there was no system of compulsory service. Initial enlistment was for one- or two-year terms, depending on the service and the assignment, and there was little difficulty in filling vacancies. Recruits were attracted by benefits, which included early retirement with pension, and by the opportunity to attend armed forces schools, which provided skills useful in civilian occupations. Noncommissioned officers (NCOs) were career soldiers, sailors, or airmen who were chosen from the recruits toward the end of the initial period of service. The small size of the armed forces permitted selection of physically qualified applicants; in keeping with the country's high literacy rate (96 percent in 1990), recruits generally had at least a basic education (see Education, ch. 2).

In 1990 over 573,000 males were fit for military service; enlisted personnel were between eighteen and forty-five years of age. A loosely organized reserve was made up of approximately 120,000 former members of the armed forces. Constituting only about 0.8 percent of the total population, the armed forces were not a drain on the country's work force.

Morale in the military services was generally adequate in 1990. The 1989 defeat of the referendum to overturn amnesty provisions for most military personnel who committed offenses during the period of military rule appeared to quell any lingering uneasiness in the armed forces over the relinquishment of power. The decrease in personnel during the 1985-87 period drew some protest, especially among those forced to leave service. Low levels of pay continued to be a major morale problem, despite a number of partially compensating benefits. The Ministry of National Defense reported in mid-1988 that from 1973 to 1988 enlisted men's salaries lost 34 percent of their purchasing power; officers' salaries, 44 percent; and auxiliary personnel's, 21.5 percent.

Military personnel, active-duty and retired, as well as their dependents, were entitled to medical care provided by the armed forces medical services. Officers could retire on partial pay after twenty years of service and on full pay after thirty years. NCOs received the same benefits after fifteen and twenty years of service, respectively. Additional allowances were provided for hazardous duty.

Military Justice

According to the constitution of 1967, the military justice system had jurisdiction over military offenders who committed crimes during wartime; in peacetime the system had jurisdiction only over military personnel charged with committing military offenses. During the period of military rule, civilians charged with crimes against the national security were tried by military courts, as were most offenses committed by military personnel. The role of the military justice system was greatly reduced because of the return to democracy, however, and since that time the Supreme Court of Justice has consistently held that in peacetime, jurisdictional disputes between the parallel civil and military court systems should be resolved in favor of the civil courts. Whenever the Supreme Court of Justice accepted a military case on appeal, the law required that two military judges serve on the court on an ad hoc basis.

The Supreme Military Tribunal, which was composed of five members, four of whom had to be military field-grade officers, was the highest military appeals court for military offenders. Beneath it were two military judges of first instance, who had original jurisdiction over serious offenses and appellate jurisdiction over less serious offenses. Those who had committed less serious offenses were first tried by lower court judges.

Defense Spending

According to the latest government figures available in 1990, the defense budget for 1986 was N$Ur22.8 billion (for value of the Uruguayan new peso—see Glossary), or between US$125 million and US$150 million, depending on the source of information. The figure represented approximately 11.8 percent of total central government expenditures, down from the 12 percent to 15 percent levels sustained in the early 1980s. When measured in current pesos, military spending rose sharply during the 1979–86 period. When factoring in inflation, however, spending rose slowly during the 1977-81 period, then fell approximately 20 percent over the 1982–86 period.

The decline in real growth in the defense budget during the 1982–86 period was accompanied by a dramatic depreciation of the peso, making the dollar value of defense spending fall by some 62 percent over the period. This decline had a serious effect on military readiness by virtually precluding importation of spare parts, replacements, or modern equipment. Between 1977 and 1983, military equipment had accounted for between 0.5 and 3.7 percent of total annual imports. From 1984 to 1987, the nation imported no military supplies. As of 1990, a frigate imported in 1988 from France represented the only significant purchase of military equipment after 1983. There were unconfirmed reports in the international press, however, that in March 1990 the nation purchased two more frigates of the same class.

When compared with other Latin American countries, the portion of the national budget devoted to defense was above average.

The military's portion of the gross national product (GNP—see Glossary) was about 2.4 percent in 1986, in the middle range for Latin American nations.

Until the late 1970s, the defense budget was augmented by large amounts of United States military assistance. Over the 1950–77 period, the country received nearly US$60 million of assistance in the form of grants and credits from the United States. During the 1977–78 period, however, the nation refused further assistance in response to harsh criticism from the administration of President Jimmy Carter over the military government's human rights abuses. The United States resumed military assistance to Uruguay in 1987, after the return to civilian rule, but on a very limited level, in keeping with the overall reduction of United States security assistance worldwide. Aid during the 1987–90 period consisted of approximately US$1 million in grants intended to maintain equipment acquired from the United States. The United States also funded the education of a small number of Uruguayan military personnel at United States military facilities under the International Military Education and Training (IMET) program. IMET assistance in United States fiscal year (FY) 1990 totaled US$124,000. The United States Department of Defense's FY 1991 request totaled US$200,000.

Uruguay did not export any military equipment. The domestic defense industry was very limited in scope and produced only the most basic military supplies, such as small-arms ammunition, uniforms, and stores. The only exception was the navy's shipyard, which built small patrol craft and was capable of providing drydock, overhaul, and repair support.

Armed Forces Organization, Training, and Equipment

Under the constitution, the president is commander in chief of the armed forces and exercises administrative control over the three services through the Ministry of National Defense. In practice, operational control passed through the service commanders, who were appointed by the president. There was a nominal chief of the joint staff but no substantive joint staff organization. In 1990 the defense minister was a former law professor who had been active in the transition to democracy. Assistants from each of the three services were assigned to the minister.

During the 1973-85 period, first the military government's Council of State and then the Council of the Nation passed several laws that limited the president's military control. Principal among these was the February 1974 decree that served as an organic law for the armed forces. Under this law, the commanders of the three services were chosen by a board of generals from each respective service. During the 1984-85 transition to civilian rule, the appointment procedure was amended so that the boards of generals chose candidates from which the president then appointed service chiefs of staff. In 1986 the reestablished General Assembly returned the power of direct appointment of the service commanders to the president.

In 1987 the General Assembly passed a new organic law for the armed forces establishing that the "basic duty of the armed forces is to defend the honor, independence, and the peace of the republic, its territorial integrity, its Constitution, and its laws." The law explicitly stated that the armed forces should always act under the supreme command of the president and the minister of national defense in keeping with constitutional measures currently in force. Training practices were modified to include courses for military cadets on the proper role of the military in a democracy. The length a service commander could serve was cut from eight to five years, and service commanders were required to retire when the term of service expired. As of 1990, the government and the armed forces appeared to be adhering to all provisions of the law.

The Ministry of National Defense was responsible for the administration of military training, health, communications, and construction, and it supervised the military retirement and pension system. The ministry supervised the triservice Military Institute for Advanced Studies, which served as a national war college to train senior officers. Also under the ministry was the General Directorate of Defense Information (Dirección General de Información de Defensa—DGID). As reorganized by the executive branch in 1989, the DGID was a triservice agency that coordinated and planned all operations of the three separate military intelligence services. Traditionally, the army's intelligence branch was the most powerful of the military intelligence services.

The country was divided into four military regions. Military Region I, headquartered at Montevideo, had responsibility for the national capital and the departments of Montevideo and Canelones (see fig. 1). Military Region II, headquartered at San José, included the departments of Colonia, Durazno, Flores, Florida, San José, and Soriano. Military Region III, headquartered at Paso de los Toros, comprised the departments of Artigas, Paysandú, Río Negro, Rivera, Salto, and Tacuarembó. Military Region IV, headquartered at Maldonado, included the departments of Cerro Largo, Lavalleja, Maldonado, Rocha, and Treinta y Tres.

Uruguay had cordial foreign military relations with both Argentina and Brazil, as well as with the United States. During the 1980s, armed forces personnel represented the nation in foreign peacekeeping activities in Cambodia, on the Angola-Namibia border, in the Sinai, and on the Iran-Iraq border. Uruguay was a member of the Inter-American Defense Board (IADB), which maintained a headquarters and staff in Washington and acted as a military advisory group to the Organization of American States (OAS), of which Uruguay was also a member.

Uruguay had a long history of military cooperation with neighboring countries. It joined with twenty other Latin American nations and the United States in 1945 to sign the Act of Chapultepec, in which each agreed to consult on any aggression against a cosignatory. Uruguay was also a signatory to the 1947 Inter-American Treaty of Reciprocal Assistance (Rio Treaty), in which the United States and Latin American and Caribbean countries committed themselves to working toward the peaceful settlement of disputes and collective self-defense in the Americas. Uruguay also was a signatory to the 1967 Treaty for the Prohibition of Nuclear Weapons in Latin America (Tlatelolco Treaty) and the Treaty on the Non-Proliferation of Nuclear Weapons. Uruguay also accepted the Biological Weapons Convention, which prohibits the development, production, or stockpiling of such weapons.

Army

In May 1990, Lieutenant General Guillermo de Nava, the army commander, defined the army's mission and the role of its members. He stressed that "for the government and the country the most important action of the army is the exact compliance with our fundamental role that is defined in the law and which consists of defending the honor, the independence, and the peace of the Republic, the integrity of its territory, its Constitution, and its laws." He also maintained that the armed forces must take action against "all types of aggression."

Army personnel in 1990 numbered some 17,200, a reduction of 22 percent from the 1983 level of 22,000. The army consisted of infantry, cavalry, artillery, engineer, signal, administrative, transport, matériel, medical, and veterinary services. The chief of the army staff presided over staff sections for personnel, intelligence, operations and instruction, logistics, and public relations.

The army's main tactical units were organized under four corps headquarters that were administrative rather than operational. Each corps was located in one of the four military regions (each army corps bore the same number as the military region). The four corps together had one independent infantry brigade, fifteen infantry battalions, six engineer battalions, six artillery battalions, and ten cavalry battalions (four horsed, three mechanized, two motorized, and one armored). Each corps was responsible for at least three infantry battalions, one engineer battalion, and one field artillery battalion, as well as logistics, signals, and support units. The number and type of cavalry battalions within each corps varied. The First Corps at Montevideo was traditionally the most powerful of the army's main command elements. Its cavalry units included one horsed battalion, one mechanized battalion with scout cars, and one motorized battalion. The artillery command of the First Corps had one antiaircraft battalion in addition to its field artillery battalion.

One independent infantry brigade headquarters that performed many of the army's administrative functions was attached to army headquarters at Montevideo. The brigade was responsible for one armored battalion, one airborne battalion, and one ranger infantry battalion. Also at the army level was one motorized cavalry battalion that functioned as a presidential bodyguard and performed ceremonial duties. One engineer brigade made up of two battalions, as well as assorted logistics and support elements, completed the units assigned to army headquarters.

The Second Corps was headquartered at San José. Under it was an armored cavalry battalion equipped with light tanks and armored personnel carriers (APCs). The Third Corps, at Paso de los Toros, had two horsed battalions and one mechanized cavalry battalion. One of its infantry battalions was equipped with APCs. The Fourth Corps was headquartered at Minas. Within the Fourth Corps, one horsed battalion and one mechanized cavalry battalion were located at Melo.

Major ground force arms were relatively heterogeneous in origin. Much was obsolete United States equipment, some acquired thirdhand from various foreign sources. The armor inventory included fifty-four light tanks, all of United States or Belgian origin (see table 19, Appendix). The army also had Belgian-, United States-, and Brazilian-made armored vehicles. APCs included United States and West German models. Artillery pieces and air defense guns were of Swedish, Argentine, and United States manufacture. In general, the entire inventory was aging and in need of modernization, but economic considerations—combined with the absence of a significant internal or external threat—made it unlikely that new equipment would be ordered in the near future.

Army officers were trained at the four-year Military Academy, from which they were commissioned as second lieutenants. The army's School of Arms and Services provided specialist training for recruits and officers. The Command and Staff School trained mid-level officers for promotion to staff or field positions.

Navy

As of 1990, naval strength stood at 4,500, which included both naval air personnel and marines. Personnel had been reduced from a high of 6,200 in 1983. The only naval base in operation was located at Montevideo, where facilities included a dry dock and a slipway. In addition to the naval staff, the navy's commander was assisted by the chief of forces afloat and the chiefs of naval education and training, naval aviation, customs, and the marine police.

The navy was active in riverine and offshore patrol, transport, and sea-and-air rescue. In the late 1980s, naval vessels seized foreign boats caught fishing illegally in the country's territorial waters. The navy also played a role in interdicting drug traffickers.

The fleet command was divided into one escort division and one patrol division. The escort division operated a newly acquired French frigate, as well as one other frigate, one destroyer escort, and one corvette, all formerly in service with the United States Navy (see table 20, Appendix). The patrol division had three relatively modern French-built large patrol craft, one antiquated Italian-built large patrol craft, two United States-built large patrol craft (delivered in February 1990), and two small patrol craft. The fleet also included one minesweeper, five amphibious landing craft, one training vessel, and a small number of support and utility craft. An additional two frigates of the same class (Rivière) as that purchased in 1988 were contracted for in February 1990. The ships were due for extensive refitting, making their delivery date uncertain.

Uruguayan Naval Aviation had 400 personnel. Operations were divided into combat, communications, and training elements. All naval aircraft were based at the naval air base at Laguna del Sauce in Maldonado Department. The marine detachment numbered 500 and was organized into a single battalion.

All naval schools were located at the Naval Training Center in the Montevideo port area. Naval officers underwent a five-year course at the Naval Academy, graduates of which were also commissioned in the National Maritime Police and the merchant marine. The senior school for naval officers was the Naval War College. Enlisted personnel were trained at the School of Naval Specialization.

The navy commanded the 1,500-strong National Maritime Police, which performed coast guard duties, supervised the nation's ports and merchant marine, and acted as a harbor police. The maritime police operated three small patrol craft and a buoy tender. Its personnel were trained by the navy.

Air Force

Air force strength in 1990 was 3,500, down from 4,400 in 1983. The air force was equipped with eighteen combat aircraft, seven of which were used principally as trainers (see table 21, Appendix). The air force generally operated out of bases at Paso de Mendoza, Carrasco, Durazno, Laguna del Sauce, Laguna Negra, and Punta del Este.

The commander of the air force was assisted by a staff with sections for personnel, intelligence, operations, and matériel. The air force was organized into tactical, training, and matériel commands. The Tactical Air Command, whose headquarters were at Carrasco Air Base outside of Montevideo, was responsible for the operation of most of the service's assets. These were apportioned between two air brigades. The first had one fighter squadron, three transport squadrons (which were also responsible for regular civilian flights), and a sea-and-air rescue group at Carrasco. The second brigade, at Durazno Air Base, had one training squadron for fighters and one liaison unit with other aircraft.

The Air Training Command, with one training squadron, was headquartered at the General Artigas Military Airport in Pando. It oversaw the Air Force Academy and the Military Air School at Pando and the Command and General Staff School at Carrasco, which provided advanced training for officers. The Air Technical School at Pando gave specialist training to officers and trained air force recruits. The school also trained paratroopers for the army. Attached to the Air Training Command were a small number of fixed-wing and rotary aircraft. The Air Matériel Command consisted of maintenance, supply, communications, and electronics elements. It also oversaw the administration and operation of military and civilian airfields.

Uniforms, Ranks, and Insignia

All three branches of the service had summer, winter, and dress uniforms. The army winter uniform was made of green gabardine, and the summer uniform was made of beige tropical worsted. For dress, a white blouse was worn in the summer. Navy and air force uniforms were similar in style and color to those of the respective United States forces. The blouse of the navy winter uniform was double breasted, and that of the summer uniform was single breasted.

Officer and enlisted ranks corresponded generally to those of the United States Armed Forces. Army officer ranks were indicated

URUGUAYAN RANK	ALFÉREZ	TENIENTE SEGUNDO	TENIENTE PRIMERO	CAPITÁN	MAYOR	TENIENTE CORONEL	CORONEL	GENERAL	TENIENTE GENERAL
ARMY									
UNITED STATES RANK TITLE	2D LIEUTENANT	1ST LIEUTENANT	1ST LIEUTENANT	CAPTAIN	MAJOR	LIEUTENANT COLONEL	COLONEL	BRIGADIER GENERAL	MAJOR GENERAL/ LIEUTENANT GENERAL
URUGUAYAN RANK	ALFÉREZ	TENIENTE SEGUNDO	TENIENTE PRIMERO	CAPITÁN	MAYOR	TENIENTE CORONEL	CORONEL	BRIGADIER GENERAL	TENIENTE GENERAL
AIR FORCE	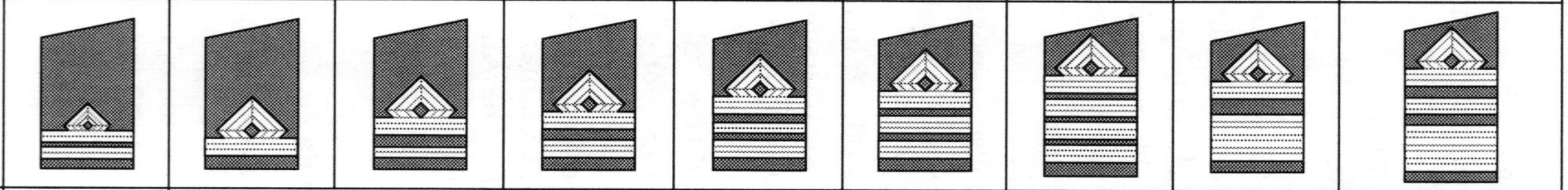								
UNITED STATES RANK TITLE	2D LIEUTENANT	1ST LIEUTENANT	1ST LIEUTENANT	CAPTAIN	MAJOR	LIEUTENANT COLONEL	COLONEL	BRIGADIER GENERAL	MAJOR GENERAL/ LIEUTENANT GENERAL
URUGUAYAN RANK	GUARDIA-MARINA	ALFÉREZ DE FRAGATA	ALFÉREZ DE NAVÍO	TENIENTE DE NAVÍO	CAPITÁN DE CORBETA	CAPITÁN DE FRAGATA	CAPITÁN DE NAVÍO	CONTR-ALMIRANTE	VICE-ALMIRANTE
NAVY	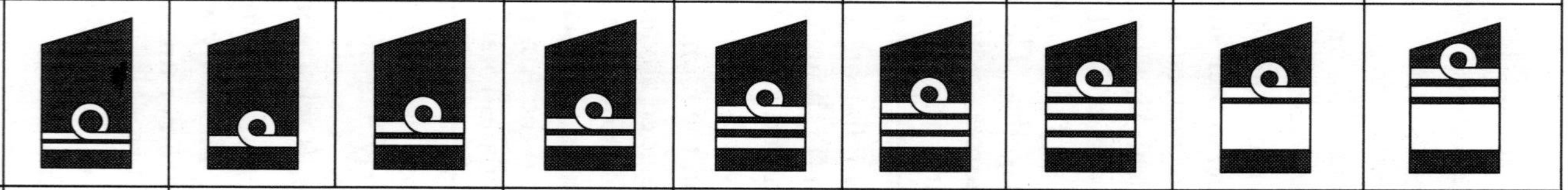								
UNITED STATES RANK TITLE	ENSIGN	LIEUTENANT JUNIOR GRADE	LIEUTENANT JUNIOR GRADE	LIEUTENANT	LIEUTENANT COMMANDER	COMMANDER	CAPTAIN	REAR ADMIRAL LOWER HALF	REAR ADMIRAL UPPER HALF VICE ADMIRAL

Figure 10. Officer Ranks and Insignia, 1990

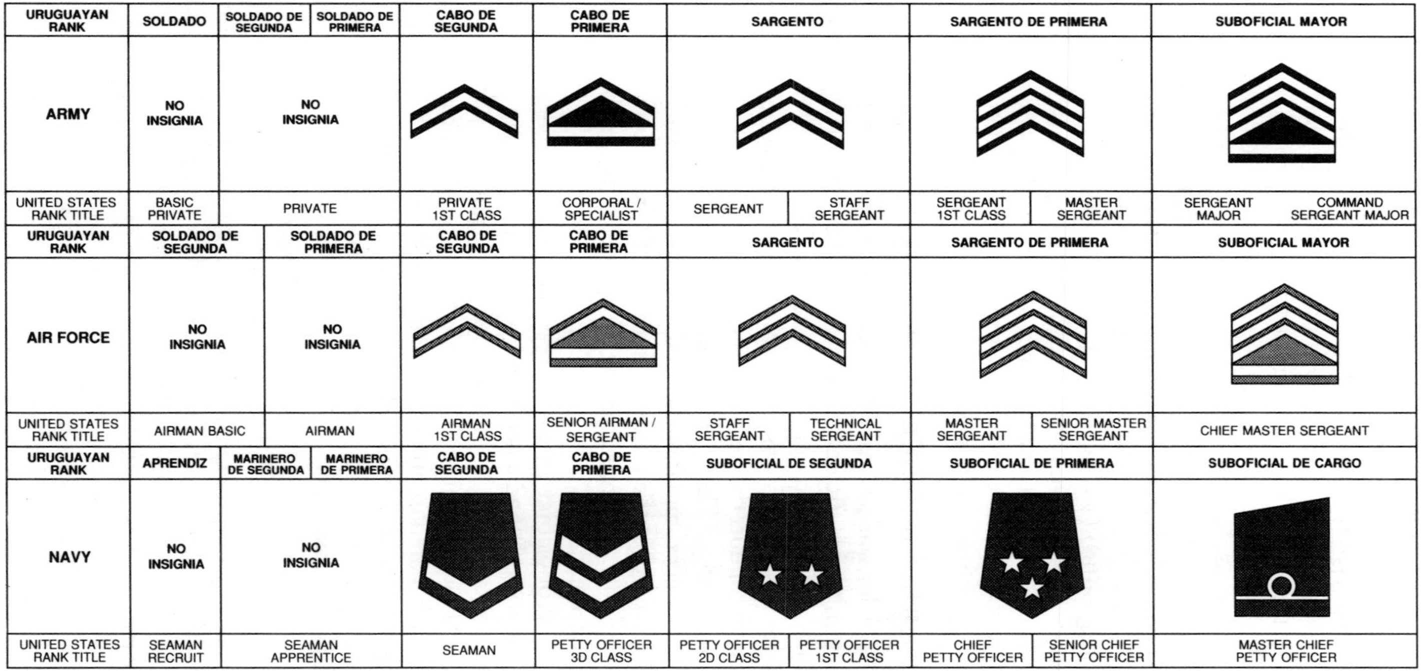

Figure 11. Enlisted Ranks and Insignia, 1990

	SOLDADO	SOLDADO DE SEGUNDA	SOLDADO DE PRIMERA	CABO DE SEGUNDA	CABO DE PRIMERA	SARGENTO	SARGENTO DE PRIMERA	SUBOFICIAL MAYOR
URUGUAYAN RANK	SOLDADO	SOLDADO DE SEGUNDA	SOLDADO DE PRIMERA	CABO DE SEGUNDA	CABO DE PRIMERA	SARGENTO	SARGENTO DE PRIMERA	SUBOFICIAL MAYOR
ARMY		NO INSIGNIA		(insignia)	(insignia)	(insignia)	(insignia)	(insignia)
UNITED STATES RANK TITLE	BASIC PRIVATE	PRIVATE	PRIVATE	PRIVATE 1ST CLASS	CORPORAL/ SPECIALIST	SERGEANT / STAFF SERGEANT	SERGEANT 1ST CLASS / MASTER SERGEANT	SERGEANT MAJOR / COMMAND SERGEANT MAJOR
URUGUAYAN RANK	SOLDADO	SOLDADO DE SEGUNDA	SOLDADO DE PRIMERA	CABO DE SEGUNDA	CABO DE PRIMERA	SARGENTO	SARGENTO DE PRIMERA	SUBOFICIAL MAYOR
AIR FORCE		NO INSIGNIA		(insignia)	(insignia)	(insignia)	(insignia)	(insignia)
UNITED STATES RANK TITLE	AIRMAN BASIC	AIRMAN	AIRMAN	AIRMAN 1ST CLASS	SENIOR AIRMAN/ SERGEANT	STAFF SERGEANT / TECHNICAL SERGEANT	MASTER SERGEANT / SENIOR MASTER SERGEANT	CHIEF MASTER SERGEANT
URUGUAYAN RANK	APRENDIZ	MARINERO DE SEGUNDA	MARINERO DE PRIMERA	CABO DE SEGUNDA	CABO DE PRIMERA	SUBOFICIAL DE SEGUNDA	SUBOFICIAL DE PRIMERA	SUBOFICIAL DE CARGO
NAVY		NO INSIGNIA		(insignia)	(insignia)	(insignia)	(insignia)	(insignia)
UNITED STATES RANK TITLE	SEAMAN RECRUIT	SEAMAN APPRENTICE	SEAMAN	PETTY OFFICER 3D CLASS	PETTY OFFICER 2D CLASS / PETTY OFFICER 1ST CLASS	CHIEF PETTY OFFICER	SENIOR CHIEF PETTY OFFICER	MASTER CHIEF PETTY OFFICER

by gold buttons and braiding on shoulder boards; piping of various colors indicated the branch of service. Army enlisted ranks were indicated by yellow chevrons. Rank insignia for officers in both the navy and the air force were indicated by gold bands on the sleeves of the winter uniform and by similar bands on the shoulder boards of the summer uniform. Air force enlisted ranks were denoted by gray chevrons on a blue background, and navy enlisted ranks were indicated by yellow chevrons and stars on a red background (except for the rank equivalent to master chief petty officer, which was designated by a narrow gold band and loop on a navy-blue background) (see fig. 10; fig. 11).

Traditionally, Uruguayan governments have not awarded military decorations. The three branches of the armed forces, however, have awarded special emblems for excellence in graduation standing at the service academies and at service schools.

Public Order and Internal Security

Public order was well established in the nation, and the government committed sufficient resources to law enforcement to maintain domestic order throughout the country. Urban and rural areas were generally safe, as was travel throughout the nation. Citizens were able to conduct day-to-day affairs in peace and without government interference. The constitution guarantees the right to privacy and due process and freedom of the press, association, assembly, and religion. After the return to civilian rule in 1985, all of these rights were routinely respected by the government and by law enforcement agencies.

Several groups that were suppressed or banned under the period of military rule had since emerged as active participants in the national political life. These included leftist political parties, students, and labor organizations. During the late 1980s, each of these groups participated in protests or demonstrations. Such actions required government permits, which were routinely granted. Demonstrations by these groups were generally peaceful and free from government harassment.

Disputes between political parties or between factions of the same party occasionally flared into violence during the late 1980s; violence was usually minor, however, taking the form of vandalism or arson against party offices. In general, few injuries and little damage were sustained. In 1985 the government legalized all political parties, and as of 1990 there were no known political prisoners or any banned or illegal political groups in the nation.

The MLN–T, also known as the Tupamaros, was a former urban guerrilla organization given amnesty in 1985. The MLN–T was established in 1962 by Raúl Sendic Antonaccio, leader of a group of students, peasants, and intellectuals who espoused an extreme nationalist and socialist ideology. Organized according to a clandestine cell-based structure, the movement conducted a guerrilla campaign from 1963 to 1973 that included bank robberies, kidnappings, sabotage, and jail breaks. The army effectively destroyed the Tupamaros in 1972, and its leaders were imprisoned for long terms or forced into exile (see The Military Government, 1973–85, ch. 1). After the remaining Tupamaro prisoners were freed under an amnesty decree in March 1985, the MLN–T publicly renounced armed struggle and committed itself to left-wing parliamentary politics. In 1990 the Tupamaros constituted a marginal political force of some several hundred members (see Political Parties, ch. 4). The group published a newspaper and operated a radio station in Montevideo.

Student organizations, repressed during the military regime, reestablished themselves in 1985 when academic freedom and university autonomy were restored. Several professors who had been dismissed for ideological reasons were allowed to return to their positions as well. During the late 1980s, students held several protests, none of which had a serious effect on public order (see Political Forces and Interest Groups, ch. 4).

Labor unions and labor activists were also targets of repression under the military regime. During the late 1980s, however, labor activity resumed, and several labor actions and strikes took place. Certain of these activities caused localized disruption of day-to-day activities, but most grievances were solved within a short time, and none led to serious violence. In 1986, during a strike by the staff of the state-owned National Administration of Fuels, Alcohol, and Portland Cement (Administración Nacional de Combustibles, Alcohol, y Portland—ANCAP), the military was called in to ensure distribution of fuel but did not act in a law enforcement capacity (see Labor, ch. 3).

Local and international human rights groups operated freely in the nation during the late 1980s, and these groups surfaced no credible reports of killings or disappearances. The constitution forbids brutal treatment of prisoners, and there were few accusations of torture of prisoners after 1985. The most dramatic exception took place in mid-1989, when the death of a bricklayer while in police custody led to charges of police brutality and mistreatment. Although the police maintained the man hanged himself in his cell, controversy over the case led to the resignation of the minister of interior and to the conviction of a deputy police chief for misconduct.

Human rights groups took serious exception to the 1986 law providing amnesty for military and police personnel charged with committing human rights abuses under the military government. According to a study by the General Assembly, some forty-six members of the military and police benefited from the amnesty. Human rights groups, however, claimed that the real number was well over 100. Military and police officers charged with corruption or with financial irregularities were not covered under the amnesty. In 1988 a former army general and a former minister of agriculture and fishing were charged with making illicit financial transactions during the period of military rule.

Crime

Official statistics on the incidence of crime during the 1980s were not available in 1990. In general, however, there did not appear to be an unusual degree of ordinary crime. Judging from reports in the national press, the level of crime was higher in urban areas, particularly in Montevideo, than in rural areas.

Smuggling was a perennial problem for law enforcement officials, and the borders with Argentina and Brazil were periodically closed during the late 1980s in an effort to control trafficking in contraband. In 1989 smuggling surged because of the strength of the Uruguayan new peso relative to Argentine and Brazilian currencies. The resulting fall in government tax revenue and legal domestic trade prompted the government to seal the borders once again. Residents of the border area protested, claiming that the government should differentiate between small- and large-scale smuggling.

During the late 1980s, the nation experienced problems with the sale and abuse of illegal narcotics and with drug trafficking. Stories in the domestic press covered a police raid on a cocaine laboratory and told of seizures of marijuana, LSD (lysergic acid diethylamide), and cocaine. In an effort to focus more resources on the problem, the government in July 1988 announced the formation of the National Council for the Prevention and Repression of Illicit Traffic and Improper Use of Drugs. The new body was responsible for coordinating the nation's antidrug campaign. After the international press reported in 1989 that Uruguayan gold merchants were involved in laundering drug money, the police began investigating possible domestic links to international drug-trafficking organizations.

The National Police

The National Police were established in 1829, one year after the country gained its independence. At that time, each department

A 1984 election campaign poster demanding amnesty for Tupamaros
Graffito denouncing Uruguay's foreign debt and the International
Monetary Fund, displayed during the 1984 election campaign
Courtesy Charles Guy Gillespie

was assigned a police chief, similar to the system in modern use. As of 1990, police forces numbered approximately 17,500, a ratio of about five police officers to each 1,000 inhabitants. At least 20 percent of the total was assigned to the capital area, in which about one-half of the country's total population lived. In all, about 40 percent of the police force was assigned to urban areas, and the remainder were assigned to rural settlements.

Article 168 of the constitution gives the president, acting through the minister of interior, responsibility for the preservation of public order. Article 173 authorizes him to appoint a chief of police for each of the departments, whom he is authorized to remove at will.

The Ministry of Interior had the responsibility for ensuring public safety throughout the nation, except for coastal areas and the shores of navigable rivers and lakes, which were the responsibility of the National Maritime Police, under the Uruguayan Navy. Police training was centralized under the administration of the ministry, which oversaw the operation of the Police Training Academy. The academy, established in 1936, had separate schools for officers and cadets and for other ranks. The course for noncommissioned officers ran for one year, and the course for cadets ran for two years. The academy also offered in-service and specialty courses of varying lengths.

Subordinate to the Ministry of Interior, the National Police were organized into four operating agencies: the Montevideo Police, the Interior Police, the National Traffic Police, and the National Corps of Firemen. Each of these agencies was administratively a separate entity, handling most personnel administration, including recruitment, separately.

The Montevideo Police had five administrative divisions: investigation, security, support services, intelligence, and legal affairs. Operationally, they were divided into the patrol services, canine corps, security and traffic bureau, criminal investigation bureau, and antismuggling brigade. The criminal investigation bureau was unique in that it conducted operations nationwide, not just in the capital area. The Montevideo Police maintained twenty-nine police stations, one of which was concerned solely with urban traffic. The Montevideo Police also worked out of police posts in small towns and villages near the capital.

The Interior Police coordinated the activities of the police forces maintained by each department. The National Traffic Police controlled traffic on the nation's roadways. The National Corps of Firemen was a centralized fire-prevention and fire-fighting agency. Its personnel underwent basic training with police personnel but

*Two Uruguayan marines demonstrate a search of a
vehicle and its occupant.
Courtesy United States Department of Defense*

followed up with specialized training and career assignments.
Detachments of the corps were assigned to police forces in each
department and in the city of Montevideo.

Two police paramilitary organizations were assigned to the capital
area. The first was the Republican Guard, which had some 500
personnel as of 1990. This unit was organized into cavalry elements
used for guard duty, parades, and ceremonial occasions. When
necessary, the Republican Guard was called on for riot duty back-
up for the regular police. The Metropolitan Guard was responsible principally for guarding municipal property, banks, and
embassies. As of 1990, its personnel numbered some 650. The
Metropolitan Guard was conceived of as a paramilitary force and
was equipped with machine guns and riot-control gear. The unit
was also charged with helping the police control disturbances and
acting as a ready reserve for emergencies of all types.

The Criminal Justice System

The constitution provides that judicial power be vested in the
Supreme Court of Justice (see The Judiciary, ch. 4). Immediately
below the Supreme Court of Justice are six appellate courts, including the appellate court on criminal matters. Its judgment is

by unanimous decision of the three justices. The next courts below the appellate courts are the courts of first instance, or lawyer courts (*juzgados letrados*), the principal courts of first instance for criminal felony cases. In 1990 Montevideo had ten courts of first instance to hear criminal cases, the departments of Paysandú and Salto had two each, and each of the other departments had one. The lower justice of the peace courts hear minor cases and have original jurisdiction over most misdemeanors.

The nation's judicial system is based on the Napoleonic Code of 1804. Once a suspect is identified, the constitution requires issuance of a written arrest warrant unless the suspect was caught during the commission of a crime. By law a suspect can be held incommunicado for twenty-four hours, after which he or she must be brought before a judge to answer charges. Judges then have twenty-four hours to decide whether to release or to charge the individual. Once charges are brought, an accused has the right to legal counsel; a public defender is appointed to represent those accused who cannot afford counsel. If the accused is charged with a crime carrying a penalty of at least two years, he or she can be confined during the investigation of the case. Bond is allowed in such cases, provided the individual is not deemed a danger to society or likely to flee.

The constitution requires that all trials be held in public to the extent that they have to be open and give a public statement of the charge. According to the Code of Criminal Procedure, however, arguments by the prosecution and the defense are submitted to the judge in writing, and these written documents are not usually made public. The defense attorney has the right to review all written documents submitted to the court. The constitution does not provide protection against self-incrimination, and at trial an accused can be required to answer any questions from the judge. Based on the written statements submitted, the judge hands down his or her decision (usually without seeing the accused parties in person); there is no provision for trial by jury.

In the second half of the 1980s, several jurists and human rights groups suggested numerous changes to the judicial procedure to increase efficiency and fairness. Among the proposed reforms were the institution of trial by jury and tightened supervision of pretrial investigations, but as of 1990 none of these changes had been made.

The principal source of the nation's criminal law was the Penal Code of 1889, which was amended in 1934 and contained three books. The first book concerned general principles of the law and the definition of offenses, which were divided according to gravity into felonies and misdemeanors. The first book also defined various punishments, which comprised incarceration in a penitentiary or prison, exile, deprivation of political rights, disqualification or suspension of professional qualifications, and fines. It also discussed extenuating circumstances for a defendant, such as age, intoxication, or insanity. The second book concerned felony crimes, including crimes against the sovereignty of the state, the political order, public order, public administration, and public health. The remaining articles in the second book dealt with crimes against persons and property. The third book concerned misdemeanor offenses. In June 1989, the Penal Code was amended to provide sanctions against committing or inciting hatred or other forms of violence against persons based on race, color, religion, or national or ethnic origin.

In addition to the Penal Code, several other statutes covered criminal offenses. Drug legislation was covered in a 1974 law that regulated the commercial sale and use of controlled substances and penalized drug abuse and drug trafficking. Juvenile offenders were treated under a 1934 code for minors that established a juvenile court in Montevideo with jurisdiction over persons under the age of eighteen; in 1990 there were four such courts in Montevideo.

The Ministry of Interior supervised the federal prisons and departmental jails. All nineteen departments maintained jails in which accused persons were temporarily housed pending trial and sentencing. All prisoners sentenced to confinement were held in one of three federal prisons or at the work colony at San José. Two of the federal prisons were for men, and the third was for women. The work colony was designed to aid in the rehabilitation of prisoners for whom agricultural work was believed to be helpful.

Although the three federal prisons existed independently of each other, a single entity in the ministry administered them. A prerelease facility housed prisoners about to complete their term of imprisonment. These individuals could bring their families to live with them until their final discharge. The prisoners themselves were in charge of the facility under the guidance of trained instructors. The prison area was surrounded by a wide moat. The prerelease facility was outside the moat. Visits to minimum security inmates took place in the open; medium security inmates were separated from visitors by a glass partition; and those in maximum security were separated by reinforced glass partitions, with telephones for communication.

The Penal Code provided that inmates of minimum security institutions could be employed in such activities as road building, quarrying, and similar public improvement projects. The obligation to work was established by law, and work was mandatory for prisoners who had not been tried. Prisoners earned small amounts for their labor; these sums were paid upon release. Prison labor was aimed at rehabilitating the individual, a principle no doubt derived from the country's tradition of extensive social services.

* * *

As of late 1990, no definitive studies dealing comprehensively with national security matters in contemporary Uruguay had been published. A general treatment of modern Uruguayan political life, touching on the military and its place in the national life, can be found in Martin Weinstein's *Uruguay: Democracy at the Crossroads.* The most complete coverage of the history and development of the armed forces is contained in the section "Uruguay" in Adrian J. English's *Regional Defence Profile, No. 1: Latin America.* For development of the armed forces since 1980, the reader must search through issues of the *Latin American Weekly Report,* the *Latin America Report* produced by the Joint Publications Research Service, and the *Daily Report: Latin America* put out by the Foreign Broadcast Information Service. Current order-of-battle information is available in the International Institute of Strategic Studies' excellent annual, *The Military Balance.* The best overview of conditions of public order is contained in the sections on Uruguay in *Country Reports on Human Rights Practices,* a report submitted annually by the United States Department of State to the United States Congress. (For further information and complete citations, see Bibliography.)

Appendix

Table 1. *Metric Conversion Coefficients and Factors*

When you know	Multiply by	To find
Millimeters	0.04	inches
Centimeters	0.39	inches
Meters	3.3	feet
Kilometers	0.62	miles
Hectares (10,000 m²)	2.47	acres
Square kilometers	0.39	square miles
Cubic meters	35.3	cubic feet
Liters	0.26	gallons
Kilograms	2.2	pounds
Metric tons	0.98	long tons
	1.1	short tons
	2,204	pounds
Degrees Celsius	9	degrees Fahrenheit
(Centigrade)	divide by 5 and add 32	

Table 2. *Population Size and Density by Department, 1985 Census*

Department	Population	Density *
Artigas	69,145	5.8
Canelones	364,248	80.3
Cerro Largo	78,416	5.7
Colonia	112,717	18.5
Durazno	55,077	4.7
Flores	24,739	4.8
Florida	66,474	6.4
Lavalleja	61,466	6.1
Maldonado	94,314	19.7
Montevideo	1,311,976	2,475.4
Paysandú	103,763	7.5
Río Negro	48,644	5.2
Rivera	89,475	9.5
Rocha	66,601	6.3
Salto	108,487	7.7
San José	89,893	18.0
Soriano	79,439	8.8
Tacuarembó	83,498	5.4
Treinta y Tres	46,869	4.9
URUGUAY	2,955,241	16.9

* Persons per square kilometer.

Source: Based on information from Uruguay, Dirección General de Estadística y Censos, *Anuario estadístico, 1988,* Montevideo, 1989.

Table 3. *Ranking of Departments by Level of Development, 1978*

Rank	Department	Index of Social and Economic Development
1	Montevideo	97.7
2	Maldonado	66.1
3	Colonia	37.6
4	Paysandú	34.0
5	Lavalleja	30.1
6	Soriano	24.9
7	Flores	24.1
8	Salto	22.6
9	Canelones	22.1
10	Rocha	19.2
11	Florida	18.6
12	Durazno	17.9
13	Río Negro	16.4
14	San José	15.7
15	Treinta y Tres	14.6
16	Artigas	12.2
17	Cerro Largo	10.9
18	Tacuarembó	10.2
19	Rivera	5.7

Source: Based on information from Danilo Veiga, "Tipología departmental y desarrollo regional en el Uruguay," Montevideo, 1978, 43.

Table 4. *Population, Selected Years, 1769–2020* *

Year	Population	Year	Population
1769	12,000	1941	2,186,000
1796	46,000	1950	2,193,000
1829	74,000	1963	2,596,000
1835	128,000	1975	2,788,000
1852	132,000	1980	2,908,000
1860	223,000	1985	2,955,000
1872	420,000	1988	3,081,000
1889	712,000	1995	3,152,000
1908	1,043,000	2000	3,264,000
1916	1,294,000	2020	3,679,000
1930	1,699,000		

* Figures for 1852, 1860, 1908, 1963, 1975, and 1985 are census results; figures for other years to 1988 are estimates; figures for 1995, 2000, and 2020 are projections. All figures are rounded off to the nearest thousand.

Table 5. Income Distribution by Area, 1986

| | Percentage Share of Household Income | | |
| | Lowest | Highest | Highest |
Area	20 Percent	20 Percent	10 Percent
Montevideo	5.5	47.3	29.9
Department capitals	6.2	45.9	29.1
Rest of interior	5.7	46.4	29.8

Source: Based on information from Pablo Martínez Bengochea and Alicia Melgar, "Evolución de precios e ingresos, 1985-1986," *Cuadernos del CLAEH* [Montevideo], 11, No. 39, 1986, 88.

Table 6. Decline of Real Wages, 1968-82
(1968 = 100)

Year	Private Sector	Public Sector	Uruguay
1968	100	100	100
1969	111	112	111
1970	111	109	110
1971	116	115	116
1972	98	94	96
1973	96	93	94
1974	96	91	93
1975	88	82	85
1976	81	79	80
1977	71	71	71
1978	68	68	68
1979	62	64	63
1980	58	67	62
1981	62	72	67
1982	62	72	67

Source: Based on information from Martin Weinstein, *Uruguay: Democracy at the Crossroads,* Boulder, Colorado, 1988, 69.

Table 7. Evolution of Real Wages, 1981-89
(fourth quarter 1984 = 100)

Year	Private Sector	Public Sector	Uruguay
1981	131	149	140
1982	130	149	140
1983	104	117	111
1984	99	102	100
1985	114	116	115
1986	123	122	122
1987	133	122	128
1988	136	123	130
1989	138	119	130

Source: Based on information from *Búsqueda* [Montevideo], No. 540, June 14-20, 1990, 29.

Table 8. Decline of Real Minimum Wage, 1981–89

Year	Index *
1981	97
1982	99
1983	85
1984	85
1985	89
1986	84
1987	86
1988	80
1989	74

* March 1973 = 100.

Source: Based on information from *Búsqueda* [Montevideo], No. 539, June 7–13, 1990, 27.

Table 9. Key Economic Indicators, 1985–89

	1985	1986	1987	1988	1989 [1]
Gross domestic product (GDP) [2]	5,204	6,382	7,734	7,944	8,800
Real GDP growth [3]	0.3	6.6	4.9	0.5	1.5
Labor force [4]	1.3	1.3	1.3	1.3	1.3
Unemployment rate [5]	13	11	9	9	9
Inflation rate [5]	72	71	57	69	85
Exchange rate [6]	101	152	227	359	606
Foreign debt [2]	4,900	5,238	5,888	6,330	6,700

[1] Preliminary.
[2] In millions of United States dollars.
[3] In percentages; real GDP growth takes inflation into account.
[4] In millions.
[5] In percentages.
[6] In Uruguayan new pesos (for value of the Uruguayan new peso—see Glossary) to United States dollars.

Table 10. Public-Sector Finances, 1983-87
(in millions of Uruguayan new pesos) *

	1983	1984	1985	1986	1987
Revenues					
Taxes					
Income	3,339	3,599	8,616	18,086	30,706
Property	1,951	1,854	4,414	9,829	19,218
Goods and services	15,718	24,037	48,750	95,781	163,145
External trade	3,851	6,129	8,936	15,937	32,927
Payroll	222	241	784	1,368	2,219
Total taxes	25,081	35,860	71,500	141,001	248,215
Nontax revenues	4,204	3,937	5,197	8,850	22,724
Total revenues	29,285	39,797	76,697	149,851	270,939
Expenditures					
General services	4,777	6,675	12,001	23,724	41,590
Defense	5,345	7,238	11,415	19,049	29,538
Education	3,108	4,090	7,689	16,261	32,037
Sanitation	2,001	2,384	4,824	10,782	18,132
Social security	13,992	17,485	28,735	44,530	83,399
Other	7,632	17,601	26,761	46,824	88,292
Total expenditures	36,855	55,473	91,425	161,170	292,988
Deficit	7,570	15,676	14,728	11,319	22,049

* For value of the Uruguayan new peso—see Glossary.

Source: Based on information from Uruguay, Dirección General de Estadística y Censos, *Anuario estadístico, 1988*, Montevideo, 1989.

Table 11. Public-Sector Expenditures,
Selected Years, 1980-87
(in percentages)

Expenditures	1980	1984	1986	1987
Capital expenditures	9.6	5.7	6.3	10.6
Current transfers and subsidies	5.3	12.2	6.7	8.0
Financial investment and net lending	2.5	3.1	2.6	n.a.
Interest payments	2.2	9.5	10.4	8.9
Purchase of goods and services	80.4	69.5	74.0	72.5
TOTAL	100.0	100.0	100.0	100.0

n.a.—not available.

Source: Based on information from Inter-American Development Bank, *Economic and Social Progress in Latin America*, Washington, 1989, 481-84.

Table 12. Public-Sector Revenues, 1980, 1984, and 1986
(in percentages)

Revenues	1980	1984	1986
Taxes			
Income	14.9	9.4	15.3
Property	4.9	4.5	5.8
Goods and services	58.4	58.2	59.9
External trade	12.8	17.4	16.4
Total taxes	91.0	89.5	97.4
Nontax revenues	9.0	10.5	2.6
TOTAL	100.0	100.0	100.0

Source: Based on information from Inter-American Development Bank, *Economic and Social Progress in Latin America,* Washington, 1989, 477–80.

Table 13. Agricultural and Fisheries Production, 1983–88
(in thousands of tons)

Product	1983	1984	1985	1986	1987	1988
Livestock products						
Beef and veal	431	302	323	330	255	301
Mutton and lamb	60	41	44	83	54	n.a.
Milk	571	521	595	640	635	n.a.
Wool	82	82	71	87	90	89
Total livestock products	1,144	946	1,033	1,140	1,034	390
Crops						
Rice	323	339	421	394	335	381
Wheat	363	419	349	246	232	414
Corn	104	112	108	103	104	118
Barley	45	80	113	80	62	124
Soybeans	12	11	21	35	63	n.a.
Total crops	847	961	1,012	858	796	931
Fisheries						
Argentine hake	80	65	97	86	84	n.a.
Atlantic croaker	25	24	19	24	28	n.a.
Striped weakfish	9	11	7	13	11	n.a.
Other	30	34	15	18	15	n.a.
Total fisheries	144	134	138	141	138	n.a.

n.a.—not available.

Source: Based on information from Uruguay, Dirección General de Estadística y Censos, *Anuario estadístico, 1988,* Montevideo, 1989.

Table 14. Selected Autonomous Entities, 1990

Acronym	Organization
AFE	Administración de los Ferrocarriles del Estado (State Railways Administration)
ANCAP	Administración Nacional de Combustibles, Alcohol, y Portland (National Administration of Fuels, Alcohol, and Portland Cement)
ANDEBU	Asociación Nacional de Broadcasters Uruguayos (National Association of Uruguayan Broadcasters)
ANEP	Asociación Nacional de Empleados Públicos (National Association of Public Employees)
ANP	Administración Nacional de Puertos (National Administration of Ports)
ANTEL	Administración Nacional de Telecomunicaciones (National Telecommunications Administration)
BPS	Banco de Previsión Social (Social Welfare Bank)
BROU	Banco de la República Oriental del Uruguay (Bank of Uruguay)
COCAP	Consejo de Capacitación Profesional (Professional Training Council)
CONADI	Comisión Nacional de Informática (National Informatics Commission)
INC	Instituto Nacional de Colonización (National Land Settlement Institute)
OSE	Administración de Obras Sanitarias del Estado (State Sanitary Works Administration)
PLUNA	Primeras Líneas Uruguayas de Navegación Aérea (Uruguayan National Airlines)
SODRE	Servicio Oficial de Difusión Radiotelevisión y Espectáculos (Official Radio and Television Service)
TAMU	Transportes Aéreos Militares Uruguayos (Uruguayan Military Air Transport)
UTE	Administración Nacional de Usinas y Transmisiones Eléctricas (National Administration for the Generation and Transmission of Electricity)

Table 15. *Manufacturing Production and Employment by Sector, 1987*

Sector	Value[1]	Employment[2]
Food and beverages	1,296	41
Textiles, apparel, and footwear	891	37
Petroleum refining	493	2
Chemicals	400	9
Transportation goods	259	3
Steel, metal, and metal products	158	7
Paper and paper products	150	4
Machinery and appliances	139	5
Tobacco products	105	1
Rubber products	97	3
Plastic products	81	4
Other	281	16
TOTAL	4,350	132

[1] In millions of United States dollars.
[2] In thousands.

Source: Based on information from Uruguay, Dirección General de Estadística y Censos, *Anuario estadístico, 1988,* Montevideo, 1989.

Table 16. *Balance of Payments, 1984-88*
(in millions of United States dollars)

	1984	1985	1986	1987	1988
Current account					
Merchandise exports	925	854	1,088	1,182	1,404
Merchandise imports	-732	-675	-814	-1,080	-1,112
Trade balance	193	179	274	102	292
Net other goods and services	-332	-309	-231	-242	-280
Net transfers	10	11	25	8	21
Current account balance	-129	-119	68	-132	33
Capital account					
Direct investment	3	-8	-5	5	-2
Portfolio investment	19	97	86	13	37
Other long-term capital	20	-29	55	22	-100
Other short-term capital	124	-134	-156	199	204
Capital account balance	166	-74	-20	239	139
Net errors and omissions	-121	259	240	-68	-209
Counterpart items	22	-23	-38	-49	19
Exceptional financing	0	0	0	40	40
Other liabilities	-1	0	0	4	15
Change in reserves	63	-43	-250	-34	-37
(- means increase)					

Source: Based on information from International Monetary Fund, *International Financial Statistics,* Washington, 1990, 552.

*Table 17. Principal Political Parties, Factions, and
Candidates, Elections of November 26, 1989*

Party	Faction	Candidate
Colorado Party (Partido Colorado)	United Batllism (Batllismo Unido—BU) (right-of-center)	Senator Jorge Batlle Ibáñez
	Colorado and Batllist Union (Unión Colorada y Batllista— UCB) (right-of-center)	Jorge Pacheco Areco
	Social Action Movement (Movimiento de Acción Social—MAS) (left-of-center)	Hugo Fernández Faingold
National Party (Partido Nacional)	Herrerist Movement (Movimiento Herrerista) (right-of-center)	Senator Luis Alberto Lacalle de Herrera
	La Rocha National Movement (Movimiento Nacional de La Rocha—MNR) (left-of-center)	Senator Carlos Julio Pereyra
	For the Fatherland (Por la Patria—PLP) (centrist)	Senator Alberto Sáenz de Zumarán
Broad Front (Frente Amplio)	Left-of-center coalition of communist and socialist parties, Tupamaros, and eleven other small parties	General (Retired) Líber Seregni Mosquera
New Sector (Nuevo Espacio)	Integration Movement (Movimiento de Integración— MI) coalition (left-of-center) *	Senator Hugo Batalla

* Coalition consisted of Christian Democratic Party (Partido Demócrata Cristiano—PDC), Civic Union (Unión Cívica—UC), and People's Government Party (Partido por el Gobierno del Pueblo—PGP).

Table 18. Principal Newspapers, 1990

Newspaper	Circulation and Frequency	Affiliation	Date Established
El Día	100,000, daily; 150,000, Sunday	Colorado	1886
El Diario	80,000, evening	Independent Colorado	1923
Diario Oficial	Morning	Official gazette	n.a.
Gaceta Comercial	4,500, morning weekly	Independent leftist	1916
La Hora	Morning	Broad Front	1984
La Mañana	40,000, morning	Independent Colorado	1917
Mundocolor	4,500, evening	n.a.	1976
La Opinión	Weekly	UCB [1]	1985
El País	130,000	Conservative Blanco	1918
La Razón	Weekly	MNR [2]	1987
Ultimas Noticias	19,000, evening	Moon Unification Church	1981

n.a.—not available.
[1] Unión Colorada y Batllista (Colorado and Battlist Union).
[2] Movimiento Nacional de La Rocha (La Rocha National Movement).

Table 19. Major Army Equipment, 1990

Type and Description	Country of Origin	In Inventory
Tanks		
M-24 Chaffee light tanks	United States	17
M-41A1 Bulldog light tanks	Belgium (United States-made)	22
Scorpion light tanks	Belgium	15 (more on order)
Armored vehicles		
M-3A1 White armored cars	United States	28
FN-4-RM-62 armored cars	Belgium	22
M113 armored personnel carriers	United States	15
Condor armored personnel carriers	West Germany	50
EE-3 Jararaca armored reconnaissance vehicles	Brazil	18
EE-9 Cascavel armored reconnaissance vehicles	-do-	15
Artillery		
FAL 7.62mm assault rifles	Argentina	n.a.
Bofors M-1902 75mm, towed	Argentina (Swedish-made)	12
M-101A1 105mm howitzers	South Korea (United States-made)	25
M-114A1 155mm, towed	-do-	5
M-1 81mm mortars	United States	40
107mm mortars	-do-	5
M-18 57mm recoilless rifles	-do-	30
M-40A1 106mm recoilless rifles	-do-	10
Antitank weapons		
Milan 106mm antitank guns	-do-	10
Air defense weapons		
M-167 Vulcan 20mm air defense guns ...	South Korea (United States-made)	6
Bofors L/60 40mm air defense guns	Sweden	2

n.a.—not available.

Table 20. *Major Navy Equipment, 1990*

Type and Description	Country of Origin	In Inventory
Escorts		
Commandant Rivière-class frigate	France	1 (2 on order)
Dealey-class frigate	United States	1
Cannon-class destroyer escort [1]	–do–	1
Auk-class corvette	–do–	1
Patrol craft		
Vigilante-class large patrol craft	France	3
Salto-class large patrol craft	Italy	1
Large patrol craft	United States	2
Small patrol craft	n.a.	2
Miscellaneous		
Adjutant-class minesweeper	United States	1
LCM 6 landing craft	–do–	2
LD–43-class landing craft	Uruguay	3
Tanker [2]	Japan	1
Training ship	Spain	1
Cohoe-class salvage vessel	United States	1
Transport vessel [2]	Denmark	1
Naval aircraft		
Grumman SA 2A/G Trackers	United States	5
Beech Super King Air 200T	–do–	1
T–28 Frennecs armed trainers	Argentina	8
Beech T–34 B/C	United States	6
Beech TC–45	–do–	2
Bell 47 helicopter	–do–	1
Bell 222 helicopter	–do–	1
CASA C–212-200 Aviocar	Spain	1
Sikorsky SH–34 helicopters	United States	2
Piper PA–18 Super Cub trainers	–do–	2
SN–7 trainers	–do–	5

n.a.—not available.
[1] To be replaced by Commandant Rivière-class frigates on order.
[2] Under civilian charter.

Table 21. Major Air Force Equipment, 1990

Type and Description	Country of Origin	In Inventory
Training		
North American AT-6A Texan	United States	7
Beech T-34A/B Mentor and T-6	-do-	24
Cessna T-41D Mescalero	-do-	6
Light attack		
FMA IA-58B Pucarás	Argentina	6
Cessna A-37B Dragonflies	United States	8
Lockheed AT-33 Shooting Stars	-do-	4
Liaison		
Cessna U-17A Skywagon	-do-	6
Cessna 182	-do-	2
Cessna 310	-do-	1
Piper PA-18 Super Cub	-do-	1
Piper PA-23	-do-	1
Beech Queen Air 80	-do-	5
Transports		
CASA C-212 Aviocar	Spain	4
Embraer EMB-110	Brazil	4
Fokker F-27	Netherlands	2
Fairchild-Hiller FH-227	United States	2
Douglas C-47	-do-	2
Survey		
Embraer EMB-110B1	Brazil	1
Commander 680	United States	1
Helicopters		
Bell 212	-do-	2
Bell UH-1B	-do-	2
Bell UH-1H	-do-	4
Hiller UH-23F	-do-	2

Bibliography

Chapter 1

Acevedo, Eduardo. *Anales históricos del Uruguay*, 1. Montevideo: Barreiro y Ramos, 1933.

————. *Anales históricos del Uruguay*, 2. Montevideo: Barreiro y Ramos, 1933.

————. *Anales históricos del Uruguay*, 4. Montevideo: Barreiro y Ramos, 1934.

————. *Anales históricos del Uruguay*, 6. Montevideo: Barreiro y Ramos, 1936.

Alisky, Marvin. *Uruguay: A Contemporary Survey*. New York: Praeger, 1962.

Alonso Eloy, Rosa, and Carlos Demassi. *Uruguay, 1958-1968: Crisis y estancamiento*. Montevideo: Ediciones de la Banda Oriental, 1986.

Amnesty International. *Political Imprisonment in Uruguay*. London: 1979.

————. *Tortured to Death in Uruguay: 22 Known Cases*. London: 1976.

————. *Uruguay Deaths under Torture, 1975-77*. London: 1978.

Artigas. Montevideo: Ediciones de "El País," 1960.

Astori, Danilo. *El Uruguay de la dictadura, 1973-1985: La política económica de la dictadura*. Montevideo: Ediciones de la Banda Oriental, 1989.

Bandera, Manuel M. de la. *La constitución de 1967*. Montevideo: Secretaría del Senado, 1967.

Baracchini, Hugo. *Historia de las comunicaciones en el Uruguay*. Montevideo: Universidad de la República, 1977.

Barbagelata, Aníbal Luis. *El constitucionalismo uruguayo a mediados del siglo XIX*. Montevideo: Fundación de Cultura Universitaria, 1978.

Barrán, José Pedro. *Apogeo y crisis del Uruguay pastoril y caudillesco, 1838-1875*. Montevideo: Ediciones de la Banda Oriental, 1974.

Barrán, José Pedro, and Benjamín Nahum. *Bases económicas de la revolución artiguista*. Montevideo: Ediciones de la Banda Oriental, 1964.

————. *Batlle: Los estancieros y el imperio británico*. Montevideo: Ediciones de la Banda Oriental, 1983.

————. *Historia rural del Uruguay moderno*. (7 vols.) Montevideo: Ediciones de la Banda Oriental, 1967-78.

Barrios Pintos, Aníbal. *Historia de la ganadería en el Uruguay, 1574–1971.* Montevideo: Biblioteca Nacional, 1978.

Blanco Acevedo, Pablo. *El federalismo de Artigas y la independencia nacional.* Montevideo: 1950.

_____. *El gobierno colonial en el Uruguay y los orígenes de la nacionalidad.* Montevideo: Barreiro y Ramos, 1944.

Bralich, Jorge. *Breve historia de la educación en el Uruguay.* Montevideo: CLEP/Ediciones de Nuevo Mundo, 1987.

Bruschera, Oscar. *Las décadas infames, 1967–1985.* (Hoy es Historia series.) Montevideo: Librería Linardi y Risso, 1986.

Caetano, Gerardo. *La agonía del reformismo, 1916–1925.* (Serie de Investigaciones, Nos. 37–38.) Montevideo: Centro Latinoamericano de Economía Humana, 1983.

Caetano, Gerardo, and Raúl Jacob. *El nacimiento del terrismo (1930–33),* 1. Montevideo: Ediciones de la Banda Oriental, 1989.

Caetano, Gerardo, and José Pedro Rilla. *Breve historia de la dictadura, 1973–1985.* Montevideo: Centro Latinoamericano de Economía Humana/Ediciones de la Banda Oriental, 1987.

_____. *El Uruguay de la dictadura, 1973–1985: La era militar.* Montevideo: Ediciones de la Banda Oriental, 1989.

Calatayud Bosch, José. *Grandeza y decadencia del Partido Nacional.* Montevideo: Ediciones Liga Federal, 1971.

Cardozo, Efraím. *El imperio del Brasil y el Río de la Plata.* Buenos Aires: 1961.

Castellanos, Alfredo Raúl. *La Cisplatina, la independencia, y la república caudillesca, 1820–1838.* Montevideo: Ediciones de la Banda Oriental, 1977.

Contribución a la historia económica del Uruguay. Montevideo: Academia Nacional de Economía, 1984.

D'Elía, Germán. *El movimiento sindical.* Montevideo: Colección "Nuestra Tierra," 1969.

_____. *El Uruguay neo-Batllista, 1946–1958.* Montevideo: Ediciones de la Banda Oriental, 1982.

Fabregat, Julio T. *Elecciones uruguayas.* Montevideo: Cámara de Senadores, 1972.

Faraone, Roque. *De la prosperidad a la ruina.* Montevideo: Editorial Arca, 1987.

_____. *El Uruguay en que vivimos, 1900–1965.* Montevideo: Editorial Arca, 1965.

Faroppa, Luis. *Políticas para una economía desequilibrada: Uruguay, 1958–1981.* Montevideo: Ediciones de la Banda Oriental, 1982.

Faroppa, Luis, Marisa Buchelli, Alberto Couriel, and Alberto Bensión. *Cuatro tesis sobre la situación económica nacional.* Montevideo:

Fundación de Cultura Universitaria/Colegio de Economistas y Contadores del Uruguay, 1973.

Finch, M.H.J. *Historia económica del Uruguay contemporáneo.* Montevideo: Ediciones de la Banda Oriental, 1980.

————. *A Political Economy of Uruguay since 1870.* New York: St. Martin's Press, 1981.

Fitzgibbon, Russell H. *Uruguay: Portrait of a Democracy.* New York: Russell and Russell, 1966.

Frega, Ana, Mónica Maronna, and Yvette Trochon. *Baldomir y la restauración democrática, 1938-1946.* Montevideo: Ediciones de la Banda Oriental, 1987.

Gallinal, Gustavo. *El Uruguay hacia la dictatura.* Montevideo: Editorial Nueva América, 1938.

Gillespie, Charles Guy, Louis Goodman, Juan Rial, and Peter Winn. *Uruguay y la democracia.* (3 vols.) (Wilson Center Latin American Program-Montevideo Series.) Montevideo: Ediciones de la Banda Oriental, 1984-85.

González, Luis E., and Jorge Notaro. *Alcances de una política estabilizadora heterodoxa: El caso uruguayo, 1974 a 1979.* Montevideo: Wilson Center-Seminar on Stabilization Policies in Latin America, 1979.

González Sierra, Yamandú. *Reseña histórica del movimiento sindical uruguayo, 1870-1984.* Montevideo: Centro Interdisciplinario de Estudios del Desarrollo, Uruguay, 1989.

Herrera, Luis Alberto de. *La misión Ponsonby.* Montevideo: Cámara de Representantes, 1988.

Isola, Ema. *La esclavitud en el Uruguay desde sus comienzos hasta su extinción, 1743-1852.* Montevideo: Comisión Nacional de Homenaje del Sesquicentenario de los Hechos Históricos de 1825, 1975.

Jacob, Raúl. *Benito Nardone: El ruralismo hacia el poder, 1945-1958.* Montevideo: Ediciones de la Banda Oriental, 1981.

————. *Breve historia de la industria en Uruguay.* Montevideo: Fundación de Cultura Universitaria, 1981.

————. *El frigorífico nacional en el mercado de carnes.* Montevideo: Fundación de Cultura Universitaria, 1979.

————. *Modelo Batllista: ¿Variación sobre un viejo tema?* Montevideo: Editorial Proyección, 1988.

————. *Uruguay, 1929-1938: Depresión ganadera y desarrollo fabril.* Montevideo: Fundación de Cultura Universitaria, 1981.

————. *El Uruguay de Terra, 1931-1938.* Montevideo: Ediciones de la Banda Oriental, 1983.

Lerin, François and Cristina Torres. *Historia política de la dictadura uruguaya, 1973-1980.* Montevideo: Ediciones del Nuevo Mundo, 1987.

Lindahl, Goran G. *Batlle: Fundador de la democracia en el Uruguay.* Montevideo: Editorial Arca, 1971.

Lista Clericetti, Julio. *Historia política uruguaya, 1938-1972.* Montevideo: J. Lista Clericetti, 1984.

López Chírico, Selva. *El estado y las fuerzas armadas en el Uruguay del siglo XX.* Montevideo: Ediciones de la Banda Oriental, 1985.

Macadar, Luis. *Uruguay, 1974-1980: (Un nuevo ensayo de reajuste económico?* Montevideo: Centro de Investigaciones Económicas/Ediciones de la Banda Oriental, 1982.

Machado, Carlos. *Historia política uruguaya, 1938-1972.* Montevideo: Ediciones de la Banda Oriental, 1972.

Machado Ferrer, Martha, and Carlos Fagúndez Ramos. *Los años duros: Cronología documentada, 1964-1973.* Montevideo: Monte-Sexto, 1987.

Manini Rios, Carlos. *Anoche me llamó Batlle.* Montevideo: Imprenta Letras: 1970.

Melgar, Walter, and Walter Cancela Vilanova. *El Uruguay de nuestro tiempo, 1958-1983—Economía: La hora del balance.* Montevideo: Centro Latinoamericano de Economía Humana, 1983.

Méndez Vives, Enrique. *El Uruguay de la modernización, 1876-1904.* Montevideo: Ediciones de la Banda Oriental, 1975.

Montero Bustamante, Raúl, and Julio M. Llamas. *Fundación de Montevideo.* (Instituto Histórico y Geográfico del Uruguay series.) Montevideo: Editorial Arca, 1976.

Mourat, Oscar. *5 perspectivas históricas del Uruguay moderno.* Montevideo: Fundación de Cultura Universitaria, 1969.

Nahum, Benjamín. *Crisis política y recuperación económica, 1930-1958.* Montevideo: Ediciones de la Banda Oriental, 1987.

Oddone, Juan Antonio. *Uruguay en los años treinta.* Montevideo: Universidad de la República, 1988.

Oddone, Juan Antonio, and Blanca Paris. *La universidad uruguaya del militarismo a la crisis, 1885-1958.* (3 vols.) Montevideo: Universidad de la República, 1971.

Pérez Santarcieri, María Emilia. *Partidos políticos en el Uruguay: Síntesis histórica de su origen y evolución.* Montevideo: Imprenta Valgraf, 1989.

Pivel Devoto, Juan E. *Historia de los partidos y de las ideas políticas en el Uruguay II: La definición de los bandos, 1829-1838.* Montevideo: Editorial Medina, 1956.

Pivel Devoto, Juan E., and Alcira Ranieri de Pivel Devoto. *Historia de la República Oriental del Uruguay, 1830-1930.* Montevideo: Editorial Medina, 1966.

Reyes Abadie, Washington. *Historia del Partido Nacional.* Montevideo: Ediciones de la Banda Oriental, 1989.

————. *Julio Herrera y Obes.* Montevideo: Ediciones de la Banda Oriental, 1977.

————. *Latorre: La forja del estado.* Montevideo: Ediciones de la Banda Oriental, 1977.

Reyes Abadie, Washington, and Andrés Vázquez Romero. *Crónica general del Uruguay.* Montevideo: Ediciones de la Banda Oriental, 1979.

Reyes Abadie, Washington, Oscar H. Bruschera, and Tabaré Melogno. *El ciclo artiquista.* Montevideo: Universidad de la República, 1965.

Rial, Juan. *Partidos políticos, democracia, y autoritarismo.* Montevideo: Centro de Informaciones y Estudios del Uruguay/Ediciones de la Banda Oriental, 1984.

————. *Uruguay elecciones de 1984: Un triunfo del centro.* Montevideo: Ediciones de la Banda Oriental, 1985.

Rodríguez, Héctor. *Nuestros sindicatos, 1865-1965.* Montevideo: Ediciones Uruguay, 1965.

Rodríguez Villamil, Silvia, and Graciela Sapriza. *La imigración europea en el Uruguay.* Montevideo: Ediciones de la Banda Oriental, 1982.

Sala de Tourón, Lucía, and Rosa Alonso. *El Uruguay comercial: Pastoril y caudillesco—Tomo I Economía.* Montevideo: Ediciones de la Banda Oriental, 1986.

Sala de Tourón, Lucía, Nelson de la Torre, and Julio C. Rodríguez. *Estructura económico-social de la Colonia.* Montevideo: Ediciones Pueblos Unidos, 1967.

Salterain Herrera, Eduardo de. *Latorre.* Montevideo: Estado Mayor del Ejército, 1975.

Solari, Aldo, and Rolando Franco. *Las empresas públicas en el Uruguay.* Montevideo: Fundación de Cultura Universitaria, 1983.

Solari, Aldo, Néstor Campiglia, and Germán Wettstein. *Uruguay en cifras.* Montevideo: Universidad de la República, 1966.

Terra, Gabriel, Jr. *Gabriel Terra y la verdad histórica.* Montevideo: 1962.

Torre, Nelson de la, Julio C. Rodríguez, and Lucía Sala de Tourón. *La revolución agraria artiguista, 1815-1816.* Montevideo: Ediciones Pueblos Unidos, 1969.

Torres Wilson, José de. *Brevísima historia del Uruguay.* Montevideo: Ediciones de la Planta, 1984.

Vanger, Milton I. *Batlle y Ordóñez: El creador de su época, 1902-1907.* Buenos Aires: Editorial Universitaria de Buenos Aires, 1968.

————. *El país modelo: José Batlle y Ordóñez, 1907-1915.* Montevideo: Editorial Arca/Ediciones de la Banda Oriental, 1983.

Vicario, Luis. *El crecimiento urbano de Montevideo.* Montevideo: Ediciones de la Banda Oriental, 1970.

Vida y cultura en el Río de la Plata, 1. (XVII Cursos Internacionales de Verano.) Montevideo: Universidad de la República, 1987.

Visca, Carlos. *Emilio Reus y su época.* Montevideo: Ediciones de la Banda Oriental, 1963.

Weinstein, Martin. *Uruguay: Democracy at the Crossroads.* Boulder, Colorado: Westview Press, 1988.

_____. *Uruguay: The Politics of Failure.* Westport, Connecticut: Greenwood Press, 1975.

_____. "Uruguay's Elections: A Prolonged Transition to Democracy," *NACLA Report on the Americas,* 18, No. 6, November–December 1984, 12–15.

Wilgus, A. Curtis. *Historical Atlas of Latin America: Political, Geographic, Economic, Cultural.* New York: Cooper Square, 1967.

Williman, José Claudio. *Santos: La consolidación del estado.* Montevideo: Ediciones de la Banda Oriental, 1979.

Winn, Peter. *El imperio informal británico en el Uruguay en el siglo XIX.* Montevideo: Ediciones de la Banda Oriental, 1975.

Wonsewer, Israel, Enrique V. Iglesias, Mario Buscheli, and Luis A. Faroppa. *Aspectos de la industrialización en el Uruguay.* Montevideo: Ediciones de la Banda Oriental, 1987.

Zubillaga, Carlos. *De la tradición a la crisis.* Montevideo: Centro Latinoamericano de Economía Humana/Ediciones de la Banda Oriental, 1985.

Zubillaga, Carlos, and Romeo Pérez. *El Uruguay de nuestro tiempo, 1958-1983: Los partidos políticos.* Montevideo: Centro Latinoamericano de Economía Humana, 1983.

Zum Felde, Alberto. *Proceso histórico del Uruguay.* Montevideo: Editorial Arca, 1967.

Chapter 2

Abadie Soriano, Roberto. "The Literacy Campaign in Uruguay," *Fundamental and Adult Education,* 10, No. 1, 1958, 11–15.

Aguiar, César A. *Salario, consumo, emigración.* Montevideo: Fundación de Cultura Universitaria, 1981.

_____. *Uruguay: País de emigración.* Montevideo: Ediciones de la Banda Oriental, 1982.

Aguirre, Rosario. *El trabajo informal urbano en Montevideo.* Montevideo: Ediciones de la Banda Oriental/Centro Interdisciplinario de Estudios del Desarrollo, Uruguay, 1986.

Bibliography

Alisky, Marvin. *Uruguay: A Contemporary Survey.* New York: Praeger, 1969.

Apezechea, Héctor, Rafael Bayace, Enrique Mazzei, and Danilo Veiga (eds.). *La nueva crisis urbana: Pobreza extrema y pequeñas empresas.* Montevideo: Ediciones de la Banda Oriental, 1985.

Ardao, Arturo. *Racionalismo y liberalismo en el Uruguay.* Montevideo: Universidad de la República, 1962.

Arocena, José. "El desarrollo de la pequeña y microempresa," *Cuadernos del CLAEH* [Montevideo], 12, No. 42, 1987, 29–36.

Astori, Danilo. *Los "Marginados" uruguayos: Teoría y realidad.* (Temas del Siglo XX series.) Montevideo: Ediciones de la Banda Oriental, 1984.

Atlas para la República Oriental del Uruguay. Montevideo: Ediciones Raschetti/Ediciones de Montevideo, 1983.

Azúa, Carlos de. *Uruguay: ¿Una sociedad amortiguadora?* Montevideo: Ediciones de la Banda Oriental, 1984.

Barrán, José Pedro, and Benjamín Nahum. *Historia rural del Uruguay moderno.* (7 vols.) Montevideo: Ediciones de la Banda Oriental, 1967–78.

Baumann, Renate. *Brazil-Argentina-Uruguay: A Integracão em debate.* São Paulo: Editôra Marco Zero, Universidade de Brasília, 1987.

Bayce, Rafael. *El sistema educativo uruguayo, 1973–85.* (2 vols.) Montevideo: Centro de Investigación y Experimentación Pedagógica/Ediciones de la Banda Oriental, 1985–88.

Bensión, Alberto, and Jorge Caumont. *Política económica y distribución del ingreso en el Uruguay, 1970–1976.* Montevideo: Acali Editorial, 1979.

Benton, Lauren. "Reshaping the Urban Core: The Politics of Housing in Authoritarian Uruguay," *Latin American Research Review,* 21, No. 2, 1986, 33–52.

Benvenuto, Luis Carlos. *Uruguay hoy.* Buenos Aires: Siglo Veintiuno, 1971.

Bon Espasandín, Mario. *Cantegriles.* Montevideo: Túpac Amaru, 1963.

Campiglia, Néstor. *Los grupos de presión y el proceso político.* Montevideo: Editorial Arca, 1969.

_____. *Migración interna en el Uruguay.* Montevideo: Universidad de la República, 1968.

_____. *Montevideo: Población y trabajo,* 7. (Nuestra Tierra series.) Montevideo: Editorial Nuestra Tierra, 1971.

Carpena, Enrique. "Clase social, ideología, y opinión pública," *Cuadernos de ciencias sociales* [Montevideo], 1, No. 1, 1970.

Castagnola, José Luis. "Participación y movimientos sociales: Notas sobre un debate conceptual y sus consecuencias políticas,"

Cuadernos del CLAEH [Montevideo], 11, No. 39, 1986, 65–79.

————. "Problemática y alternativas culturales de los nuevos movimientos sociales," *Cuadernos del CLAEH* [Montevideo], 11, No. 42, 1987, 65–81.

Centro de Investigaciones Económicas. *La crisis uruguaya y el problema nacional.* Montevideo: Ediciones de la Banda Oriental, 1984.

Collado, E.G., and Simon G. Hanson. "Old Age Pensions in Uruguay," *Hispanic American Historical Review,* 16, No. 2, May 1936, 173–89.

Cortiñas Peláez, León. "Autonomy and Student Co-Government in the University of Uruguay," *Comparative Education Review,* 7, No. 2, October 1963, 166–72.

Das, Man Singh, and Clinton J. Jesser (eds.). *The Family in Latin America.* Ghaziabad, India: Vikas, 1980.

Davis, J. Merle. *The Evangelical Church in the River Plate Republics.* New York: International Missionary Council, 1943.

Davis, Jack Emory. *The Spanish of Argentina and Uruguay: An Annotated Bibliography for 1940–1978.* New York: Mouton, 1982.

D'Elía, Germán. *El movimiento sindical.* Montevideo: Colección "Nuestra Tierra," 1969.

D'Elía, Germán, and Armando Miraldi. *Historia del movimiento obrero en el Uruguay: Desde sus orígenes hasta 1930.* (Temas del Siglo XX series.) Montevideo: Ediciones de la Banda Oriental, 1984.

Elizaincín, Adolfo. "The Emergence of Bilingual Dialects on the Brazilian-Uruguayan Border," *Linguistics* [Berlin], No. 177, 1976, 123–34.

Errandonea, Alfredo. "Apuntes sobre la conformación de las clases sociales en el medio rural uruguayo," *Cuadernos de ciencias sociales* [Montevideo], 1, No. 1, 1970, 9–54.

————. *Las clases sociales en el Uruguay.* (Enciclopedia Uruguaya series.) Montevideo: Centro Latinoamericano de Economía Humana/Ediciones de la Banda Oriental, 1989.

————. "Las clases sociales en la sociología uruguaya: Un tema bloqueado," *Cuadernos del CLAEH* [Montevideo], 11, No. 39, 1986, 23–42.

————. "Conflicto de clases," *Cuadernos del CLAEH* [Montevideo], 13, Nos. 45–46, 1988, 175–92.

Errandonea, Alfredo, and Daniel Costabile. *Sindicato y sociedad en el Uruguay.* Montevideo: Fundación de Cultura Universitaria, 1968.

Faroppa, Luis. *Perspectivas para un país en crisis,* 47. (Nuestra Tierra series.) Montevideo: Editorial Nuestra Tierra, 1969.

Filgueira, Carlos H. "Burocracia y clientela: Una política de absorción de tensiones,'' *Cuadernos de ciencias sociales* [Montevideo], 1, No. 1, 1970.

_____. ''Imbalance y movilidad en la estructura social: El caso uruguayo,'' *Cuadernos de ciencias sociales* [Montevideo], 3, No. 3, 1973.

_____. ''Indicadores comparativos de los departamentos del Uruguay.'' Montevideo: Centro de Informaciones y Estudios del Uruguay, 1976.

_____. *Movimientos sociales en el Uruguay de hoy.* Montevideo: Ediciones de la Banda Oriental/CLACSO, 1985.

Filgueira, Nea (ed.). *La mujer en el Uruguay: Ayer y hoy,* 15. (Temas del Siglo XX series.) Montevideo: Ediciones de la Banda Oriental, 1984.

Finch, M.H.J. *A Political Economy of Uruguay since 1970.* New York: St. Martin's Press, 1981.

Finch, M.H.J., and Alicia Casas de Barrán (comps.). *Uruguay,* 102. (World Bibliographical Series.) Oxford: Clio Press, 1989.

Fitzgibbon, Russell H. ''The Political Impact of Religious Development in Uruguay,'' *Church History,* 22, No. 1, March 1953, 21–32.

_____. *Uruguay: Portrait of a Democracy.* New York: Russell and Russell, 1966.

Fortuna, Juan Carlos. ''Las políticas sociales en la crisis uruguaya.'' Montevideo: Centro de Informaciones y Estudios del Uruguay, 1985.

Fortuna, Juan Carlos, and Suzana Prates. ''Informal Sector Versus Informalized Labor Relations in Uruguay.'' Chapter 4 in Alejandro Portes, Manuel Castells, and Lauren Benton (eds.), *The Informal Economy.* Baltimore: Johns Hopkins University Press, 1989.

Ganón, Isaac. *Estructura social del Uruguay.* Montevideo: Editorial AS, 1966.

Gillespie, Charles Guy, Louis Goodman, Juan Rial, and Peter Winn. *Uruguay y la democracia.* (3 vols.) (Wilson Center Latin American Program-Montevideo Series.) Montevideo: Ediciones de la Banda Oriental, 1984–85.

González, Luis E. ''Acerca de tres análisis marxistas del batllismo,'' *Cuadernos de ciencias sociales* [Montevideo], 2, No. 2, 1972.

_____. ''Los sindicatos en la arena política,'' *Cuadernos de marcha* [Montevideo], No. 9, July 1986, 23–27.

_____. ''La transformación del sistema político uruguayo.'' (Master's thesis.) Bariloche, Argentina: Fundación Bariloche, 1976.

_____. "Uruguay, 1980–1981: An Unexpected Opening," *Latin American Research Review*, 18, No. 3, 1983, 63–76.

Grupo de Estudios Urbanos. *Una ciudad sin memoria*. Montevideo: Ediciones de la Banda Oriental, 1983.

Guarnieri, Juan Carlos. *Diccionario del lenguaje Rioplatense*. Montevideo: Ediciones de la Banda Oriental, 1979.

Handelman, Howard. "Labor-Industrial Conflict and the Collapse of Uruguayan Democracy," *Journal of Interamerican Studies and World Affairs*, 23, No. 4, November 1981, 371–94.

Hanson, Simon Gabriel. *Utopia in Uruguay: Chapters in the Economic History of Uruguay*. n.p.: n. pub., 1938. Reprint. Westport, Connecticut: Hyperian Press, 1979.

Hayes, Robert C. *Labor Law and Practice in Uruguay*, 88. Washington: Department of Commerce, Bureau of Labor Statistics, 1971.

Hensey, Frederick Gerald. *The Socio-Linguistics of the Brazilian-Uruguayan Border*. The Hague: Mouton, 1972.

Hensey, Fritz. "Fronterizo: A Case of Phonological Restructuring." Pages 47–59 in Jacob Ornstein (ed.), *Three Essays on Linguistic Diversity*. The Hague: Mouton, 1975.

Hugarte, Renzo P., and Daniel Vidari. *El legado de los inmigrantes*, 29 and 39. (Nuestra Tierra series.) Montevideo: Editorial Nuestra Tierra, 1969.

Instituto de Ciencias Sociales. "Bibliografía sobre estratificación y estructura de clases en el Uruguay," *Cuadernos de ciencias sociales* [Montevideo], 1, No. 1, 1970.

Instituto de Economía. *El proceso económico del Uruguay*. Montevideo: Universidad de la República, 1969.

Inter-American Development Bank. *Economic and Social Progress in Latin American*. Washington: 1989.

Katzman, Rubén. "Youth and Unemployment in Montevideo," *CEPAL Review* [Santiago, Chile], No. 29, August 1986, 119–31.

Klaczko, Jaime, and Juan Rial. *Uruguay: El país urbano*. Montevideo: Ediciones de la Banda Oriental/CLACSO, 1981.

Kurian, George Thomas. "Uruguay." Pages 1596–1601 in George Thomas Kurian (ed.), *World Education Encyclopedia*. New York: Facts on File, 1988.

Liebman, Arthur, Kenneth N. Walker, and Myron Glazer. *Latin American University Students*. Cambridge: Harvard University Press, 1972.

Longhi Zunino, Augusto. *Las clases sociales y el futuro nacional*, 5. (Uruguay Hoy series.) Montevideo: Centro Interdisciplinario de Estudios del Desarrollo, Uruguay, 1988.

Marsilio, Horacio de. *El lenguaje de los uruguayos*, 24: (Nuestra Tierra series.) Montevideo: Editorial Nuestra Terra, 1969.

Martin, Percy A., and Earl Smith. "Labor Legislation in Uruguay," *Monthly Labor Review*, 25, October 1927, 726–33.

Martínez Bengochea, Pablo, and Alicia Melgar. "Evolución de precios e ingresos, 1985–1986," *Cuadernos del CLAEH* [Montevideo], 11, No. 39, 1986, 81–106.

Martorelli, Horacio. *Poder, política, y sociedad.* Montevideo: Ediciones de la Banda Oriental, 1983.

_____. *La sociedad rural uruguayo,* 5. (Colección Temas Nacionales series.) Montevideo: Fundación de Cultura Universitaria/Centro Interdisciplinario de Estudios del Desarrollo, Uruguay, 1982.

May, Jacques Meyer, and Donna L. McLellan. "Uruguay." Pages 359–419 in Jacques Meyer May and Donna L. McLellan (eds.), *The Ecology of Malnutrition in Eastern South America.* New York: Hafner Press, 1974.

Mazzei, Enrique, and Danilo Veiga. "Heterogeneidad y diferenciación social en sectores de pobreza extremo." Montevideo: Centro de Informaciones y Estudios del Uruguay, 1985.

_____. *Indicadores socioeconómicos del Uruguay.* Montevideo: Centro de Informaciones y Estudios del Uruguay, 1989.

Mecham, J. Lloyd. "Separation in Uruguay." Pages 252–60 in J. Lloyd Mecham (ed.), *Church and State in Latin America.* Chapel Hill: University of North Carolina Press, 1966.

Melgar, Alicia. *Distribución del ingreso en el Uruguay,* 18. Montevideo: Centro Latinoamericano de Economía Humana, 1981.

_____. "El mercado de trabajo en el Uruguay: Recesión y reactivación." Montevideo: Centro de Investigaciones Económicas, 1987.

Melgar, Alicia, and Fabio Villalobos. *La desigualdad como estrategía,* 5. (Colección Argumentos series.) Montevideo: Centro Latinoamericano de Economía Humana/Ediciones de la Banda Oriental, 1986.

Meo Zilio, Giovanni, and Ettore Rossi. *El elemento italiano en el habla de Buenos Aires y Montevideo.* Florence: Valmartina, 1970.

Mesa-Lago, Carmelo (ed.). *Social Security in Latin America: Pressure Groups, Stratification, and Inequality.* Pittsburgh: University of Pittsburgh Press, 1978.

Mizrahi, Roberto. "La economía del sector informal: La dinámica de las pequeñas unidades y su viabilidad," *Cuadernos del CLAEH* [Montevideo], 11, No. 40, 1986, 5–22.

Nichols, Madaline Wallis. *The Gaucho: Cattle Hunter, Cavalryman, Ideal of Romance.* Durham: Duke University, 1942. Reprint. New York: Gordian Press, 1968.

Notaro, Jorge. *La política económica en el Uruguay, 1968–1984.*

Montevideo: Centro Interdisciplinario de Estudios del Desarrollo, Uruguay, 1984.

Oddone, Juan Antonio. *La formación del Uruguay moderno.* Buenos Aires: Editorial Universitaria de Buenos Aires, 1966.

Oddone, Juan Antonio, and Blanca Paris. *La universidad uruguaya del militarismo a la crisis, 1885-1958.* (3 vols.) Montevideo: Universidad de la República, 1971.

Panizza, Francisco. "El clientelismo en la teoría política contemporánea," *Cuadernos del CLAEH* [Montevideo], 12, No. 44, 1987, 63-70.

Pedretti de Bolón, Alma. *El idioma de los uruguayos: Unidad y diversidad.* Montevideo: Ediciones de la Banda Oriental, 1983.

Pendle, George. *Uruguay: South America's First Welfare State.* (2d ed.) London: Oxford University Press, 1957.

Pereda Valdés, Ildefonso. *El Negro en el Uruguay.* Montevideo: Revista del Instituto Histórico y Geográfico del Uruguay, 1965.

Pérez, Romeo. "Lo social y lo político en la dinámica de los movimientos sociales urbanos," *Cuadernos del CLAEH* [Montevideo], 12, No. 42, 1987, 29-38.

Pérez, Romeo, and Piedro Cueva. "Movimientos sociales urbanos y sistema político: El caso de Paso Carrasco," *Cuadernos del CLAEH* [Montevideo], 11, No. 40, 1986, 23-43.

Petrucelli, José Luis. "Consequences of Uruguayan Emigration," *International Migration Review,* 13, No. 3, Fall 1979, 519-26.

Picerno, Alfredo, and Pablo Mieres (eds.). *Uruguay: Indicadores básicos.* Montevideo: Centro Latinoamericano de Economía Humana, 1983.

Portes, Alejandro. "Latin American Urbanization During the Years of Crisis," *Latin American Research Review,* 24, No. 3, 1989, 7-44.

Portes, Alejandro, Silvia Blitzer, and John Curtis. "The Urban Informal Sector in Uruguay," *World Development,* 14, No. 6, June 1986, 727-41.

Porzecanski, Arturo C. "The Case of Uruguay." Pages 70-112 in Carmelo Mesa-Lago (ed.), *Social Security in Latin America: Pressure Groups, Stratification, and Inequality.* Pittsburgh: University of Pittsburgh Press, 1978.

Prates, Suzana. "El trabajo de la mujer en una época de crisis (o cuando se pierde ganando)." In Nea Filgueira (ed.), *La Mujer en el Uruguay: Ayer y hoy,* 15. (Temas del Siglo XX series.) Montevideo: Ediciones de la Banda Oriental, 1984.

Rama, Carlos M. *Las clases sociales en el Uruguay.* Montevideo: El Siglo Ilustrado, 1960.

_____. "The Passing of the Afro-Uruguayans from Caste Society into Class Society." Pages 28–50 in Magnus Mörner (ed.), *Conference on Race and Class in Latin America.* New York: Columbia University Press, 1970.

Rama, Germán W. *El ascenso de las clases medias,* 36. (Enciclopedia Uruguaya series.) Montevideo: Editores Reunidos, 1968.

_____. *El club político.* Montevideo: Editorial Arca, 1971.

Real de Azúa, Carlos. *La clase dirigente,* 34. (Nuestra Tierra series.) Montevideo: Editorial Nuestra Tierra, n.d.

_____. *El impulso y su freno.* Montevideo: Ediciones de la Banda Oriental, 1964.

_____. "El poder de la cúpide: Elites, sectores dirigentes, y clase dominante," *Cuadernos del CLAEH* [Montevideo], 42, No. 2, 1987, 42–57.

Rial, Juan. "Immigración y urbanización en el Río de la Plata con especial referencia a la corriente española y el caso de Montevideo, Uruguay." (Documentos de Trabajo series, 89). Montevideo: Centro de Informaciones y Estudios del Uruguay, n.d.

_____. *Población y desarrollo de un pequeño país: Uruguay, 1830–1930.* Montevideo: Acali Editorial, 1983.

Rial, Juan, and Jaime Klaczko. *Uruguay: El país urbano.* Montevideo: Ediciones de la Banda Oriental, 1981.

Rodé, Patricio. "Las políticas sociales en el proceso de redemocratización," *Cuadernos del CLAEH* [Montevideo], 10, No. 35, 1985, 23–42.

Rodríguez, Héctor. *Nuestros sindicatos, 1865–1965.* Montevideo: Ediciones Uruguay, 1965.

Rodríguez Villamil, Silvia, and Graciela Sapriza. *La inmigración europea en el Uruguay.* Montevideo: Ediciones de la Banda Oriental, 1982.

Rosario Beisso, María del, and José Luis Castagnola. "Identidades sociales y cultura política en Uruguay," *Cuadernos del CLAEH* [Montevideo], 12, No. 44, 1987, 9–18.

Rothman, Ana M. "Evolution of Fertility in Argentina and Uruguay." Pages 712–32 in International Union for the Scientific Study of Population (eds.), *International Population Conference,* 1. Liège, Belgium: 1971.

Royol, José. *La salud pública,* 48. (Nuestra Tierra series.) Montevideo: Editorial Nuestra Tierra, 1969.

Sanguinetti Freire, Alberto. "Social Legislation in Uruguay," *International Labour Review* [Geneva], 59, No. 3, March 1949, 271–96.

Santa Ana, Julio de. *Aspectos religiosos de la sociedad uruguaya.* Montevideo: Centro de Estudios Cristianos, 1965.

Sierra, Gerónimo de. "El batllismo: Su naturaleza y su función de clase (conjunto de hipótesis)," *Cuadernos de ciencias sociales* [Montevideo], 1, No. 1, 1972.

––––––. "Estructura económica y estructura de clases en el Uruguay," *Cuadernos de ciencias sociales* [Montevideo], 1, No. 1, 1970.

––––––. *Sociedad y política en el Uruguay de la crisis.* Montevideo: Librosur, 1985.

Solari, Aldo. *El desarrollo social del Uruguay en la postguerra.* Montevideo: Editorial Arca, 1967.

––––––. "El envejecimiento de la población uruguaya 30 años después," *Cuadernos del CLAEH* [Montevideo], 12, No. 43, 1987, 7–26.

––––––. *Estudios sobre la sociedad uruguaya, 1.* Montevideo: Editorial Arca, 1964.

––––––. *Sociología rural latinoamericana.* Buenos Aires: Editorial Universitaria de Buenos Aires, 1963.

––––––. *Sociología rural nacional.* (2d ed.) Montevideo: Facultad de Derecho y Ciencias Sociales, 1958.

––––––. *Uruguay en cifras.* Montevideo: Universidad de la República, 1966.

Solari, Aldo, and Rolando Franco. "Equality of Opportunities and Elitism in the Uruguayan University," *NorthSouth,* 6, No. 11, 1981, 1–16.

––––––. "The Family in Uruguay." Pages 46–83 in Man Singh Das and Clinton J. Jesser (eds.), *The Family in Latin America.* Ghaziabad, India: Vikas, 1980.

Solari, Aldo, Néstor Campiglia, and Susana Prates. "Education, Occupation, and Development," *International Social Science Journal* [Geneva], 19, No. 3, 1967, 404–15.

Soler Roca, Miguel. *Uruguay: Análisis crítico de los programas escolares de 1949, 1957, y 1979.* Barcelona: Imprenta Juvenil, 1984.

Taglioretti, Graciela. *Women and Work in Uruguay.* Paris: United Nations Educational, Scientific, and Cultural Organization, 1983.

Terra, Juan Pablo. "Distribución social del ingreso en Uruguay." (Investigaciones series, 31.) Montevideo: Centro Latinoamericano de Economía Humana, n.d.

––––––. *La vivienda, 38.* Montevideo: Editorial Nuestra Tierra, 1969.

Terra, Juan Pablo, and Mabel Hopenhaym. *La infancia en el Uruguay (1973-1984).* Montevideo: Centro Latinoamericano de Economía Humana/United Nations Children's Fund/Ediciones de la Banda Oriental, 1986.

Traversoni, Alfredo, and Diosma Piotti. *Nuestro sistema educativo hoy.* Montevideo: Ediciones de la Banda Oriental, 1984.

United Nations Development Programme. *Human Development Report, 1990.* New York: Oxford University Press, 1990.

Ures, Jorge. "La relación clase-voto en Montevideo en las elecciones del 28 de noviembre de 1971," *Revista uruguaya de ciencias sociales* [Montevideo], 1, No. 1, April–June 1972.

Uruguay. Dirección General de Estadística y Censos. *Anuario estadístico, 1988.* Montevideo: 1989.

Van Aken, Mark J. "The Radicalization of the Uruguayan Student Movement," *The Americas (Academy of American Franciscan History),* 33, No. 1, 1976, 109–29.

Veiga, Danilo. "Socioeconomic Structure and Population Displacements: The Uruguayan Case," *NorthSouth,* 6, No. 12, 1981, 1–25.

_____. "Tipología departmental y desarrollo regional en el Uruguay." (Documentos de Trabajo, 11.) Montevideo: Centro de Informaciones y Estudios del Uruguay, 1978.

Villalobos, Fabio. "Las políticas de ajuste el proceso de industrialización: Uruguay, 1980–1985," *Cuadernos del CLAEH* [Montevideo], 11, No. 38, 1986, 85–105.

Villegas, Juan S.J. *La iglesia en el Uruguay: Libro conmemorativo en el primero centenario de la erección del obispado de Montevideo.* Montevideo: Instituto Teológico del Uruguay, 1978.

Weinstein, Martin. *Uruguay: Democracy at the Crossroads.* Boulder, Colorado: Westview Press, 1988.

_____. *Uruguay: The Politics of Failure.* Westport, Connecticut: Greenwood Press, 1975.

Wonsewer, Israel, and Anna María Teja. *La emigración uruguaya, 1963–75.* Montevideo: Centro de Investigaciones Económicas/Ediciones de la Banda Oriental, 1983.

Wood, James R., and Eugene A. Weinstein. "Industrialization Values and Occupational Evaluation in Uruguay," *American Journal of Sociology,* 72, No. 1, July 1966, 47–57.

World Bank. *Uruguay Economic Memorandum.* Washington: 1979.

Zum Felde, Alberto. *Proceso histórico del Uruguay.* Montevideo: Editorial Arca, 1967.

(Various issues of the following periodical were also used in the preparation of this chapter: *Búsqueda* [Montevideo].)

Chapter 3

Academia Nacional de Economía. *Contribución a la historia económica del Uruguay.* Montevideo: 1984.

Alonso, José M. "El agro en el Uruguay del futuro." Pages 47–65 in José M. Alonso (ed.), *Ambiente y desarrollo.* (Temas del Siglo series.) Montevideo: Ediciones de la Banda Oriental, 1985.

Bergstein, Jonas. "Foreign Investment in Uruguay: A Law and Development Perspective," *University of Miami Inter-American Law Review,* 20, Spring 1989, 351-92.

"Betting on Blanco," *Economist,* 309, Nos. 75-78, December 2, 1989, 50.

Blejer, Mario I., and José Gil Díaz. "Domestic and External Factors in the Determination of the Real Interest Rate: The Case of Uruguay," *Economic Development and Cultural Change,* 34, No. 3, April 1986, 589-606.

Bolton, Brian. "Latin America 250," *South: The Third World Magazine* [London], No. 102, April 1989, 45-51.

Bronstein, Arturo S. "The Evolution of Labour Relations in Uruguay: Achievements and Challenges," *International Labour Review* [London], 128, No. 2, March-April 1989, 195-212.

Burton, Robert Henderson, II. "Uruguay: A Study of Arrested Economic Development." (Ph.D. dissertation.) New Orleans: Department of Economics, Louisiana State University, 1967.

Buzzetti, José L. *Historia económica y financiera del Uruguay.* Montevideo: Talleres de la Paz, 1969.

Caneela Vilanova, Walter. *El Uruguay actual: Un enfoque económico.* Montevideo: Fundación de Cultura Universitaria, 1979.

Centro de Investigaciones Económicas. *La Crisis uruguaya y el problema nacional.* Montevideo: Ediciones de la Banda Oriental, 1984.

Daroczi, Isabel, Elena García, and Miguel Liguera. *Atlas para la República Oriental del Uruguay.* Montevideo: Ediciones Rashetti/Ediciones de Montevideo, 1983.

Díaz Alejandro, Carlos. "Latin America in the 1930s." Pages 17-49 in Rosemary Thorp (ed.), *Latin America in the 1930s.* London: Macmillan Press for Oxford University, 1984.

Economist Intelligence Unit. *Country Report: Uruguay, Paraguay* [London], No. 1, 1987, 6-23.

_____. *Country Report: Uruguay, Paraguay* [London], Nos. 1-4, 1989.

_____. *Country Report: Uruguay, Paraguay* [London], No. 1, 1990.

Europa World Year Book, 1989. London: Europa, 1989.

Faraone, Roque. *Introducción a la historia del Uruguay, 1825-1973.* Montevideo: Editorial Arca, 1974.

Finch, M.H.J. *A Political Economy of Uruguay since 1870.* New York: St. Martin's Press, 1981.

Furtado, Celso. *Economic Development of Latin America.* (2d ed.) (Trans., Suzette Macedo.) (Cambridge Latin America Series.) London: Cambridge University Press, 1976.

Gauhar, Altaf. "Consensus Politics Sanguinetti Style," *South* [London], No. 88, February 1988, 15–17.

Instituto de Economía. *La Crisis Económica.* (Nuestra Tierra series.) Montevideo: Universidad de la República, 1988.

_____. *Uruguay '87.* Montevideo: Universidad de la República, 1987.

Inter-American Development Bank. *Economic and Social Progress in Latin America.* Washington: 1989.

International Monetary Fund. *International Financial Statistics.* Washington: 1990.

Jane's World Railways, 1989–90. (Ed., Geoffrey Allen.) Coulsdon, Surrey, United Kingdom: Jane's Information Group, 1989.

Katzman, Rubén. "Youth and Unemployment in Montevideo," *CEPAL Review* [Santiago, Chile], No. 29, August 1986, 119–31.

Kneit, Julio. *Uruguay 1985: La luz tras las tinieblas.* Montevideo: Prisma, 1985.

Kurian, George Thomas. *Encyclopedia of the Third World, 3.* (3d ed.) New York: Facts on File, 1987.

Larrain, Felipe B. "La reforma financiera uruguaya de los setenta: De la liberalización a la crisis," *Trimestre económico* [Mexico City], 55, July–September 1988, 605–47.

Macadar, Luis. "Uruguay: Crisis externa e inserción subregional— El comercio con Argentina y Brazil, 1975–84," *Integración latinoamericana* [Buenos Aires], 12, No. 127, September 1987, 3–19.

Melo, Jaime de. "Financial Reforms, Stabilization, and Growth under High Capital Mobility: Uruguay, 1974–83." Pages 229–49 in Michael Connolly and Claudio González-Vega (eds.), *Economic Reform and Stabilization in Latin America.* New York: Praeger, 1987.

Millot, Julio, Carlos Silva, and Lindor Silva. *El desarrollo industrial del Uruguay: De la crisis de 1929 a la posguerra.* Montevideo: Universidad de la República, 1973.

"Montevideo's Mixed Blessings," *South* [London], No. 89, March 1988, 80–81.

Pascale, Graziano. "Lacalle: En la vía de la integración," *Visión* [Montevideo], 74, No. 6, February 19, 1990, 8–10.

Portes, Alejandro. "The Urban Informal Sector in Uruguay: Its Internal Structure, Characteristics, and Effects," *World Development* [Oxford], 14, No. 6, June 1986, 727–41.

Reyes Abadie, Washington, and José C. Williman. *Economía del Uruguay en el siglo XIX, 32.* (Nuestra Tierra series.) Montevideo: Universidad de la República, 1969.

Rial Roade, Juan. (Trans., Lisa Ebener and Gerald M. Greenfield.) "Uruguay." Pages 701–25 in Gerald M. Greenfield and Sheldon L. Maram (eds.), *Latin American Labor Organizations.* Westport, Connecticut: Greenwood Press, 1987.

Sachs, Jeffrey. "Recent Studies in the Latin American Debt Crisis," *Latin American Research Review,* 23, No. 3, 1988, 170–79.

Sanders, Thomas G. *Uruguay's Return to Democracy.* (Universities Field Staff International, UFSI Reports, Latin America, No. 22.) Indianapolis: 1985.

Sjaastad, Larry A. "Debt, Depression, and Real Rates of Interest in Latin America." Pages 21–39 in Philip L. Brock, Michael B. Connolly, and Claudio González-Vega (eds.), *Latin American Debt and Adjustment.* New York: Praeger, 1989.

Spiller, Pablo T. "Uruguay." Pages 70–72 in Nicolás Ardito Barleta, Mario Blejer, and Luis Landau (eds.), *Economic Liberalization and Stabilization Policies in Argentina, Chile, and Uruguay.* Washington: World Bank, 1983.

United Nations. Economic Commission for Latin America and the Caribbean. *Economic Panorama of Latin America, 1988.* Santiago, Chile: 1988.

United States. Central Intelligence Agency. *The World Factbook, 1989.* Washington: 1989.

————. Department of Commerce. *Foreign Economic Trends and Their Implications for the United States: Uruguay.* Washington: September 1988.

————. Department of Commerce. *Foreign Economic Trends and Their Implications for the United States: Uruguay.* Washington: January 1990.

Uruguay. Dirección General de Estadística y Censos. *Anuario estadístico, 1988.* Montevideo: 1989.

————. Ministerio de Economía y Finanzas. *Uruguay: Un retrato económico.* Montevideo: 1988.

————. Presidencia de la República. *Cuatro años de democracia.* (Serie informe del poder ejecutivo a la Asamblea General.) Montevideo: 1989.

"Uruguay Sets a Fragile Example," *Economist* [London], 308, No. 7569, September 24, 1988, 96.

Wilkie, James, and Enrique Ochoa. *Statistical Abstract of Latin America,* 27. Los Angeles: Latin American Center, University of California at Los Angeles, 1989.

Williman, José Claudio. *Historia económica del Uruguay.* Montevideo: Ediciones de la Plaza, 1986.

World Bank. *World Debt Tables.* (External Debt of Developing Countries Series.) Washington: 1989.

World Radio TV Handbook. (Ed., Andrew Sennitt.) Hvidovre, Denmark: Billboard, 1990.

(Various issues of the following periodicals were also used in the preparation of this chapter: *Business Latin America,* July 1989, January–March 1990; *Búsqueda* [Montevideo], 1989–90; *Christian Science Monitor,* November 1989; *Euromoney* [London], March 1989; *Guía financiera* [Montevideo], February-March 1989; *Latin American Economic Report* [London], 1988–90; *Latin American Monitor* [London], July–August 1989; *Latin American Regional Reports: Southern Cone* [London], 1988–90; *Latinamerica Press* [Lima], November 1989; *Los Angeles Times,* April 1989; and *New York Times,* November 1989.)

Chapter 4

Alisky, Marvin. *Uruguay: A Contemporary Survey.* New York: Praeger, 1969.

Blaustein, Albert P., and Gisbert H. Flanz. *Constitutions of the Countries of the World.* Dobbs Ferry, New York: Oceana, 1982.

Bronstein, Arturo S. "The Evolution of Labour Relations in Uruguay: Achievements and Challenges," *International Labour Review* [London], 128, No. 2, March–April 1989, 195–212.

Bruschera, Oscar. *Evolución institucional del Uruguay en el siglo XX.* (Cuadernos Uruguayos series.) Montevideo: Ediciones del Nuevo Mundo, 1988.

Day, Alan J. (ed.). *Political Parties of the World.* Chicago: St. James Press, 1988.

Europa World Year Book, 1989. London: Europa, 1989.

Finch, M.H.J. "Democratisation in Uruguay," *Third World Quarterly* [London], 7, No. 3, July 1985, 594–609.

Finch, M.H.J., and Alicia Casas de Barrán (comps.). *Uruguay,* 102. (World Bibliographical Series.) Oxford: Clio Press, 1989.

Fitzgibbon, Russell H. *Uruguay: Portrait of a Democracy.* New York: Russell and Russell, 1966.

Gillespie, Charles Guy. "Democratic Consolidation in the Southern Cone and Brazil: Beyond Political Disarticulation?" *Third World Quarterly* [London], 11, No. 2, April 1989, 92–113.

_____. *Negotiating Democracy: Politicians and Generals in Uruguay.* (Cambridge Latin American Studies, 72.) Cambridge: Cambridge University Press, 1991.

_____. "Party Strategies and Redemocratization: Theoretical and Comparative Perspectives on the Uruguayan Case." (Ph.D. dissertation, Yale University, 1987.) Ann Arbor: Dissertation Abstracts International, DA8917178.

————. "Uruguay's Return to Democracy," *Bulletin of Latin American Research* [London], 4, No. 2, 1985, 99–197.

González, Luis Eduardo. "Political Structures and the Prospects for Democracy in Uruguay." (Ph.D. dissertation, Yale University, 1988.) Ann Arbor: Dissertation Abstracts International, DA8917181.

————. "Uruguay, 1980–1981: An Unexpected Opening," *Latin American Research Review*, 18, No. 3, 1983, 63–76.

Hobday, Charles. *Communist and Marxist Parties of the World.* (Keesing's Reference Publication Series.) Burnt Mill, Harlow, Essex, United Kingdom: Longman Group, 1986.

Instituto de Comunicación y Desarrollo. *Mass media: La guía.* Montevideo: November 1987.

Kaufman, Edy. *Uruguay in Transition.* New Brunswick, New Jersey: Transaction Books, 1979.

Khachaturov, K. "Soviet-Uruguayan Relations: Yesterday and Today," *International Affairs* [Moscow], No. 9, September 1986, 67–74.

Kurian, George Thomas. *Encyclopedia of the Third World,* 3. (3d ed.) New York: Facts on File, 1987.

"The Legal System of Uruguay." Pages 237–56 in Kenneth Robert Redden (ed.), *Modern Legal Systems Cyclopedia,* 10. Buffalo: William S. Hein, 1985.

Lindahl, Goran G. *Uruguay's New Path: A Study in Politics During the First Colegiado, 1919–33.* Stockholm: Broderna Lagerstrom, 1962.

McDonald, Ronald H. "Confrontation and Transition in Uruguay," *Current History,* 84, No. 498, February 1985, 57–60, 87–88.

————. "The Dilemma of Normalcy in Uruguay," *Current History,* 87, No. 525, January 1988, 25–28, 35–36.

————. "Legislative Politics in Uruguay: A Preliminary Statement." Pages 113–35 in Winston A. Agor (ed.), *Latin American Legislatures: Their Role and Influence.* New York: Praeger, 1971.

————. "The Struggle for Normalcy in Uruguay," *Current History,* 81, No. 472, February 1982, 69–73, 85–86.

McDonald, Ronald H., and J. Mark Ruhl. *Party Politics and Elections in Latin America.* Boulder, Colorado: Westview Press, 1989.

Mieres, Pablo. "Un sistema de partidos en transición: Notas preliminares a propósito de los resultados de las elecciones nacionales de 1989," *Cuadernos del CLAEH* [Montevideo], 15, No. 53, 1990, 5–22.

Pendle, George. *Uruguay: South America's First Welfare State.* (3d ed.) London: Oxford University Press, 1965. Reprint. Westport, Connecticut: Greenwood Press, 1985.

Portillo, Alvaro, and Enrique Gallicchio. *Montevideo: Geografía electoral.* Montevideo: Centro Uruguaya Independiente, 1988.

Porzecanski, Arturo C. ''Authoritarian Uruguay,'' *Current History,* 76, No. 416, February 1977, 73–75, 85–86.

Quagliotti de Bellis, Bernardo. ''El Uruguay internacional: Reseña histórica,'' *Geosur: Asociación Sudamericana de Estudios Geopolíticos e Internacionales* [Montevideo], 19, Nos. 111–12, July–August 1989, 3–18.

Rama, Germán W. *La democracia en Uruguay: Una perspectiva de interpretación.* Buenos Aires: Grupo Editor Latinoamericano, 1987.

Sanders, Thomas G. *Uruguay's Return to Democracy.* (Universities Field Staff International, UFSI Reports, Latin America, No. 22.) Indianapolis: 1985.

Solari, Aldo. *Partidos políticos y sistema electoral.* Montevideo: El Libro Libre/Fundación Uruguaya para el Fomento de la Cultura, la Ciencia, y la Tecnología, 1988.

Taylor, Philip B., Jr. *Government and Politics of Uruguay.* Westport, Connecticut: Greenwood Press, 1984.

United States. Department of State. *Country Reports on Human Rights Practices for 1988.* (Report submitted to United States Congress, 101st, 1st Session, Senate, Committee on Foreign Relations, and House of Representatives, Committee on Foreign Affairs.) Washington: GPO, February 1989.

Uruguay. *Constitución de la República del Uruguay y actas institucionales vigentes.* Montevideo: Corporación Gráfica, 1980.

Uruguay. Presidencia de la República. Oficina Nacional del Servicio Civil. ''Las políticas y líneas acción de la Oficina Nacional del Servicio Civil, 1985–1988,'' *Revista de administración pública uruguaya* [Montevideo], 4, No. 10, May 1989, 14–45.

Weinstein, Martin. ''Consolidating Democracy in Uruguay: The Sea Change of the 1989 Elections.'' (Working Paper Series, 4.) New York: Bildner Center for Western Hemisphere Studies, City University of New York, January 1990.

_____. *Uruguay: Democracy at the Crossroads.* Boulder, Colorado: Westview Press, 1988.

_____. *Uruguay: The Politics of Failure.* Westport, Connecticut: Greenwood Press, 1975.

Weschler, Lawrence. ''The Great Exception, I-Liberty,'' *New Yorker,* 65, April 3, 1989, 43–50, 67–85.

_____. ''The Great Exception, II-Impunity,'' *New Yorker,* 65, April 10, 1989, 85–102, 105–8.

_____. *A Miracle, a Universe: Settling Accounts with Torturers.* New York: Pantheon Books, 1990.

Yearbook on International Communist Affairs, 1989. (Ed., Richard F. Staar.) Stanford, California: Hoover Institution Press, 1989.

(Various issues of the following periodicals were also used in the preparation of this chapter: *Búsqueda* [Montevideo], 1986, 1988–89; Foreign Broadcast Information Service, *Daily Report: Latin America,* 1985–90; *Latin American Weekly Report* [London], 1989–90; *Latinamerica Press,* 1987–90; *New York Times,* 1989–90; and *Washington Post,* 1989–90.)

Chapter 5

Andrade, John. *World Police and Paramilitary Forces.* New York: Stockton Press, 1985.

Blaustein, Albert P., and Gisbert H. Flanz. *Constitutions of the Countries of the World.* Dobbs Ferry, New York: Oceana, 1982.

Copley, Gregory R. *Defense and Foreign Affairs Handbook.* Washington: Perth, 1987.

Couhat, Jean Labayle (ed.). *Combat Fleets of the World, 1988–89.* Annapolis: Naval Institute Press, 1988.

Day, Alan J. (ed.). *Political Parties of the World.* Chicago: St. James Press, 1988.

DMS-Market Intelligence Reports: Foreign Military Markets—Latin America and Australasia. Alexandria, Virginia: Jane's Information Group, 1989.

English, Adrian J. "Uruguay." Pages 421–40 in Adrian J. English (ed.), *Armed Forces of Latin America: Their Histories, Development, Present Strength, and Military Potential.* London: Jane's, 1984.

———. "Uruguay." Pages 262–71 in Adrian J. English (ed.), *Regional Defence Profile, No. 1: Latin America.* London: Jane's, 1988.

González, Luis E. "Uruguay, 1980–1981: An Unexpected Opening," *Latin American Research Review,* 18, No. 3, 1983, 63–76.

Hobday, Charles. *Communist and Marxist Parties of the World.* (Keesing's Reference Publications Series.) Burnt Mill, Harlow, Essex, United Kingdom: Longman Group, 1986.

Hoskey, James L. (ed.). *Lambert's Worldwide Directory of Defense Authorities with International Defense Organizations and Treaties.* Washington: Lambert, 1983.

Ingleton, Roy D. *Police of the World.* New York: Scribner's, 1979.

International Monetary Fund. *Government Finance Statistics Yearbook, 1988.* Washington: 1988.

———. *International Financial Statistics Yearbook, 1989.* Washington: 1989.

Jane's All the World's Aircraft, 1989–90. (Ed., John W.R. Taylor.) London: Jane's, 1990.

Jane's Fighting Ships, 1989–90. (Ed., John Moore.) London: Jane's, 1989.

Keegan, John (ed.). *World Armies.* New York: Facts on File, 1984.

Kurian, George Thomas. *Encyclopedia of the Third World, 3.* (3d ed.) New York: Facts on File, 1987.

Lindahl, Goran G. *Uruguay's New Path: A Study in Politics During the First Colegiado, 1919–33.* Stockholm: Broderna Lagerstrom, 1962.

The Military Balance, 1982–1983. London: International Institute for Strategic Studies, 1982.

The Military Balance, 1989–1990. London: International Institute for Strategic Studies, 1989.

Pendle, George. *Uruguay.* (3d ed.) London: Oxford University Press, 1965. Reprint. Westport, Connecticut: Greenwood Press, 1985.

Porzecanski, Arturo C. *Uruguay's Tupamaros: The Urban Guerrilla.* New York: Praeger, 1973.

Rama, Germán W. *La democracia en Uruguay: Una perspectiva de interpretación.* Buenos Aires: Grupo Editor Latinoamericano, 1987.

Sivard, Ruth Leger. *World Military and Social Expenditures, 1989.* Leesburg, Virginia: World Priorities, 1989.

Stockholm International Peace Research Institute. *SIPRI Yearbook, 1989: World Armaments and Disarmament.* Oxford: Oxford University Press, 1989.

United States. Arms Control and Disarmament Agency. *World Military Expenditures and Arms Transfers, 1988.* Washington: 1988.

———. Department of State. *Country Reports on Human Rights Practices for 1986.* (Report submitted to United States Congress, 100th, 1st Session, Senate, Committee on Foreign Relations, and House of Representatives, Committee on Foreign Affairs.) Washington: GPO, February 1987.

———. Department of State. *Country Reports on Human Rights Practices for 1987.* (Report submitted to United States Congress, 100th, 2d Session, House of Representatives, Committee on Foreign Affairs, and Senate, Committee on Foreign Relations.) Washington: GPO, February 1988.

———. Department of State. *Country Reports on Human Rights Practices for 1988.* (Report submitted to United States Congress, 101st, 1st Session, Senate, Committee on Foreign Relations, and House of Representatives, Committee on Foreign Affairs.) Washington: GPO, February 1989.

———. Department of State. *Country Reports on Human Rights Practices for 1989*. (Report submitted to United States Congress, 101st, 2d Session, House of Representatives, Committee on Foreign Affairs, and Senate, Committee on Foreign Relations.) Washington: GPO, February 1990.

Uruguay. *Código del proceso penal de la República Oriental del Uruguay*. Montevideo: Fundación de Cultura Universitaria, 1985.

———. *Código penal de la República Oriental del Uruguay*. Montevideo: Fundación de Cultura Universitaria, 1986.

———. *Constitutión de la República del Uruguay y actas institucionales vigentes*. Montevideo: Corporación Gráfica, 1980.

Vanger, Milton I. *The Model Country: José Batlle y Ordóñez of Uruguay, 1907-1915*. Hanover, New Hampshire: University Press of New England, 1980.

Weinstein, Martin. *Uruguay: Democracy at the Crossroads*. Boulder, Colorado: Westview Press, 1988.

———. *Uruguay: The Politics of Failure*. Westport, Connecticut: Greenwood Press, 1975.

Willis, Jean L. *Historical Dictionary of Uruguay*. Metuchen, New Jersey: Scarecrow Press, 1974.

Wilson, Carlos. *The Tupamaros: The Unmentionables*. Boston: Branden Press, 1974.

Yearbook on International Communist Affairs, 1989. (Ed., Richard F. Staar.) Stanford, California: Hoover Institution Press, 1989.

(Various issues of the following periodicals were also used in the preparation of this chapter: Foreign Broadcast Information Service, *Daily Report: Latin America;* Joint Publications Research Service, *Latin America Report; Latin American Weekly Report* [London]; *Latin America Regional Reports: Southern Cone* [London]; and *Washington Post*.)

Glossary

ALADI (Asociación Latinoamericana de Integración)—Latin American Integration Association. Headquartered in Montevideo, ALADI was established in August 1980 to replace the twenty-year-old Latin American Free Trade Association (LAFTA). ALADI's members included Argentina, Bolivia, Brazil, Chile, Colombia, Ecuador, Mexico, Paraguay, Peru, Uruguay, and Venezuela. Instead of uniform tariff cuts, ALADI advocated a regional tariff preference for goods originating in member states and tariffs scaled according to a member country's level of economic development: most developed, intermediate, or least developed.

autonomous entities (*entes autónomos*)—Autonomous government agencies or state enterprises performing various industrial, commercial, or social services. The constitution stipulated that these bodies were to have a degree of autonomy or decentralization as established by laws enacted with the approval of an absolute majority of the full membership of each chamber of the General Assembly. They were administered by five- to seven-member boards of directors or directors general. Members were either elected by the Senate or appointed by the president with the consent of the Senate. The degree of autonomy or decentralization varied. For example, the constitution stipulated that postal, customs, port authority, and public health services were not to be fully decentralized, but rather granted only as much autonomy as was compatible with control by the executive. The autonomous agencies could be divided into two general classifications: the first was concerned with education, welfare, and culture; the second, with industry and commerce. In the first classification, autonomous agencies supervised the University of the Republic and the councils for secondary and elementary education, as well as the training for teachers. Others were concerned with radio, television, the theater, housing, welfare, and social security. In the second classification, agencies supervised the waterworks, fishing industry, ports, national merchant marine, and production of petroleum products, cement, alcoholic beverages, and electric power. In the commercial field, autonomous agencies supervised the Central Bank of Uruguay, the Social Welfare Bank, the State Insurance Bank, and the Mortgage Bank.

A three-fifths vote of the full membership of both chambers of the General Assembly was required for the passage of a law to allow the admission of private capital in the organization or expansion of the assets of any of the autonomous entities, and the contribution of private capital, if allowed, was never to be greater than that of the national government. The state could also participate in the industrial, agricultural, or commercial activities of enterprises formed by workers' cooperatives, if it had the consent of the enterprise. The autonomous entities could not conduct any business not specifically assigned to them by law, nor could they expend any of their resources for purposes foreign to their usual activities.

consumer price index (CPI)—A statistical measure of sustained change in the price level weighted according to spending patterns.

Enterprise for the Americas Initiative—A plan announced by President George H.W. Bush on June 27, 1990, calling for the United States to negotiate agreements with selected Latin American countries to reduce their official debt to the United States and make funds available through this restructuring for environmental programs; to stimulate private investment; and to take steps to promote extensive trade liberalization with the goal of establishing free trade throughout the Western Hemisphere.

fiscal year—Same as calendar year.

GATT (General Agreement on Tariffs and Trade)—An intergovernmental agency related to the United Nations and headquartered in Geneva, GATT was established in 1948 as a multilateral treaty with the aim of liberalizing and stabilizing world trade. GATT's fundamental principles included nondiscriminatory trade among members, protection of domestic trade through the customs tariff, and agreement on tariff levels through negotiations among the contracting parties. The Uruguay Round of major multilateral trade negotiations, the eighth such round of negotiations, began at Punta del Este in September 1986.

GDP (gross domestic product)—A measure of the total value of goods and services produced by the domestic economy during a given period, usually one year. Obtained by adding the value contributed by each sector of the economy in the form of profits, compensation to employees, and depreciation (consumption of capital). The income arising from investments and possessions owned abroad is not included. Hence, the term *domestic* is used to distinguish GDP from GNP (*q.v.*).

GNP (gross national product)—The total market value of all final goods and services produced by an economy during a year. Obtained by adding GDP (*q.v.*) and the income received from abroad by residents, less payments remitted abroad to nonresidents.

IMF (International Monetary Fund)—Established along with the World Bank (*q.v.*) in 1945, the IMF is a specialized agency affiliated with the United Nations that takes responsibility for stabilizing international exchange rates and payments. The main business of the IMF is the provision of loans to its members when they experience balance of payments difficulties. These loans often carry conditions that require substantial internal economic adjustments by the recipients.

import-substitution industrialization—An economic development strategy that emphasizes the growth of domestic industries, often by import protection using tariff and nontariff measures. Proponents favor the export of industrial goods over primary products.

peso—The traditional unit of currency, first issued in 1862. Replaced by the Uruguayan new peso (*q.v.*) in 1975 at the rate of 1,000 old pesos for each new peso. The term *peso* is often used as a short form to refer to the Uruguayan new peso in the post-1975 era.

terms of trade—The number of units that must be given up for one unit of goods by each party, e.g., nation, to a transaction. The terms of trade are said to move in favor of the party that gives up fewer units of goods than it did previously for one unit of goods received and against the party that gives up more units of goods for one unit of goods received. In international economics, the concept of ''terms of trade'' plays an important role in evaluating exchange relationships between nations.

Uruguayan new peso (N$Ur)—The Uruguayan unit of currency, consisting of 100 centésimos. Often referred to in short form as the peso. The Uruguayan new peso was introduced in 1975 to replace the old peso at the rate of 1,000 old pesos for each new peso. Since 1975 the exchange rate, linked to the United States dollar, has been frequently adjusted, with the value of the new peso declining. The average exchange rate per US$1 was N$Ur101 in 1985; N$Ur152 in 1986; N$Ur227 in 1987; N$Ur359 in 1988; N$Ur606 in 1989; and N$Ur1,171 in 1990. So extreme has the devaluation of the peso been that in 1991 Uruguayan authorities began to consider introducing another new peso, equal in value to 1,000 units of the existing new peso.

value-added tax (VAT)—An incremental tax applied to the value added at each stage of the processing of a raw material or the production and distribution of a commodity. It is calculated as the difference between the product value at a given stage and the cost of all materials and services purchased as inputs. The VAT is a form of indirect taxation, and its impact on the ultimate consumer is the same as that of a sales tax.

World Bank—Informal name used to designate a group of three affiliated international institutions: the International Bank for Reconstruction and Development (IBRD), the International Development Association (IDA), and the International Finance Corporation (IFC). The IBRD, established in 1945, has the primary purpose of providing loans to developing countries for productive projects. The IDA, a legally separate loan fund administered by the staff of the IBRD, was set up in 1960 to furnish credits to the poorest of developing countries on much easier terms than those of conventional IBRD loans. The IFC, founded in 1956, supplements the activities of the IBRD through loans and assistance designed specifically to encourage the growth of productive private enterprises in less developed countries. To participate in the World Bank group, member states must first belong to the IMF (*q.v.*).

Index

abortion, 78
Acción, 34
Accounts Tribunal, 164–65, 170; duties of, 164; members of, 164–65
acquired immune deficiency syndrome (AIDS), 82–83
Act of Chapultepec, 192, 218
Administración Nacional de Combustibles, Alcohol, y Portland. *See* National Administration of Fuels, Alcohol, and Portland Cement
Administración Nacional de Puertos. *See* National Administration of Ports
Administración Nacional de Telecomunicaciones. *See* National Telecommunications Administration
Administración Nacional de Usinas y Transmisiones Eléctricas. *See* National Administration for the Generation and Transmission of Electricity
Advanced Democracy Party, 177
Advance Grouping, 26
AEBU. *See* Uruguayan Association of Bank Employees
Africa: immigrants from, 65; relations with, 197
agricultural: enterprises, 120; expansion, 35, 56; exports, 124; markets, liberalization of, 44; practices, 99; reform, 10, 24
agricultural production, 123–25; of citrus, 125; of corn, 124–25; decline in, 112; labor force in, 120; land area dedicated to, 123; increase in, 119; methods, 118, 124; as percentage of gross domestic product, 109, 118; stagnation in, 118–19; subsidies, 124; of wheat, 124
agricultural products: citrus, 125; corn, 124–25; as inputs to manufacturing, 118; prices, 28; rice, 124; as source of foreign exchange, 119; wheat, 124
agriculture, 118–27; decline of, 97; effect of erosion on, 124; and industry, link between, 109; in interior, 56–57; labor force in, 115; land tenure, 120; land use, 119–20; in littoral, 57; and manufacturing, relationship between, 118; under military government, 45; re-

search and development in, 24
Aguerrondo, Mario, 40, 41
Aguirre Ramírez, Gonzalo, 175, 182
AIDS. *See* acquired immune deficiency syndrome
air force, 139, 209–10, 213, 221; aircraft of, 208; commands of, 221; equipment of, 204, 208, 209–10; mission of, 204; number of personnel in, 221; organization of, 221; origins of, 209; training, 221
Air Force Academy, 209, 221
Air Technical School, 221
ALADI. *See* Latin American Integration Association
Alfonsín, Raúl, 146
Algeria, 197
Alliance for Progress, 39
Allies, 192
Alvarez Armelino, Gregorio, xxix, 46, 158, 189
Amézaga, Juan José, 32
Amézaga administration, 33–34; civil liberties restored under, 33
amnesty: for military, xxix–xxx, 179–80, 186, 212, 226; for political prisoners, 158, 204; for Tupamaros, 92, 158, 177, 189, 224
Amnesty International, xxix, 43, 179–80
amnesty law, 179–80, 186, 212; referendum on, 180
ANCAP. *See* National Administration of Fuels, Alcohol, and Portland Cement
ANDEBU. *See* National Association of Uruguayan Broadcasters
Animal Welfare Ecological Green Party (EE-PV), 176
ANP. *See* National Administration of Ports
ANR. *See* National Republican Association
Antarctica, 196
ANTEL. *See* National Telecommunications Administration
Aquí, 190
Arce, Líber, 40
architecture, 59–60
Argentina, xxix, 11; competition with,

Socialist Workers' Party (PST), 177
social reform, 27; under Amézaga, 33;
under Batlle y Ordóñez, xxvii, 22,
24–26, 27, 103, 104; end to, 25–26;
during Great Depression, 28; weakened
by Terra, 30
social rights, 29
social security system, 27, 80; abuse of,
84–85; categories of benefits in, 85;
government spending on, 80; pensions,
84–86; reform of, xxxii; spending on,
xxxv, 85
social services: control of, 45; cutbacks in,
xxiv
Social Welfare Bank, 39, 84, 134
social welfare programs, xxiii, xxviii, 4,
22, 37, 97, 99; opposition to, 36;
proposals to restructure, xxxiv–xxxv;
supported by exports, 99, 111
Sociedad de Defensa de la Tradición
Familia y Propriedad. *See* Society for
the Defense of Family Tradition and
Property
Society for the Defense of Family Tradi-
tion and Property (TFP), 176
Solano López, Francisco, 15, 207
Soriano, xxv
Soriano Department, 56, 57; develop-
ment in, 62; farming in, 119
Sosa, Julio María, 26
Sosism, 26
South Africa, 197
South Atlantic War, 195
Southern Cone Common Market (Mer-
cosur), xxxii–xxxiii; reaction to, xxxii–
xxxiii
The Southern Star/La Estrella del Sur, xxvi
Soviet Union, 187; relations with, 31,
193, 196; Sanguinetti's visit to, 152,
196
Soviet-Uruguayan Cultural Center, 196
Spain: discovery of Uruguay by, 3; emi-
gration to, 69; immigration from,
xxvii, 15, 16, 51, 102; independence
from, xxvi; invasion of, by Napoleon,
8; relations with, 31; rivalry of, with
Portugal, xxv, 3, 204
Spanish military, xxv
State Electric Power and Telephone Company, 28
State Electric Power Company, 22, 28
state enterprises. *See* autonomous entities
State Insurance Bank, 134, 147

State Railways Administration (*see also*
North Tramway and Railway Company), 24, 39
State Security Law (1972), 42
Stock Exchange, 59
strike insurance, 37
strikes, 210; of 1950s, 37; of 1960s, 116;
of 1973, 42; of 1980s, 115, 117, 187,
225; of 1990s, xxxiv, 188; by public
employees, 116, 188; repressed, 26
student demonstrations, 40, 43, 46, 88,
210, 225
student organizations, 225
students, 87, 188–89; influence of, 188–
89; number of, 88; political activity of,
224, 225
Students' Social and Cultural Association
for Public Education (ASCEEP), 46
sub-lemas. See political parties, factions of;
see under individual parties
suffrage (*see also* voting): under 1830 constitution, 11; under 1934 constitution,
29; universal male, 26; women's, xxvii,
29, 78, 159
Supreme Court of Justice, 154, 155, 157,
165, 215, 229–30; appointment of
judges by, 167, 168; appointment of
members of, 164, 166; members of,
166; powers of, 166, 204; regeneration
of, 166; women on, 159
Supreme Military Tribunal, 215
Switzerland, 51
"Switzerland of South America," xxiii,
34, 36, 51, 100
Syria: immigration from, 27

Tacuarembó Department, 56; development in, 62; drought in, 124; ranches
in, 119, 122
Taiwan, 196
Tajes, Máximo, 19
TAMU. *See* Uruguayan Military Air
Transport
Tanzania, 197
tariff barriers, xxxii, 97; effect of, on
domestic industry, 106, 127; lowered
under military regime, 108
tariff reduction agreements, 146
Tarigo, Enrique E., 174
taxes, 18, 24, 80; increased under Lacalle,
xxx; increased under Sanguinetti, 113

Published Country Studies

(Area Handbook Series)

550-65	Afghanistan		550-87	Greece
550-98	Albania		550-78	Guatemala
550-44	Algeria		550-174	Guinea
550-59	Angola		550-82	Guyana and Belize
550-73	Argentina		550-151	Honduras
550-169	Australia		550-165	Hungary
550-176	Austria		550-21	India
550-175	Bangladesh		550-154	Indian Ocean
550-170	Belgium		550-39	Indonesia
550-66	Bolivia		550-68	Iran
550-20	Brazil		550-31	Iraq
550-168	Bulgaria		550-25	Israel
550-61	Burma		550-182	Italy
550-50	Cambodia		550-30	Japan
550-166	Cameroon		550-34	Jordan
550-159	Chad		550-56	Kenya
550-77	Chile		550-81	Korea, North
550-60	China		550-41	Korea, South
550-26	Colombia		550-58	Laos
550-33	Commonwealth Caribbean, Islands of the		550-24	Lebanon
550-91	Congo		550-38	Liberia
550-90	Costa Rica		550-85	Libya
550-69	Côte d'Ivoire (Ivory Coast)		550-172	Malawi
550-152	Cuba		550-45	Malaysia
550-22	Cyprus		550-161	Mauritania
550-158	Czechoslovakia		550-79	Mexico
550-36	Dominican Republic and Haiti		550-76	Mongolia
550-52	Ecuador		550-49	Morocco
550-43	Egypt		550-64	Mozambique
550-150	El Salvador		550-35	Nepal and Bhutan
550-28	Ethiopia		550-88	Nicaragua
550-167	Finland		550-157	Nigeria
550-155	Germany, East		550-94	Oceania
550-173	Germany, Fed. Rep. of		550-48	Pakistan
550-153	Ghana		550-46	Panama